SECONDARY SCIENCE TEACHING FOR ENGLISH LEARNERS

D1707685

SECONDARY SCIENCE TEACHING FOR ENGLISH LEARNERS

Developing Supportive and Responsive Learning Contexts for Sense-Making and Language Development

Edward G. Lyon, Sara Tolbert, Jorge Solís,
Patricia Stoddart, and George C. Bunch

ROWMAN & LITTLEFIELD
Lanham • Boulder • New York • London

Published by Rowman & Littlefield
A wholly owned subsidiary of The Rowman & Littlefield Publishing Group, Inc.
4501 Forbes Boulevard, Suite 200, Lanham, Maryland 20706
www.rowman.com

Unit A, Whitacre Mews, 26-34 Stannary Street, London SE11 4AB

Copyright © 2016 by Rowman & Littlefield

All rights reserved. No part of this book may be reproduced in any form or by any electronic or mechanical means, including information storage and retrieval systems, without written permission from the publisher, except by a reviewer who may quote passages in a review.

British Library Cataloguing in Publication Information Available

Library of Congress Cataloging-in-Publication Data

Names: Bunch, George C.
Title: Secondary science teaching for English learners : developing
    supportive and responsive learning contexts for sense-making and language
    development / George C. Bunch [and four others].
Description: Lanham, Maryland : Rowman & Littlefield, 2016. | Includes
    bibliographical references.
Identifiers: LCCN 2016004260 | ISBN 9781442231276 (e-book)
Subjects: LCSH: Science—Study and teaching (Secondary) | English
    language—Study and teaching (Secondary)—Foreign speakers.
Classification: LCC Q181 .S3895 2016 | DDC 507.1/2—dc23
LC record available at http://lccn.loc.gov/2016004260

♾™ The paper used in this publication meets the minimum requirements of
American National Standard for Information Sciences—Permanence of Paper
for Printed Library Materials, ANSI/NISO Z39.48-1992.

Printed in the United States of America

Contents

Foreword   vii
    Dr. Okhee Lee

Acknowledgments   xi

Introduction: Preparing the Next Generation of Secondary
    Science Teachers   xiii
    Edward G. Lyon

Part I: Foundations for Language, Literacy, and Science Integration

1   The New Vision for Secondary Science Education:
    Connecting Language and Literacy to Science Learning   3
    Patricia Stoddart

2   Responsive Approaches for Teaching English Learners
    in Secondary Science Classrooms: Foundations of the
    SSTELLA Framework   21
    Jorge Solís and George C. Bunch

**Part II: Supportive and Responsive Science Teaching Practices
for English Learners**

3   The SSTELLA Framework: A Synergistic and Reciprocal
    Relationship between Language Development and Science
    Learning for Secondary Students   51
    Sara Tolbert and Patricia Stoddart

4 Contextualizing Science Activity   59
   Sara Tolbert

5 Scientific Sense-Making through Scientific and
   Engineering Practices   79
   Edward G. Lyon and Sara Tolbert

6 Scientific Discourse through Scientific and Engineering Practices   103
   Edward G. Lyon and Jorge Solís

7 English Language and Disciplinary Literacy Development
   in Science   131
   Jorge Solís

**Part III: Applying SSTELLA Practices to Curricular and
Assessment Planning**

8 Explaining the Antibiotic Resistance of MRSA: A Biology Unit
   to Integrate Scientific Practices with Disciplinary Literacy   157
   Edward G. Lyon

9 Deconstructing the "Explaining the Antibiotic Resistance
   of MRSA" Unit   171
   Sara Tolbert and Edward G. Lyon

10 Responsive Approaches to Assessing English Learners
   in Science Classrooms   185
   Edward G. Lyon

Appendix A   SSTELLA Practices Progression   215

Index   221

About the Authors   227

Foreword

Dr. Okhee Lee

THIS BOOK HAS many admirable features that will undoubtedly make distinct contributions to the field of science education. Below, I highlight each of these features and present implications of this work for the research agenda, classroom practices, and educational policies that will push the field forward.

First, the book is timely. The teaching profession has been struggling in recent years to respond to several imperatives that converge on education of English learners (ELs). ELs make up the fastest growing student population across the nation, even in those states that have not traditionally experienced significant growth of ELs. At the same time, achievement and opportunity to learn gaps in subject areas, including science, persist between ELs and non-ELs. Concern about these gaps between ELs and non-ELs is intensified with implementation of the Common Core State Standards (CCSS) and the Next Generation Science Standards (NGSS) as these new standards are both academically rigorous and language intensive. As such, the new standards present learning opportunities and demands to all students, especially ELs who are learning rigorous academic standards in a language (i.e., English) they are still acquiring.

This book provides solutions to the challenge of educating ELs in science classrooms, especially at the secondary level where the research literature is limited in meeting the wide range of prior science knowledge and home language literacy that secondary ELs bring to their science classrooms. As science education is in transition from the previous standards to the NGSS, this book provides insights into what effective implementation of the NGSS and simultaneous promotion of language and literacy development might look like with ELs. The book offers the hope that rigorous science learning and rich language use with ELs is possible, which could result in closing science achievement gaps.

Second, the book blends theory and practice. Grounded in a sociocultural perspective, the SSTELLA Framework emphasizes contextualizing science activities and scaffolding language practices. Contextualizing science activities in the context of ELs' homes and communities creates science learning that is personally meaningful and real for students. Contextualization also elicits ELs' funds of knowledge (cultural resources) and everyday language, including home language (linguistic resources). Scaffolding language practices is critical as engagement in the NGSS science and engineering practices involves both scientific sense-making and scientific discourse. As such, contextualizing science and scaffolding language have synergistic and reciprocal relationships, as the authors emphasize.

Based on this theoretical grounding of the SSTELLA Framework, the book offers rich and extensive classroom vignettes making the SSTELLA Framework come alive. Teachers' instructional moves and students' responses illustrate that the NGSS along with the CCSS offer opportunities for science learning and language and literacy development for all students and ELLs in particular. The consistency of this "can do" message across science disciplines, grade levels, language proficiency levels, classrooms with different compositions of ELs, and geographic locations (Arizona, California, and Texas) is all the more impressive.

Third, the book is comprehensive in addressing teaching, learning, assessment, instructional materials, and teacher education in the areas of science education and language and literacy education. The book starts with a call for new ways of conceptualizing science learning and language and new ways of integrating science and language in response to the rapid growth of ELs who face academic rigor and intense language presented by the NGSS and the CCSS. Then, the book provides detailed accounts of how the SSTELLA Framework addresses teaching, learning, assessment, instructional materials, and teacher education in science and language in a synergistic and reciprocal manner. This portrayal enables readers to realize how science and language integration with ELs occurs, what it looks like, and how the SSTELLA Framework can be applied to their own work.

Finally, the book is unique in respecting the experiences and voices of experts from a variety of disciplinary backgrounds. The breadth, depth, and up-to-date knowledge that this book provides of the research literature across a wide range of theoretical and practical issues in science learning and language learning with ELs is possible because of the interdisciplinary approach incorporated into the SSTELLA Framework. The team of SSTELLA researchers, who are also the authors of this book, sends the message that complex educational issues require sophisticated solutions through interdisciplinary contributions. While the research team consists of intergenerational scholars, it speaks well for the field that the lead authors bring fresh perspectives on teaching and learning of science and language with secondary ELs.

The authors offer forward thinking on NGSS implementation along with the CCSS for ELs at a time when science education is transitioning from the previous standards to the new standards. It would be valuable for the field to learn from the SSTELLA project. How does the field respond to the contextualization of the phenomenon (for science) and problem (for engineering) in local settings of ELs' homes and communities? How does the field respond to scaffolding of language practices while secondary ELs engage in science and engineering practices? Provided with professional development opportunities, can secondary science teachers implement the SSTELLA Framework in their classrooms? How much professional development is needed, and is it within the reach of typical secondary science teachers? What kinds of instructional materials are needed to support teachers?

As the SSTELLA Framework is implemented across three large states (Arizona, California, and Texas), I commend the research team's decision to ground their work in the NGSS even in those states that have not and are not likely to adopt the NGSS. This raises an interesting and intriguing set of questions for the field. On the one hand, what would be the influence of the Framework document (National Research Council, 2012) and the NGSS in those states that have not and may not adopt the NGSS? On the other hand, in those states that have adopted the NGSS, what would the SSTELLA Framework look like if it fully incorporated three major instructional shifts: (1) a focus on explaining phenomena (for science) or designing solutions to problems (for engineering); (2) three-dimensional learning by blending science and engineering practices, crosscutting concepts, and disciplinary core ideas; and (3) coherence (or learning progressions) from K-12?

The book is forward thinking and thought provoking. Readers will find the book worthy of reading. Moreover, readers will be compelled to implement the SSTELLA Framework in their own work.

Acknowledgments

THE SECONDARY SCIENCE TEACHING with English Language and Literacy Acquisition (SSTELLA) Project was funded by the National Science Foundation DR K–12 program, Award #1316834. There are many individuals we acknowledge that have contributed to the ideas in this book.

First, we acknowledge contributions and inspiration from collaborators that are also part of the Teacher Education and English Learners (TEEL) consortium/center including Doris Ashm Marco Bravo, Eduardo Mosqeuda, Isabel Quita, Alberto Rodriquez, Jerome Shaw, Joanna Sherman-Gardiner, and David Whitenack.

We thank science method instructors who have helped us translate research into instructional activities for novice teachers, including Kim Bilica, Joyce Hill, and Barry Roth.

We are grateful for our advisory board members who provide continual feedback and encouragement: Gene Garcia, Norma Gonzalaz, Okhee Lee, and Mark Windschitl.

Thank you to graduate and postdoctoral students who have made intellectual contributions to the work: joe Chee, Joanne Couling, Corey Knox, IvanSalinas, Vicki Lynton, and Preetha Menon.

Finally we thank all participating novice teachers and mentor teachers who have made the work become a reality in secondary science classrooms."

Introduction

Preparing the Next Generation of Secondary Science Teachers

Edward G. Lyon

Setting the Context

THE LANDSCAPE OF secondary science classrooms in the United States has changed, even since the turn of the twenty-first century.[1] Demographically, from 2002 to 2012, the percentage of Latino/a students enrolled in preK–12 public classrooms increased from 17 to 24 percent (approximately 11.8 million total Latino/a students in 2012). In 2014, the number of racial/ethnic minority school children (primarily Latino/a, African American, and Asian American) exceeded the number of White students for the first time, and by 2023, it is projected that 30 percent of preK–12 students will be Latino/a. Roughly 22 percent of school-aged children speak a language other than English at home.

According to U.S. Census data, the number of households in which a language other than English is spoken increased by nearly 160 percent from 1980 to 2010 (Ryan, 2013). While the most common language other than English spoken at home is Spanish, the number of households in which Chinese (all dialects) is spoken has increased by 435 percent during the same time period, and Chinese-language households represent the third largest language group in the United States behind English and Spanish. However, Southeast Asian languages such as Vietnamese are also increasingly spoken at home (i.e., there was a 600 percent increase in households where Vietnamese is spoken at home between 1980 and 2010) (Ryan, 2013).

This book, *Secondary Science Teaching for English Learners: Developing Supportive and Responsive Learning Contexts for Sense-Making and Language*

Development, addresses science learning for students of all languages, recognizing that different languages and dialects present different challenges and opportunities for learning science.

The number of students receiving some form of language assistance in schools (i.e., English as a Second Language or bilingual education) has represented a significant proportion of preK–12 students for over a decade (9.1 percent in 2012). A third of all EL's are found in secondary (grade 6–12) school settings. This latter subpopulation of students, referred to as English learners (or ELs) throughout this book,[2] represents close to one in every four students in California alone. The highest percentage of ELs in U.S. public schools is located in the West (National Center for Education Statistics, 2015). However, the highest rate of growth for ELs is actually occurring in states outside of the West, such as Kansas, which experienced the largest percentage point increase (4.9 percent) between 2002–2003 and 2012–2013 (National Center for Education Statistics, 2015). All in all, the increasing enrollment of EL students is a national trend, with thirty-nine states in the United States experiencing an increase in percentages of EL students between 2002–2003 and 2012–2013 (National Center for Education Statistics, 2015).

Classroom teachers, regardless of their experience, where they teach, or whom they teach, face considerable pressures to take a diverse group of students, with a range of both educational and lived experiences, and provide supportive and responsive learning contexts for all of them. Science teachers are expected to contribute to college readiness for all students and help prepare scientifically and technologically literate individuals who can enter the workforce with twenty-first-century skills such as critical thinking, problem solving, data analysis, and team collaboration (Darling-Hammond, 2006).

However, not all teachers have equal access to resources and instructional supports to enhance such goals in a time where increasing attention is being given to inequities in science, technology, engineering, and mathematics (STEM) learning opportunities. And unfortunately, less attention has been placed on researching effective approaches to supporting this next generation of science teachers, especially novice teachers.[3]

For one, the next-generation secondary science teacher is increasingly likely, even if teaching in a rural or suburban environment, to teach students, such as ELs, who have been traditionally underserved and marginalized in school settings (National Center for Education Statistics, 2015). It has been shown that a minority of novice or experienced teachers currently feels prepared to teach ELs (California Legislative Analyst's Office [LAO], 2007–2008; Gándara, Maxwell-Jolly, & Driscoll, 2005; National Center for Educational Statistics, 2001) and that preservice teacher education programs often do not have an explicit focus throughout all courses and field experiences in teaching subject matter to ELs. Consequently, each year thousands of new teachers enter the profession with little confidence and few tools to teach ELs, and may hold onto deficit perspectives about what ELs can and cannot do in mainstream classrooms.

This book offers a vision for how secondary science teachers, particularly novice ones, can be equipped with tools, both conceptual and practical, to teach effectively and responsively in multilingual science classrooms. These tools promote contextualized inquiry-based science instruction to support science learning and language and literacy development. Instead of just listing strategies for science teachers to emulate in the classroom, this book explicates a model of science teaching that brings together a core set of supportive and responsive science teaching practices. In turn, this model of science teaching informs science curriculum, instruction, and assessment. This book also facilitates a professional understanding of supportive and responsive science teaching for ELs for a range of communities *beyond* teachers, including but not limited to school and district administrators, science teacher educators, professional development consultants, new teacher induction coaches, curriculum developers, and district science coordinators.

Given the need for approaches that are responsive to the institutional and policy contexts that characterize public schooling, we situate our recommendations for science teaching within new priorities for science education and content-area literacy in the United States. We draw heavily on the National Research Council's (2012) *Framework for K–12 Science Education: Practices, Crosscutting Concepts, and Core Ideas*, which sets the stage for the Next Generation Science Standards (NGSS), adopted by thirteen states by 2015 with implementation starting in even more states.

We also position science teaching as integrated with principles from the Common Core State Standards (CCSS) for English Language Arts & Literacy in History/Social Studies, Science, and Technical Subjects (Common Core State Standards Initiative, 2010), now being implemented in forty-three U.S. states. Finally, we situate English language development in terms of approaches for developing ELs' discipline-specific language *practices*, as described by scholars (Lee et al., 2013) and outlined in the document *Framework for English Language Proficiency Development Standards corresponding to the Common Core State Standards and the Next Generation Science Standards* (Council of Chief State School Officers, 2012). Chapter 2 offers a more detailed argument for the focus on discipline-specific language practices that goes beyond commonly used sheltered instruction for ELs.

We bring together priorities in science education and content-area literacy through a model of science teaching that explicates the reciprocal and synergistic relationship between language and content. Our model draws on decades of research into how students learn science, acquire a second language, and more recently how science learning and second language acquisition are related experiences, many of which are described in chapter 1. Most recently, From 2008 to 2012, the Effective Science Teaching for English Language

Learners (ESTELL) Project, funded by the National Science Foundation (NSF), drew on the considerable research into integrating science learning with language and literacy development, including principles outlined in the Center for Research on Education, Diversity, and Excellence (CREDE), to prepare elementary preservice teachers through a redesigned elementary science method course and professional development support for their mentors. The ESTELL Project focused on five instructional practices: collaborate inquiry, contextualization, scientific discourse, English language and literacy development, and complex (scientific) thinking. Results showed that preservice teachers, when exposed to these practices, showed significantly higher performance in EL-related practices than a control group of preservice teachers in a business-as-usual teacher education program (Stoddart, Bravo, Mosqueda, & Solis, 2013). Gains were also evident for EL students of ESTELL-trained teachers (Shaw, Lyon, Stoddart, Mosqueda, & Menon, 2014). Given the effectiveness of various projects at the elementary level, researchers, many of whom were involved in the ESTELL Project, pursued another NSF-funded project to design a similar set of practices at the secondary level. The new effort, Secondary Science Teaching with English Language and Literacy Acquisition (or SSTELLA), aimed to (1) develop tools and offer support to better prepare a new generation of secondary science teachers—teachers that recognize and respond to how ELs learn in science and how ELs have been traditionally underserved and marginalized in school settings—and (2) research the impact of these tools and support on science teachers' beliefs, knowledge, and practices of teaching science to ELs. SSTELLA Project research and development has been informed by a conceptual framework that at its core emphasizes four interrelated instructional practices:

- contextualizing science activity;
- scientific sense-making through scientific and engineering practices;
- scientific discourse; and
- English language and disciplinary-literacy development.

At the writing of this book, preliminary data points toward particular components of these practices that are implemented at a higher level by novices participating in the project intervention and potentially connected to explicit modeling by science method instructors. The work has been carried out programs in California, Arizona, and Texas with vastly different contexts, including plans implementation of Common Core and Next generation Science Standards. Findings are preliminary; nevertheless, the work is grounded in empirical research that has deeply studied individual practices in a range of contexts. Instead of reporting findings this book describes the theory and historical-political-social context guiding SSTELLA as well as ways to use

SSTELLA to inform science activities, units, and even a plan for assessing student learning, all in the service of supporting ELs.

The book is organized into three parts. Part I (chapters 1 and 2) previews the current educational landscape and lays the theoretical foundations of an integrated approach to science learning and language and literacy development, as well as what it means to teach ELs responsively through *disciplinary* language and literacy development. Part II (chapters 3–7) introduces readers more formally to the SSTELLA framework and details each of the four instructional practices to help readers develop an understanding of the practice, its role in supporting ELs, and its connection to CCSS and NGSS, as well as guidance for implementing the practice in multilingual classrooms. Finally, part III (chapters 8–10) applies the SSTELLA framework to the process of science curriculum and assessment planning. In particular, a high school biology unit is described (chapter 8) and deconstructed in terms of SSTELLA practices (chapter 9). Chapter 10 examines how to plan a system of assessment through the same biology unit informed by STELLA. We conclude by revisiting the integrated nature of content-area learning and language and literacy development.

All authors are investigators on the SSTELLA Project. Although the entire book is a collaborative effort among authors (both in intellectual thinking throughout the life of the SSTELLA project and in writing), chapters were assigned to individuals' areas of expertise. All chapters were reviewed by each other as well as additional scholars of the field. Many other individuals on the SSTELLA Project, such as science method instructors and doctoral students, have also contributed their intellectual thinking and tools developed as part of the project (see the acknowledgments in this book).

Secondary Science Teaching for English Learners is designed as a resource for those who may work with, support, or inform secondary science teachers, including but not limited to science teacher educators teaching a science method course, supervisors or teacher mentors of teacher candidates, professional development consultants, curriculum developers, or school/district administrators.

The various chapters, however, are directed at science teachers or candidates themselves to support their development as science teachers in multilingual classrooms. Therefore, many of the chapters present teachers with vignettes to situate both the theory and practice presented within authentic teaching scenarios. Many chapters also provide discussion questions through which teachers and teacher candidates can reflect more deeply and make connections to their own experiences as educators of students who are ELs. Although we focus on preservice education, we have also used this approach with experienced science teachers.

Furthermore, the SSTELLA framework has been used in professional development workshops with cooperating teachers and teacher supervisors, so that these mentors of preservice teachers are better prepared to model, coach, and provide meaningful feedback to teacher candidates during field experiences in linguistically diverse science classrooms. Working closely with mentors increases coherence between coursework and field experiences.

The remainder of this chapter provides a rationale for focusing on teaching *practices* in science teacher preparation and outlines how novices might come to develop these practices through modeling, noticing, and approximating in a science method course. Our goal is to facilitate the development of teacher expertise through three core "teacher as learner" practices: *experiencing*, *noticing*, and *approximating* (Lampert et al., 2013), as well as facilitate a professional understanding of how practices connect to research and national priorities (e.g., standards) in the service of supporting all students in science, particularly ELs.

A Focus on Core Teaching Practices in Science Teacher Education

Teaching is complex. Teachers must have knowledge about their content, knowledge about how to teach content, and knowledge about whom they will be teaching. More importantly, teachers need to understand the connection between content knowledge and pedagogical knowledge (pedagogical content knowledge, or PCK) with particular classroom contexts, and how scientific concepts can be situated within the complex science-related social issues.

For example, just knowing about "what causes the seasons" and "ways to promote collaborative learning through group jobs" is not the same as knowing how collaborative learning environments can lead students to understand what causes the seasons, or how changing seasonal patterns are linked to climate change. However, demonstrating content or pedagogical content knowledge is not the same as engaging in the actual day-to-day intellectual activities of teaching in which knowledge is situated in real life.

Education scholars have been working to develop and investigate a proposed *core* set of ambitious teaching practices in various disciplines that can *best* leverage learning opportunities for a diverse group of students (Grossman & McDonald, 2008; Ball & Forzani, 2009). According to Windschitl, Thompson, Braaten, and Stroupe (2012) these practices would need to (1) be accessible to learners of teaching, even novice ones, (2) be applicable to the everyday work of teaching, and (3) function synergistically to form a cohort model of teaching and learning—so that instructional approaches are grounded in theory of how students learn science, and as prioritized in this book, how students develop disciplinary language and literacy. In science education, Windschitl et al. have argued for a core, drawing on a model-based inquiry approach, consisting of "Constructing the Big Idea," "Eliciting Students' Ideas to Adapt Instruction," "Helping Students Make Sense of Material Activity," and "Pressing for Evidence-Based Explanations."

The SSTELLA framework builds from and extends this core to identify what practices might best leverage learning for ELs in secondary science classrooms. Thus, SSTELLA also stresses big ideas in science, which students can make sense out of when engaged in scientific practices, such as arguing from evidence and constructing explanations. SSTELLA integrates these ideas with a focus on language and literacy development to ensure that sense-making activities and language and literacy opportunities are both contextualized and scaffolded. The key is that this core foregrounds *discipline-specific* practices (a core in mathematics would look different from a core in science) over *generic* teacher behaviors (e.g., "wait time"). Translating these concepts to teacher education means actually engaging preservice teachers *in* the practices versus just talking about the practices.

Research indicates that novices develop teaching expertise by experiencing, noticing/analyzing, and approximating the instructional practices they are being prepared to teach (Abell & Cennamo, 2004; Roth et al., 2011; Sherin, 2004). The figure below represents this cycle centered on core SSTELLA practices. Science teacher educators facilitate this cycle throughout coursework and connection to field experience, as suggested next.

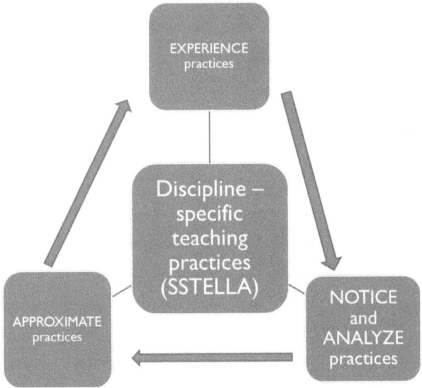

FIGURE I.1
Cycle of "Teacher as Learner"

Experiencing SSTELLA Practices

In a secondary science method course, one way for novices to experience SSTELLA practices is by the instructor actually teaching a science lesson (or part of one) in class with the preservice teachers participating as students. In chapter 8, we outline an instructional unit on teaching natural selection through antibiotic resistance of MRSA (Methicillin-resistant Staphylococcus aureus) that was developed for the purpose of implementation in secondary science methods. Although the unit integrates all SSTELLA practices, it was intended to model a focused practice—disciplinary literacy development for ELs.

The same unit segment was implemented in professional development for experienced secondary science teachers who became mentors for preservice teachers participating in SSTELLA—thus giving mentors and mentees a common experience in which to understand and discuss SSTELLA practices. While experiencing modeled lessons, novices wear multiple hats. They are (1) participating in learning (or relearning) the science content and practices themselves, (2) imagining what middle school or high school students might be experiencing while learning the content, and (3) observing what the instructor does to teach the science (e.g., how does she facilitate questions and answers? Scaffold students' use of evidence?).

Method instructors may also take advantage of videos of classroom teaching to model practices. For instance, as part of the SSTELLA project, video cases were developed depicting experienced secondary science teachers in classrooms with ELs modeling targeted SSTELLA practices. The advantage of videos is that novices can observe teaching in a *real-life* context (more authentic than a lesson modeled in the method class) with opportunities to "replay" events for further noticing and analysis.

Although modeled lessons and video exemplars might be designed to highlight individual practices, such as those forming the SSTELLA framework, the instructor should remind novices that the practices are connected and interdependent. Thus, videos depicting parts of an entire instructional unit portray the integrated nature of practices. In addition, a video shown later in the course can refer back to videos shown earlier in the course to revisit themes across practices. For example, a video targeting model-based inquiry might revisit the theme of "framing a lesson" by referring back to a previously shown video on contextualizing science activities.

Noticing and Analyzing SSTELLA Practices

Preparing novices to become reflective practitioners requires that teacher educators help them "hone in on what is important in a very complex situation" (van Es & Sherin, 2002, p. 573). Both instructor-led lessons and videos can be effective as "cases" to develop this ability to notice and analyze teaching practices. In particular, video cases allow focused attention on specific classroom events, in this case, the SSTELLA practices (Abell & Cennamo, 2004; Ash, 2007; Roth et al., 2011; Sherin, 2004). For the SSTELLA Project, "staged" clips—depicting more traditional teaching methods (i.e., didactic, not contextualized) in conjunction with the exemplar—allowed novices to discern practices and allowed teacher educators to scaffold novices' abilities to notice and interpret science teaching practices in linguistically diverse secondary classrooms.

Method instructors in the SSTELLA Project were often concerned with how to use video cases effectively to promote noticing and analysis. Van Es and Sherin (2002) outline three important characteristics of noticing (pp. 573–75):

1. Noticing involves identifying *what is important* in a teaching situation.
2. Noticing involves *making connections* between specific events and broader principles of teaching and learning.
3. Noticing involves using what *one knows about the context* to reason about a situation.

Novices and instructors must work to establish norms for analyzing videos before using them. Novices must be clear about what noticing involves—it is more than just showing examples of highly refined teaching practice. Noticing with video can be a learning tool to understand the various complex events, interactions, and decisions that characterize science teaching. Norms may include how to participate in the discussion and how to distinguish between *observing* what happens and *making inferences* about teachers and teaching. For example, the goal is never to make value judgments about teachers (i.e., whether they are a "good" or "bad" teacher). Instead, the focus is on what happens (with evidence) in the context of a focused topic (e.g., contextualizing instruction).

As an example, a pair of SSTELLA videos that we have developed depicts a teacher, Mr. L, introducing students to the geologic timeline to help students explore the relationship between geologic time and biological evolution—with a particular focus on the significance of the Cambrian Explosion in the field of evolutionary biology. This video is used purposefully to help novices notice various ways to contextualize instruction, and what it looks like *not* to contextualize instruction (e.g., how students respond differently to the contextualized versus decontextualized lesson, etc.).

Instructors assign teachers the videos to watch before class (each between five and ten minutes long) and then provide targeted prompts for the teachers to respond to and discuss in class. The instructor uses these prompts to help teachers understand what is important to be noticing in terms of contextualized science activity. The instructor also works with novices to generate ideas for alternative approaches in a similar or different context such as a different grade level, subject, or bilingual classroom. The same protocol can be used to deconstruct an instructor-modeled lesson. In both cases, a lesson plan might supplement the video and modeled lesson to provide a more holistic context for the activities. This noticing and analysis contributes to the development of teachers' expertise so that they can begin to approximate the practices (on their way to fully implementing while teaching).

Approximating SSTELLA Practices

Beyond explicit modeling and noticing, novices need opportunities to practice instructional approaches with the student population they are being prepared to teach with effective mentoring and support (Joyce & Showers, 1995; Loucks-Horsley, Hewson, Love, & Styles, 1998; Speck & Knipe, 2001). Both method course activities and field experiences (observation, co-teaching, and student teaching) can provide these opportunities to approximate actual teaching practices.

Approximation in Method Course Activities

A staple of many method courses is some form of microteaching, where novices (individually, in pairs, or in small groups) design a lesson (including a lesson plan) and teach to their peers. Microteaching is advantageous in providing a flexible and safe environment for teachers to hone in on practices and to receive instructor coaching and instructor/peer feedback on these practices.

Before engaging in the development of a "full lesson," teachers might also be called on to approximate *targeted practices* that would be shorter in length. For example, after modeling and noticing/analyzing how to frame a lesson through personally relevant experiences, the teachers might be tasked to take a traditional opening to a lesson (maybe bell work that reviews factual information from the previous day), modify it in ways that will be discussed in chapter 4 ("Contextualizing Science Activity"), and then practice teaching this revised opening to their peers.

Novice science teachers may receive opportunities to develop single-day lessons throughout their teacher education program, but from our experiences are less likely to have opportunities to deconstruct or plan entire curricular units. Thus, another approach is to break the novices into subject-specific groups (i.e., life science, earth science, physical science) and ask them to outline an eight- to ten-day unit plan around a single core idea aligned with NGSS or appropriate state science standards.

As will be discussed in chapters 5 ("Scientific Sense-Making through Scientific and Engineering Practices") and 10 ("Responsive Approaches to Assessing English Learners in Science Classrooms"), we encourage units that explicate (1) a central "big idea," (2) a culminating performance task, and (3) daily learning objectives in addition to the daily classroom activities. From these units, individual novices can develop a full single-day lesson plan to teach in class. From our experiences, it is important not to make novices feel that they should engage in the most ambitious levels of each SSTELLA practice in a single lesson. For one reason—the lesson's focus might preclude deep opportunities for particular practices.

We do feel that every lesson should be *contextualized* somehow, and that novices should try to incorporate elements of other SSTELLA practices (help students make sense of complex science ideas, engage students in the discourse of science, and promote language and literacy development). However, their lesson might focus *deeply* on sense-making (providing a supportive environment for students to engage in the practices of scientists and engineers), discourse (engaging students in talk, including argumentation to make sense of the science), or language and literacy (with ample opportunities to be supported in reading or writing authentic texts).

Effective coaching and feedback on microteaching is essential. Novices can submit drafts of lessons to the instructor for feedback, as well as submit drafts to "critical friends" (such as the other novices in the unit team) for peer feedback. After the lesson (or series of lessons), the instructor facilitates a debrief so that novices identify successes and possible areas of improvement, specifically for the targeted SSTELLA practice (as opposed to focusing predominantly on general strategies like "where to stand in the classroom" and "getting students' attention").

Throughout this process, the instructor scaffolds the development of teacher expertise by communicating clear criteria for implementing different levels of each practice, and by providing multiple opportunities for focused feedback on each novice teacher's understanding and implementation of the practices. We find this to be a more supportive context for learning, rather than providing less structured opportunities for "just getting up there and trying."

In the appendix, we provide the SSTELLA Practices Progression, which outlines each subpractice across increasingly higher levels of implementation. This progression provides a more concrete context for understanding the practices, and can be a useful tool for science teacher educators in helping novices notice and approximate the practices.

Approximation in Fieldwork

A limitation of micro-teaching in a method course is that novices do not get opportunities to interact with actual secondary science students and thus opportunities to elicit and respond to actual student ideas. Therefore, field placement greatly enhances teacher learning by doing and increases knowledge about student concepts and experiences. However, there may be several hurdles for science teacher educators to build on field experience opportunities—do novices have a field placement while taking a methods course? How frequently? Do novices have opportunities to develop their own lesson and take full responsibility of a lesson? If no, then requiring students to teach an entire lesson using the SSTELLA framework may not be possible.

As a compromise, students could lead more focused activities in their field placement to enact and thus analyze very particular instructional moves. For example, novices could facilitate a "science talk" for the purpose of (1) approximating discourse moves such as asking open-ended questions, encouraging student-student talk, and probing for evidence and (2) analyzing teacher and student discourse moves in relation to discussing big ideas in science. This activity has the advantage of taking less instructional time and supplementing a cooperating teacher's lesson (not replacing it). Novices can still apply what they have learned from noticing and interpreting videos of other teachers throughout the course to analyze the science talk. In some programs novices participate in site-based learning experiences where they observe a classroom in groups, then work with student groups to approximate talk moves, and conclude the experience outside of the classrooms through a debrief with the method instructor and classroom teacher to notice particular instructional decision, student ideas, and reflect on engaging in talk moves.

Closing Remarks

We hope this book serves as an important tool to bridge professional understanding of effective science teaching practices for ELs to the explicit modeling, noticing, and approximating of these practices. We provided insights and guidance to move the next generation of secondary science teachers from "qualified" science teachers to supportive and responsive science teachers who come to understand the importance of providing rigorous, authentic, and meaningful instruction for all students, particularly ELs.

Notes

1. All statistics from Kena et al. (2014).
2. English learner (EL), English language learner (ELL), or limited English proficient students (LEPS) are terms used in many official state and federal policies to

refer to students acquiring a second language in school. We acknowledge that these terms are problematic because these students are very diverse from age of arrival to the United States, to proficiency in the primary language, and prior academic preparation among other significant differences. ELs cannot be defined as a homogeneous or absolute group; moreover, state assessments used to classify EL designations and levels differ from state to state. The term *EL* moreover is a restrictive identifier that fails to acknowledge non-English primary languages and the emergence of bilingual abilities. However, it is the term we anticipate most readers will have familiarity with, which is why we do not use terms that are more recently being used in research and some schooling and policy contexts, such as *emergent bilinguals*.

3. The term *novices* will be used throughout this book to indicate teachers who are beginning a career in science teaching. Although most of our focus is on novices in their teacher preparation program (preservice teachers or teacher candidates), novices in their first several years of teaching also need considerable, albeit different, support and mentoring.

References

Abell, S. K., & Cennamo, K. S. (2004). Videocases in elementary science teacher preparation. In J. Brophy (Ed.), *Advances in research on teaching: Using video in teacher education* (Vol. 10, pp. 103–30). New York, NY: Elsevier JAI.

Ash, D. (2007). Using video data to capture discontinuous science meaning making in non-school settings. In R. Goldman, R. Pea, B. Barron, & S. J. Derry (Eds.), *Video research in the learning sciences* (pp. 207–26). Mahwah, NJ: Erlbaum.

August, D., Carlo, M., Dressler, C., & Snow, C. (2005). The critical role of vocabulary development for English language learners. *Learning Disabilities Research & Practice, 20*, 50–57.

Ball, D. L., & Forzani, F. M. (2009). The work of teaching and the challenge for teacher education. *Journal of Teacher Education, 60*(5), 497–511.

California Legislative Analysts Office (LAO) 2007-08 Budget Book—Education Analyses, February 21, 2007. *California Legislative Analyst's Office report, 2007-08.*

National Governors Association Center for Best Practices & Council of Chief State School Officers. (2010). *Common Core State Standards for English language arts and literacy in history/social studies, science, and technical subjects.* Washington D.C.: Authors.

Darling-Hammond, L. (2006). Constructing 21st-century teacher education. *Journal of Teacher Education, 57*(3), 300–314.

Gándara, P., Maxwell-Jolly, J., & Driscoll, A. (2005). *Listening to teachers of English language learners: A survey of California's teachers' challenges, experiences, and professional development needs.* Santa Cruz, CA: Center for the Future of Teaching and Learning.

Grossman, P., & McDonald, M. (2008). Back to the future: Directions for research in teaching and teacher education. *American Educational Research Journal, 45*(1), 184–205.

Joyce, B., & Showers, B. (1995). *Student achievement through staff development.* White Plains, NY: Longman.

Kena, G., Aud, S., Johnson, F., Wang, X., Zhang, J., Rathbun, A., Wilkinson-Flicker, S., & Kristapovich, P. (2014). The condition of education 2014 (NCES 2014-083). Washington, DC: U.S. Department of Education, National Center for Education Statistics.

Lampert, M., Franke, M. L., Kazemi, E., Ghousseini, H., Turrou, A. C., Beasley, H., . . . & Crowe, K. (2013). Keeping it complex using rehearsals to support novice teacher learning of ambitious teaching. *Journal of Teacher Education, 64*(3), 226–43.

Lee, O., Maerten-Rivera, J., Penfield, R. D., LeRoy, K., & Secada, W. G. (2008). Science achievement of English language learners in urban elementary schools: Results of a first-year professional development intervention. *Journal of Research in Science Teaching, 45*(1), 31–52.

Lee, O., Quinn, H., & Valdes, G. (2013). Science and language for English language learners in relation to Next Generation Science Standards and with implication for Common Core State Standards for NEglish language arts and mathematics. *Educational Researcher, 42*(4), 223–33.

Loucks-Horsley, S., Hewson, P. W., Love, N., & Stiles, K. E. (1998). *Designing professional development for teachers of science and mathematics.* Thousand Oaks, CA: Corwin Press.

National Center for Education Statistics. (2015). *The condition of education 2015* (NCES 2015-144), English Language Learners. Washington, DC: U.S. Department of Education.

National Research Council. (2012). *A framework for K–12 science education: Practices, crosscutting concepts, and core ideas.* Washington, DC: National Academy Press.

Roth, K. J., Garnier, H. E., Chen, C., Lemmens, M., Schwille, K., & Wickler, N. I. Z. (2011). Videobased lesson analysis: Effective science PD for teacher and student learning. *Journal of Research in Science Teaching, 48*, 117–48.

Ryan, C. (2013). *Language use in the United States: 2011, American community survey reports.* U.S. Department of Commerce. Economics and Statistics Administration. U.S. Census Bureau.

Shaw, J. M., Lyon, E. G., Stoddart, T., Mosqueda, E., & Menon, P. (2014). Improving science and literacy learning for English language learners: Evidence from a pre-service teacher preparation intervention. *Journal of Science Teacher Education, 25*(5), 621–43.

Sherin, M. G. (2004). New perspectives on the role of video in teacher education. In J. Brophy (Ed.), *Advances in research on teaching: Using video in teacher education* (Vol. 10, pp. 1–27). New York, NY: Elsevier JAI.

Speck, M., & Knipe, C. (2001). *Why can't we get it right? Professional development in our schools.* Thousand Oaks, CA: Corwin Press.

Stoddart, T., Bravo, M. A., Mosqueda, E., & Solis, J. L. (2013). Restructuring pre-service teacher education to respond to increasing student diversity. *Research in Higher Education Journal, 9*, 1–14.

Stoddart, T., Pinal, A., Latzke, M., & Canaday, D. (2002). Integrating inquiry science and language development for English language learners. *Journal of Research in Science Teaching, 39*(8), 664–87.

van Es, E. A., & Sherin, M. G. (2002). Learning to notice: Scaffolding new teachers' interpretations of classroom interactions. *Journal of Technology and Teacher Education, 10*(4), 571–96.

Villegas, A. M., & Lucas, T. (2002). *Educating culturally responsive teachers: A coherent approach.* Albany, NY: State University of New York Press.

Wilson, S. M., Floden, R. E., & Ferrini-Mundy, J. (2001). *Teacher preparation research: Current knowledge, gaps, and recommendations.* Document R-1-3, 1–83. Center for the Study of Teaching and Policy.

Windschitl, M., Thompson, J., Braaten, M., & Stroupe, D. (2012). Proposing a core set of instructional practices and tools for teachers of science. *Science Education,* 96(5), 878–903.

I

FOUNDATIONS FOR LANGUAGE, LITERACY, AND SCIENCE INTEGRATION

1

The New Vision for Secondary Science Education

Connecting Language and Literacy to Science Learning

Patricia Stoddart

Overview

THIS CHAPTER INTRODUCES readers to recent shifts in secondary science education, namely the development of Next Generation Science Standards (NGSS) and Common Core State Standards (CCSS), including standards for Literacy in Science and Technical Subjects. Throughout, I build an argument that the relationship between language, literacy, and science learning is reciprocal and synergistic. Contextualized, inquiry-based science is a vehicle for developing all students', but particularly english learners' (ELs'), academic language and literacy. Simultaneously, students' use of language in these meaningful and authentic contexts allows for deeper understanding of core ideas in science and engagement with the practices of scientists and engineers. This chapter sets the stage to understand more responsive approaches to teaching ELs in secondary science classrooms, which will be the focus of chapter 3.

Introduction: Shifts in the National Standards Movement

There have been two significant recent shifts in the national standards movement as this book was being written in 2015. First, there has been a nation-wide effort toward developing common standards in core academic subjects, commonly referred to as the "Common Core" (or CCSS) for mathematics and English language arts (ELA), including literacy in social studies, science, and technical subjects (National Governors Association Center for Best Practices and Council of Chief State School Officers, 2010).

The vision for a common set of science standards was developed through the National Research Council's (2012) document, *A Framework for K–12 Science Education: Practices, Crosscutting Concepts, and Core Ideas* (or the *Framework*), which subsequently informed the Next Generation Science Standards, or NGSS (Achieve, 2013). Second, informed by research on teaching and learning, both CCSS and NGSS recognize for the first time the critical role played by academic language and literacy in the learning of school subjects by *all* students. These new standards offer an unprecedented opportunity to improve the development of K–12 students' understanding of subject matter in general but in particular create the means to begin to close the achievement gap between ELs and native English speakers.

Research on student learning has long recognized the central role language and literacy play in the learning of school subjects (Bunch, 2013; Cazden, 2001; Halliday, 1993; Halliday & Martin, 1993; Mehan, 1979; Schleppegrell, 2004; Vygotsky, 1987; Wells, 1999). Now recognition of this fundamental relationship is embedded in the new standards. The NGSS based on the *Framework* identifies core science ideas and cross-cutting themes that students would learn in cognitively more complex ways as they progress through their K–12 science education. NGSS views science activities (reflected in scientific and engineering practices) as *language intensive* practices.

This recognition of the role of academic language and literacy in content learning is echoed in the Common Core State Standards for ELA, mathematics, and literacy in social studies, science, and technical subjects (Common Core State Standards, 2010a, 2010b). In the NGSS, science content and language intersect as students, for example, construct oral and written explanations and engage in argument from evidence (Cheuk, 2012; Lee, Quinn, & Valdés, 2013), two practices that echo CCSS for ELA. Concurrently, the ELA literacy standards for science and technical subjects require that students engage with technical (e.g., lab reports, scientific research articles) and nontechnical (e.g., newspaper articles, letters to the editor) texts that are discipline specific by writing arguments, translating written information into visual forms (e.g., tables, graphs), and comparing/contrasting findings presented in various sources. These new standards require that all teachers of all school subjects must also be teachers of academic language.[1]

Language and Subject Matter

The acquisition and use of academic language and literacy is fundamental to the learning of school subjects. Each subject matter, including mathematics, science, and social studies, has its own linguistic register, that is, norms and patterns of language use essential to the practice of the discipline (Halliday, 1978). To acquire disciplinary knowledge (i.e., theories, principals, facts), a student must, therefore, learn to read, write, and speak the language of the subject domain. In essence, each K–12 student must become multilingual. In any given day, she or he is required to speak math, science, social studies, or English literature with teachers who are fluent in that disciplinary language but do not view themselves as teachers of a second language.

The majority of secondary school teachers view their responsibility as presenting the subject matter content and covering the set curriculum, not teaching language and literacy (Stoddart et al., 2002). They assume these skills have been taught in the elementary school grades or in a different class. The language and literacy practices needed to learn secondary school subjects are quite different from the basic reading and writing skills taught in grades K–6. As the content gets more specialized and advanced in the transition from elementary to secondary school, there is a transition in the language and literacy demands for students related to the acquisition of new academic genres (Abreu, Bishop, & Presmeg, 2002; Queen, 2002).

It is important for teachers to understand the many types of language that a student uses inside and outside the classroom, how these language forms influence their learning, and how they are developed (Bunch, 2013; Cummins, 1994). On a daily basis, K–12 students use social language—the everyday language all humans use to communicate and interact socially with others in their environment—for example, the language of the home, street, bus, playground, and popular culture. To succeed in school, however, students need to become proficient in the language of the education system, which is used for formal academic learning, that is, academic language.

Academic English is the language of U.S. classrooms, of the academic disciplines (science, history, literary analysis), of texts and literature, and of extended, reasoned discourse (Gersten, Baker, Shanahan, Linan-Thompson, Collins, & Scarcella, 2007). It is more abstract and decontextualized than conversational English and students need time and support to become proficient in all academic areas. In most classrooms academic language is not explicitly taught so acquiring the academic language and literacy of each subject domain is a challenge for the majority of students.

Academic Language

Developing proficiency in academic language includes learning to listen, speak, read, write, and reason about subject-area content material. It refers to abstract, complex, and challenging language that will eventually permit you to participate successfully in the mainstream classroom. Academic language is the set of words, grammar, and organizational strategies used to describe complex ideas, higher-order thinking processes, and abstract concepts and involves more than the acquisition of vocabulary but includes understanding disciplinary approaches to reasoning such as comparing, classifying, synthesizing, evaluating, and inferring (Zwiers, 2008). It is both general and content specific. Some academic words and linguistic processes are used across all content areas (such as *interpret, analyze, source*), whereas others pertain to specific subject areas (*photosynthesis, mitosis, density*, and *inertia* for science; *constitution, revolutionary*, and *medieval* for history; *investment, recovery*, and *income* for economics).

The learning of academic language is complicated by the fact that many English words have more than one meaning. Johnson, Moe, and Baumann (1983) found that among the identified nine thousand critical words for elementary grade students, 70 percent had more than one meaning. Science terms often carry an everyday meaning and specific science meaning (e.g., *property, test, volume, matter*).

Multiple meaning words can be found across content areas, where within each domain, a different specialized meaning is intended. *Solution* in science, for example, can mean when one thing is dissolved in another. In math, the term refers to the answer and steps taken to solve a problem, while in social studies the intended meaning can be the act of ending a dispute or the payment of a debt. In science, precision with specialized language is essential for understanding and "doing" science. *Observe* and *see* seem to be interchangeable, but in science the word *observe* means to use all of your senses and to look closely at something, often for long periods of time.

It is also important to remember that academic language is more than specific content vocabulary words related to particular topics but involves such things as relating an event or a series of events to someone who was not present, being able to make comparisons between alternatives and justify a choice, knowing different forms and inflections of words and their appropriate use, and possessing and using content-specific vocabulary and modes of expression in different academic disciplines such as mathematics and social studies (Goldenberg, 2008, p. 9). This level of language learning is essential for students to succeed in school and students need time and support to become proficient in all academic areas.

The Challenge for English Learners

ELs face a significant challenge in learning academic subjects because they must learn the subject matter content at the same time they are developing a second language. Large proportions of ELs are designated as "long-term ELs" (Short, 2011), meaning they struggle with the academic aspects of language that may impede them from accessing content-area subject matter, such as math, science, and social studies in an English instructional medium (August & Shanahan, 2006; Hakuta, Butler, & Witt, 2000). Wong Fillmore (2007), for example, found that when ELs have not learned the academic language used in mathematics courses and in instructional texts, they will "need help learning it or they will find language to be an insuperable barrier to learning" (p. 337).

Even in schools recognized for working effectively with ELs, it can take three to five years to develop English oral proficiency and four to seven years to develop academic English proficiency (Hakuta et al., 2000). As ELs are developing their English proficiency, a widening gap continues to grow between ELs and native English speakers, since ELs simultaneously attend to language and content learning.

This problem is exacerbated by the separation between the teaching of subject matter and the teaching of language and literacy to ELs. Many ELs do not have access to rigorous subject-matter instruction and are relegated to remedial instructional programs because it is assumed that proficiency in English is a prerequisite to learning content (Garcia, 1993; Garrison & Kerper Mora, 1999; Gutierrez, 2002; Lee, 2005; Moll, 1992; Moschkovich, 1999).

The consequence of this separation between subject matter instruction and English language development (ELD) is that the majority of language minority students do not have access to rigorous subject-matter instruction or the opportunity to develop academic language—the specialized, cognitively demanding language functions and structures that are needed to understand, conceptualize, symbolize, discuss, read, and write about topics in academic subjects (Cummins, 1981; Lacelle-Peterson & Rivera 1994; McGroaty, 1992; Minicucci & Olsen, 1992; Oakes, 1990; Pease-Alvarez & Hakuta, 1992). In most ELD classes, ELLs acquire basic social communication skills but less readily acquire the complex subject-specific language skills required for academic success. It is not surprising that the academic progress of language minority students is significantly behind that of their native English-speaking peers.

The most recently published National Association for Educational Progress report shows that in core academic subjects—mathematics, science, and reading—the scores of Latino students are on average twenty points below those of White students. Gaps in achievement actually increase from elementary school to secondary school (National Center for Education Statistics, 2011). ELs performed well below their English-speaking peers under each state's prior standards (Goldenberg, 2013).

One solution is to teach academic subjects to ELLs in their native language while they acquire English language proficiency (Cummins, 1989; Garcia, 1997). However, a chronic shortage of bilingual teachers, particularly those who are also qualified to teach subject matter such as science or mathematics, means that few ELLs receive content instruction in their primary language (California Department of Education, 2014). An alternative approach, the essence of this book, is to integrate the teaching of academic subjects with second language acquisition (Baker & Saul, 1994; Casteel & Isom, 1994; Lee & Fradd, 1998; Mohan, 1990; Rosebery, Warren, & Conant, 1992; Snow, Met, & Genesee, 1991).

Integrating the Teaching of Subject Matter and Academic Language and Literacy

Research on second language immersion programs finds that contextualized, content-based instruction in students' second language can enhance the language proficiency of ELLs with no detriment to their academic learning (Cummins, 1981; Genesee, 1987; Lambert & Tucker, 1972; McKeon, 1994; Met, 1994; Swain & Lapkin, 1985). The subject-matter content provides a meaningful context for the learning of language structure and functions, and the language processes provide the medium for analysis and communication of subject-matter knowledge. The context of language use refers to the degree to which language provides learners with meaningful cues that help them interpret the content being communicated—visual cues, concrete objects, and hands-on activities.

In primary language development, children begin to understand utterances by relating them to sensory motor activities and the physical context (Krashen, 1985). In the development of a second language this relationship needs to be explicitly communicated in instruction. The use of language in the teaching of school subjects, however, is often decontextualized. Context-reduced or decontextualized language occurs when there is little other than the spoken language to provide information (McKeon, 1994). Examples include lectures, many of which provide little or no support for meaning, or students reading a book with no illustrations, having only the text to rely on to facilitate comprehension. This poses particular problems for students developing English language proficiency who rely heavily on context cues to understand a lesson. Since much of school language is context-reduced, ELLs often find themselves in a world of meaningless words.

A significant amount of recent research has demonstrated that integrating the teaching of academic language and literacy into subject-matter instruction significantly increases the achievement of ELs in learning across the subject areas, including science (August, Branum-Martin, Cardenas-Hagan, & Francis, 2009; Lee & Buxton, 2013; Lee, Maerten-Rivera, Penfield, LeRoy, & Secada, 2008; Stoddart, Pinal, Latzke, & Canaday, 2002) and mathematics (Abedi & Herman, 2010; Abt Associates Inc. & Education Development Center Inc., 2011; Beal, Adams, & Cohen, 2010; Friend, Most, & McCrary, 2009).

The Reciprocal Relationship between Science Learning and Language/Literacy Development

In a typical secondary science class, there are often more new vocabulary and technical science terms presented than there are in a foreign language class (Lee, 2013). Typically, science teachers have presented scientific vocabulary and concepts via decontextualized lectures and/or "cookbook"-style labs. Students are expected to memorize terms and engage in teacher-directed lab activities without a coherent understanding of the epistemic or conceptual learning goals, or how and why we come to develop science concepts via science and engineering practices (Duschl, 2008; National Research Council, 2007).

Research in science education has indicated that this approach not only impedes conceptual understanding, but is also inauthentic to science and engineering disciplines and/or how we employ science and engineering in the service of understanding and solving complex real-world problems (Achieve, 2013; American Association for the Advancement of Science, 1993; National Research Council, 1996, 2000, 2007, 2012).

Context-reduced or decontextualized language occurs when the teacher provides little more than the spoken language to deliver information (McKeon, 1994). Examples include (1) direct instruction with no visuals, gestures, graphical/multimedia representations, or change in speech to increase accessibility to content, (2) opportunities for students to read without illustrations, reading strategies, or interaction with other students to facilitate comprehension, (3) or even labs or problems to solve (e.g., stoichiometry, laws of motion) without any embedded context to help students see real-world applications and relevance to their own lives outside of school. In primary language development or the learning of a second language words acquire meaning by being related to a specific physical object (a ball, dog, tree, the sky), an action (Daddy gone, shake hands, drink milk), or a social context (party, picnic, school)—they are given context.

The context of language use refers to the degree to which language provides learners with meaningful cues that help them interpret the content being communicated—visual cues, concrete objects, and hands-on activities. In primary language development, children begin to understand utterances by relating them to sensory motor activities and the physical context (Krashen, 1985). In the development of academic language this relationship needs to be explicitly communicated in instruction.

Science instruction has the potential to provide a supportive environment for the contextualized use of language. Inquiry-based science activities (described more in chapter 5) engage students in the exploration of scientific phenomena whereby language is explicitly linked to objects, processes, hands-on experimentation, and naturally occurring events in the environment. In other words, language and content are contextualized (Baker & Saul, 1994; Casteel & Isom, 1994; Lee & Fradd, 1998; Rodriguez & Bethel, 1983; Rosebery et al., 1992; Stoddart et al., 1999).

Thus, learners engage in authentic communicative interactions, such as describing, hypothesizing, modeling, analyzing, explaining, and justifying, which all promote purposeful language (Lee & Fradd, 1998). Students can communicate their understanding, both to the teacher and to each other, in a variety of formats, for example, in writing, orally, drawing, and creating tables and graphs (Lee & Fradd, 1998).

The opportunity for language development through use in a scientific context can be a language learning experience at the same time as it can be a science learning experience (Rosebery et al., 1992). In science, language serves to structure the way concepts are developed, organized, and communicated (Kaplan, 1986; Lemke, 1990; Newman & Gayton, 1964). Inquiry involves more than hands-on activities; it also involves active thinking and discourse around activities. Rosebery et al. (1992) emphasize argumentation and collaborative inquiry as ways that students can use language authentically to examine scientific claims and the very nature of science: "The heart of the approach is for students to formulate questions about phenomena that interest them; to build and criticize theories; to collect, analyze and interpret data; to evaluate hypotheses through experimentation, observation and measurement; and to communicate their findings" (Rosebery et al., 1992, p. 65).

The relationship between science learning and English language and literacy development, therefore, can be viewed as reciprocal and synergistic. Through the *contextualized* and *authentic* use of language in scientific practices, students develop and practice complex language forms and functions. Simultaneously, through the use of language functions such as explanations and arguments in science investigations, students make sense of abstract core science ideas and enhance their conceptual understanding as well as understanding of the nature of science (Driver, Newton, & Osborne, 2000; Stoddart et al., 2002).

Empirical Evidence for the Integrated Approach

In promoting a specific model of science instruction, it is important to evaluate the empirical evidence that demonstrates that the approach positively impacts the science achievement of diverse learners. Over the past fifteen years (from 2000), a number of projects have demonstrated just this. The projects (1) LASERS, (2) Seeds of Science/Roots of Reading, (3) the Imperial Valley Project in Science, (4) SIFA, (5) P-SELL, and (6) CREDE have produced research on the relationship between the integration of science, language, and literacy instruction and EL student achievement in science, language development, reading, and writing. These studies have all reported significant improvements in EL science and literacy achievement as a result of the interventions.

LASERS (Language Acquisition through Science Education in Rural Schools), funded by the National Science Foundation (NSF), is a local systemic change project with seven school districts in central California with large numbers of ELs. The project used inquiry science as a context for implementing pedagogy that integrated language and literacy development into cognitively demanding science learning through cooperative learning and cultural and linguistic contextualization (Stoddart et al., 1999; Stoddart, 2005; Stoddart et al., 2002). In LASERS, the development of scientific understanding was promoted through the integration of contextualized science inquiry and discourse supported by elementary teachers through hands-on science activities and science talk. In a series of studies using both performance and standardized assessment, ELs in LASERS classrooms showed significant achievement gains. In three consecutive summer schools, twelve hundred limited English proficient students made significant gains in academic language and science concepts measured on the Woodcock Munoz standardized assessment of academic language and concept maps (Stoddart et al., 1999). Students were also tracked over three years in two participating schools districts. Students (n = 1,300) who were in a LASERS-trained teachers' classroom for one and two years scored significantly higher on the SAT-9 in reading, language, mathematics, and science than students who were not in a LASERS teacher classroom (Stoddart, 2005).

The NSF-funded Seeds of Science/Roots of Reading project involved science educators and literacy educators in creating and testing an integrated literacy-science curriculum. Reading instruction (texts, routines for reading, word level skills, vocabulary, and comprehension instruction) was integrated into inquiry-based science (Cervetti, Pearson, Barber, Hiebert, & Bravo, 2007).

The integrated curriculum was tested in twenty second and third grade classrooms over the course of either four or eight weeks against twenty-four comparison classrooms (twelve where science was taught alone and twelve where literacy was taught alone). Students were assessed pre- and post-instruction on science understanding, science vocabulary, and reading comprehension in science. The researchers found positive outcomes for ELs not only in the area of science understanding but also in literacy and vocabulary development when measured against the comparison groups. ELs made equivalent gains on all science measures and most literacy measures to their English-speaking counterparts.

Analysis of the Science Instruction for All (SIFA) project data describes the impact of an instructional intervention designed and implemented to promote achievement of science and literacy among culturally and linguistically diverse students located in the greater San Francisco Bay Area (Baquedano-López, Solís, & Kattan, 2005; Bravo & Garcia, 2004; García & Baquedano-López, 2007; Ku, Bravo, & Garcia, 2004; Ku, Garcia, & Corkins, 2005; Solís, 2005).

Over the course of three years, the SIFA study implemented a curricular intervention in six schools and with twenty-one teachers in third and fourth grade classrooms, in which each classroom received a year of literacy and science integrated instruction. The study focused on two science units at grades 3 and 4 where science and literacy assessments were administered at the onset and end of the intervention. The results indicate participating students, regardless of linguistic and cultural background, experienced significant growth in their science achievement and understandings of scientific writing. The curriculum had a positive effect on the students' achievement and learning of science among students whose home language was either Chinese or Spanish.

Similar positive student learning outcomes were found in the Imperial Valley Project in Science, where Amaral, Garrison, and Klentschy (2002) studied the effects of instruction that allowed students to conduct firsthand science investigations and keep a science journal to reflect on science activities and develop writing proficiency. The instructional focus was based on the idea that hands-on science activities establish an authentic purpose and offer increased opportunities for the development of writing skills (Holliday, Yore, & Alvermann, 1994).

The P-SELL project implemented an integrated science and literacy curriculum for third grade ELs in urban elementary schools within an environment increasingly driven by high-stakes testing and accountability and examined students' science achievement at the end of the first-year implementation. The study involved 1,134 third grade students at seven treatment schools and 966 third grade students at eight comparison schools. Students who received the integrated science and language curriculum showed a statistically significant increase in science achievement than students in the comparison group

(Lee et al., 2008). Furthermore, the subpopulation of 818 ELs in P-SELL classrooms showed significant improvements in science understanding compared to control group students (Lee et al., 2008).

Theory into Practice

Findings from the research and development projects just described provide compelling evidence that integrating the teaching of academic language and literacy into science teaching has a positive impact on the achievement of ELs. However, as can be seen from the context of the studies, little attention has been given to ELs in secondary science classrooms. Currently, most secondary science teachers do not view themselves as teachers of academic language and literacy. Covering the extensive science curriculum in states across the country demands considerable time and attention.

The challenge is to demonstrate to teachers that language and literacy development is a critical and productive component of science teaching that facilitates understanding of core science ideas. Integration of language and literacy development with science learning requires more than mandates. Teachers need explicit models and exemplars of practice to scaffold their innovation. This book provides not only the why—the rationale for the use of integrated pedagogy—but also the how with a road map for classroom implementation.

The need for these changes is urgent. The rapidly changing language populations in U.S. classrooms provide a demographic imperative for change. Language minority groups have traditionally been underserved in science, technology, engineering, and mathematics (STEM) education and are underrepresented in STEM degrees and careers (National Academy of Sciences, 2010; Oakes, Joseph, & Muir, 2004; Rodriguez, 2004). On the National Association for Educational Progress, the science scores of Latino students are on average twenty points below those of White students and this achievement gap has persisted for over forty years (National Center for Education Statistics, 2006b, 2011).

This bimodal pattern of K–12 and college student achievement in STEM subjects is strongly correlated with the bimodal distribution of workers in the labor force, with minority groups being overrepresented in low-skill, low-paid occupations and underrepresented in high-tech and professional occupations (Maldanado & Farmer, 2006; National Council of La Raza, 2007). This racial and economic stratification exacerbated by the education system presents a significant challenge to the stability of U.S. society.

In the next chapter, we discuss who exactly ELs are, research and policies around the teaching of ELs in content-area classrooms, and how a *responsive* approach to teaching ELs forms the foundation of the reciprocal relationship between science learning and language/literacy development.

Note

1. For this chapter, we use the term *academic* language and literacy, meaning the variety of ways language is used to learn school subjects. In the subsequent chapter, we detail exactly what type of language is used in the context of learning science, which we refer to as *disciplinary language.*

References

Abedi, J., & Herman, J. (2010). Assessing English language learners' opportunity to learn mathematics: Issues and limitations. *Teachers College Record, 112*(3), 723–46.

Abreu, G., Bishop, A., & Presmeg, N. (2002). Mathematics learners in transition. In *Transitions between contexts of mathematical practices* (pp. 7–21). Dordrecht, Netherlands: Springer.

Abt Associates Inc. & Education Development Center Inc. (2011). Math and science education with English language learners: Contribution of the DR K–12 program. Working paper. Retrieved from http://abtassociates.com/Working-Papers/2012/Math-and-Science-Education-with-English-Language-L.aspx

Achieve. (2013). *Next generation science standards.* Washington, DC: Author.

Amaral, O. M., Garrison, L., & Klentschy, M. (2002). Helping English learners increase achievement through inquiry-based science instruction. *Bilingual research journal, 26*(2), 213–39.

American Association for the Advancement of Science. (1993). *Benchmarks for science literacy.* Retrieved from www.project2061.org/publications/bsl

August, D., & Shanahan, T. (2006). Executive summary: Developing literacy in second-language learners: Report of the National Literacy Panel on Language-Minority Children and Youth. Retrieved February 16, 2009, from www.bilingual-education.org/pdfs/PROP2272.pdf

August, D., Branum-Martin, L., Cardenas-Hagan, E., & Francis, D. J. (2009). The impact of an instructional intervention on the science and language learning of middle grade English language learners. *Journal of Research on Educational Effectiveness, 2*(4), 345–76.

Baker, L., & Saul, W. (1994). Considering science and language arts connections: A study of teacher cognition. *Journal of Research in Science Teaching, 31*(9), 1023–37.

Baquedano-Lopez, P., Solís, J. L., & Kattan, S. (2005). Adaptation: The language of classroom learning. *Linguistics and Education, 6*, 1–26.

Beal, C. R., Adams, N. M., & Cohen, P. R. (2010). Reading proficiency and mathematics problem solving by high school English language learners. *Urban Education, 45*(1), 58–74.

Bishop, A. J., & Presmeg, N. (2002). Mathematical acculturation, cultural conflicts, and transition. In G. D. Abreu, A. J. Bishop, & N. Presmeg (Eds.), *Transitions between contexts of mathematical practices* (pp. 193–212). Dordrecht, Netherlands: Kluwer Academic Publishers.

Bravo, M., & Garcia, E. (2004). *Learning to write like scientists: English language learners science inquiry and writing understanding in responsive learning contexts.* National Clearinghouse for English Language Acquisition.

Bunch, G. C. (2013). Pedagogical language knowledge: preparing mainstream teachers for English learners in the new standards era. *Review of Research in Education, 37*(1), 298–341.

California Department of Education. (2014). Data & statistics reports. Retrieved from www.cde.ca.gov/ds

Casteel, C. P., & Isom, B. A. (1994). Reciprocal processes in science and literacy learning. *The Reading Teacher, 47*(7), 538–45.

Cazden, C. B. (2001). *Classroom discourse: The language of teaching and learning* (2nd ed.). Portsmouth, NH: Heinemann.

Cervetti, G. N., Pearson, P. D., Barber, J., Hiebert, E., & Bravo, M. A. (2007). Integrating literacy and science: The research we have, the research we need. In M. Pressley, A. K. Billman, K. Perry, K. Refitt, & J. Reynolds (Eds.), *Shaping literacy achievement.* New York, NY: Guilford.

Cheuk, T. (2012). Relationships and convergences found in the Common Core State Standards in Mathematics (practices), Common Core State Standards in ELA/Literacy(student portraits), and a framework for K–12 science education (science & engineering practices). Unpublished work. Stanford University, Understanding Language Initiative.

Common Core State Standards Initiative. (2010a). *Application of Common Core State Standards for English language learners.* Retrieved from www.corestandards.org

Common Core State Standards Initiative. (2010b). *Common Core State Standards for English language arts & literacy in history/social studies, science, and technical subjects.* Retrieved from www.corestandards.org

Common Core State Standards. (2015). *K–12 standards English language arts.* District of Columbia and the Department of Defense Education Activity (DoDEA).

Cummins, J. (1981). *Bilingualism and minority-language children.* Toronto, Canada: OISE Press.

Cummins, J. (1989). *Empowering minority students.* Sacramento, CA: California Association for Bilingual Education.

Cummins, J. (1994). Knowledge, power, and identity in teaching English as a second language. In F. Genesee (Ed.), *Educating second language children: The whole child, the whole curriculum, the whole community* (pp. 33–58). Cambridge, UK; New York, NY: Cambridge University Press.

Doherty, R. W., Hilberg, R. S., Epaloose, G., & Tharp, R. G. (2002). Standards performance continuum: Development and validation of a measure of effective pedagogy. *Journal of Educational Research, 96*, 78–89.

Doherty, R. W., & Pinal, A. (2004). Joint productive activity, cognitive reading strategies, and achievement. *TESOL Quarterly, 38.*

Driver, R., Newton, P., & Osborne, J. (2000). Establishing the norms of scientific argumentation in classrooms. *Science Education, 84*(3), 287–312.

Duschl, R. (2008). Science education in three-part harmony: Balancing conceptual, epistemic, and social learning goals. *Review of Research in Education, 32*(1), 268–91.

Friend, J., Most, R., & McCrary, K. (2009). The impact of a professional development program to improve urban middle-level English language learner achievement. *Middle Grades Research Journal, 4*(1), 53–75.

García, E. (1988). Effective schooling for Hispanics. *Urban Education Review, 67*(2), 462–73.

García, E. (1993). Language, culture and education. *Review of Research in Education,* 51–98.

García, E. (1997). The education of Hispanics in early childhood: Of roots and wings. *Young Children,* 5–14.

Garcia, E., & Baquedano-Lopez, P. (2007). Science instruction for all: An approach to equity and access in science education. *Language Magazine, 6*(6), 24–31.

Garrison, L., & Kerper Mora, J. (1999). Adapting mathematics instruction for English-language learners: the Language-Concept Connections. *Changing the Faces of Mathematics: Perspectives on Latinos,* 35–48.

Genesee, F. (1987). *Learning through two languages: Studies of immersion and bilingual education* (Vol. 163). Cambridge, MA: Newbury House.

Genesee, F. H. (1991). Second language learning in school settings: Lessons from immersion. In *Bilingualism, multiculturalism, and second language learning: The McGill conference in honour of Wallace E. Lambert* (pp. 183–201). Hillsdale, NJ: Lawrence Erlbaum Associates.

Gersten, R., Baker, S. K., Shanahan, T., Linan-Thompson, S., Collins, P., & Scarcella, R. (2007). Effective literacy and English language instruction for English learners in the elementary grades. IES practice guide. NCEE 2007-4011. Washington, DC: National Center for Education Evaluation and Regional Assistance, Institute of Education Sciences, U.S. Department of Education.

Goldenberg, C. (2008). Teaching English language learners: What the research does—and does not—say. *American Educator, 32*(2), 8–11.

Goldenberg, C. (2013). Unlocking the research on English learners: What we know—and don't yet know—about effective instruction. *American Educator, 37*(2), 4.

Goldman, R., Pea, R., Barron, B., & Derry, S. J. (Eds.). (2007). *Video research in the learning sciences.* Mahwah, NJ: Erlbaum.

Gutiérrez, K. D. (2002). Studying cultural practices in urban learning communities. *Human Development, 45*(4), 312–21.

Hakuta, K., Butler, Y. G., & Witt, D. (2000). How long does it take English learners to attain proficiency? The University of California Linguistic Minority Research Institute Policy report 2000-1. *Adolescence, 40,* 503–12.

Halliday, M. A. (1978). *Language as social semiotic: The social interpretation of language and meaning.* London: Arnold.

Halliday, M. A. (1993). Towards a language-based theory of learning. *Linguistics and Education, 5*(2), 93–116.

Holliday, W. G., Yore, L. D., & Alvermann, D. E. (1994). The reading–science learning–writing connection: Breakthroughs, barriers, and promises. *Journal of Research in Science Teaching, 31*(9), 877–93.

Johnson, D. D., Moe, A. J., & Baumann, J. F. (1983). *The Ginn word book for teachers, a basic lexicon: A reference tool for classroom teachers.* Lexington, MA: Ginn.

Kaplan, R. B. (1986). Culture and the written language. In J. M. Valdes (Ed.), *Culture bound: Bridging the culture gap in language teaching* (pp. 8–19). New York, NY: Cambridge University Press.

Krashen, S. (1985). The input hypothesis: Issues and implications. New York, NY: Longman.

Ku, Y. M., Bravo, M. A., & Garcia, E. (2004) Science instruction in culturally and linguistically diverse classrooms. *NABE Journal of Research and Practice, 2*(1).

Ku, Y. M., Garcia, E., & Corkins, J. (2005). Impact of the instructional intervention on science achievement of culturally and linguistically diverse students. Paper presented at the American Educational Research Association, Montreal, Canada.

Lacelle-Peterson, M. W., & Rivera, C. (1994). Is it real for all kids? A framework for equitable assessment policies for English language learners. *Harvard Educational Review, 64*(1), 55–76.

Lambert, W. E., & Tucker, G. R. (1972). *Bilingual education of children: St. Lambert experiment.* Rowley, MA: Newbury House.

Lee, O. (2005). Science education with English language learners: Synthesis and research agenda. *Review of Educational Research, 75*(4), 491–530.

Lee, O., & Buxton, C.A. (2013). Integrating science and English proficiency for English language learners. *Theory Into Practice, 52*(1), 36–42.

Lee, O., & Fradd, S. H. (1998). Science for all, including students from non-English-language backgrounds. *Educational Researcher, 27*(4), 12–21.

Lee, O., Maerten-Rivera, J., Penfield, R., LeRoy, K., & Secada, W. (2008). Science achievement of English language learners in urban elementary schools: Results of a first-year professional development intervention. *Journal of Research in Science Teaching, 45*(1), 31–52.

Lee, O., Quinn, H., & Valdés, G. (2013). Science and language for English language learners in relation to Next Generation Science Standards and with implications for Common Core State Standards for English language arts and mathematics. *Educational Researcher, 42*(4), 223–33.

Lemke, J. (1990). *Talking science: Language, learning, and values.* Norwood, NJ: Ablex.

Maldonado, C., & Farmer, E. I. (2007). Examining Latinos' involvement in the workforce and postsecondary technical education in the United States. *Journal of Career and Technical Education, 22*(2).

McGroaty, M. (1992). The societal context of bilingual education. *Educational Researcher, 21*, 7–10.

McKeon, D. (1994). Language, culture and schooling. In F. Genessee (Ed.), *Educating second language children: The whole child, the whole curriculum, the whole community* (pp. 15–32). New York, NY: Cambridge University Press.

Mehan, H. (1979). *Learning lessons: Social organization in the classroom.* Cambridge, MA: Harvard University Press.

Met, M. (1994). Teaching content through a second language. In F. Genesee (Ed.), *Educating second language children: The whole child, the whole curriculum, the whole community* (pp. 159–82). New York, NY: Cambridge University Press.

Minicucci, C., & Olsen, L. (1992). *Programs for secondary limited English proficient students: A California study* (No. 5). National Clearinghouse for Bilingual Education.

Mohan, B. A. (1990). LEP students and the integration of language and content: Knowledge structures and tasks. Washington, DC: U.S. Department of Education, Office of Educational Research and Improvement, Educational Resources Information Center.

Moll, L. C. (1992). Bilingual classroom studies and community analysis: Some recent trends. *Educational Researcher, 21*(2), 20–24.

Moschkovich, J. (1999). Supporting the participation of English language learners in mathematical discussions. *For the Learning of Mathematics,* 19(1), 11–19.

National Academy of the Sciences. (2010). *Expanding underrepresented minority participation: America's science and technology talent at the crossroads.* (A research report co-sponsored by the Committee on Underrepresented Groups and the Expansion of Science and Engineering Workforce Pipeline; Committee on Science, Engineering, and Public Policy; Policy and Global Affairs; National Academy of Sciences; National Academy of Engineering, Institute of Medicine). Washington, DC: National Academies Press. Retrieved from www.nap.edu/catalog/12984.html

National Center for Education Statistics. (2006a). *The condition of education in 2006* (NCES 2006-071). Washington, DC: U.S. Department of Education, Institute of Education Sciences.

National Center for Education Statistics. (2006b). *The nation's report card: Science 2005* (NCES 2006–466). Washington, DC: U.S. Department of Education, U.S. Government Printing Office.

National Center for Education Statistics. (2011). *The nation's report card: Science 2009.* Washington, DC: U.S. Department of Education.

National Council of La Raza. (2007). *The status of Latinos in the labor force.* Retrieved February 15, 2009, from http://nclr.forumone.com/content/publications/down load/50719

National Governors Association Center for Best Practices and Council of Chief State School Officers. (2010). *Council of Chief State School Officers.* Retrieved from www. ccsso.org/Contact_Us.html#sthash.CGBr7WNL.dpuf

National Research Council. (1996). *National science education standards.* Washington, DC: National Academy Press.

National Research Council. (2000). *The digital dilemma: Intellectual property in the information age.* Washington, DC: National Academy Press.

National Research Council. (2007). *Taking science to school: Learning and teaching science in grades K–8.* Washington, DC: National Academy Press.

National Research Council. (2010). *A framework for K–12 science education.* Washington, DC: National Academies Press.

National Research Council. (2012). *A framework for K–12 science education: Practices, crosscutting concepts, and core ideas.* Washington, DC: National Academies Press.

Newman, S. S., & Gayton, A. H. (1964). Yokuts narrative style. In D. Hymes (Ed.), *Language and culture in society* (pp. 372–81). New York, NY: Harper-Row.

Next Generation Science Standards. (2010). National Academy of Sciences managed the first of two steps in the creation of the *Next Generation Science Standards* by developing *A framework for K–12 science education*. Washington, DC: National Academies Press.

Next Generation Science Standards. (2013). *A science framework for K–12 science education*. Developed by the National Research Council. Washington, DC: National Academies Press.

Oakes, J. (1990). Multiplying inequalities: The effects of race, social class, and tracking on opportunities to learn mathematics and science. Santa Monica, CA: Rand Corp.

Oakes, J., Joseph, R., & Muir, K. (2004). Access and achievement in mathematics and science: Inequalities that endure and change. In J. Banks & C. Banks (Eds.), *Handbook of research on multicultural education* (2nd ed., pp. 69–90). San Francisco, CA: Jossey Bass.

Pease-Alvarez, L., & Hakuta, K. (1992). Enriching our views of bilingualism and bilingual education. *Educational Researcher, 21*(2), 4–19.

Queen, J. A. (2002). *Student transitions from middle to high school: Improving achievement and creating a safer environment*. Larchmont, NY: Eye on Education.

Rodriguez, A. J. (2004). *Turning despondency into hope: Charting new paths to improve students' achievement and participation in science education*. Southeast Eisenhower Regional Consortium for Mathematics and Science Education SERVE. Tallahassee, FL. Retrieved from www.serve.org/Eisenhower

Rodriguez, I., & Bethel, L. J. (1983). An inquiry approach to science and language teaching. *Journal of Research in Science Teaching, 20*(4), 291–96.

Rosebery, A. S., Warren, B., & Conant, F. R. (1992). Appropriating scientific discourse: Findings from language minority classrooms. *Journal of the Learning Sciences, 21*, 61–94.

Schleppegrell, M. J. (2004). *The language of schooling: A functional linguistics perspective*. Mahwah, NJ: Lawrence Erlbaum.

Snow, M. A., Met, M., & Genesee, F. (1991). A conceptual framework for the integration of language and content instruction. In P. A. Richard-Amato & M. A. Snow (Eds.), *The multicultural classroom* (pp. 27–38). Los Angeles, CA: Longman.

Solis, J. L. (2005). Locating student classroom participation in science inquiry and literacy activities. In J. Cohen, K. McAlister, K. Rolstad, & J. MacSwan (Eds.), *ISB4: Proceedings of the 4th International Symposium on Bilingualism*. Somerville, MA: Cascadilla Press.

Stoddart, T. (2005). *Improving student achievement with the CREDE Five Standards Pedagogy*. Technical Report No. (J1). Santa Cruz, CA: University of California, Center for Research on Education, Diversity and Excellence.

Stoddart, T., Canaday, D., Clinton, M., Erai, M., Gasper, E., Latzke, M., Pinales, A., & Ryan, J. (1999). *Language acquisition through science inquiry*. Symposium presented at the annual meeting of the American Educational Research Association, Montreal, Canada.

Stoddart, T., Pinal, A., Latzke, M., & Canaday, D. (2002). Integrating inquiry science and language development for English language learners. *Journal of Research in Science Teaching, 39*(8), 664–87.

Swain, M., & Lapkin, S. (1985). *Evaluating bilingual education: A Canadian case study.* Clevedon, England: Multilingual Matters.

Vygotsky, L. S. (1987). The collected works of L. S. Vygotsky: The fundamentals of defectology (Volume 2). Edited by Robert W. Rieber and Aaron S. Carton. New York, NY: Plenum Press.

Wells, G. (1999). *Dialogic inquiry: Towards a socio-cultural practice and theory of education.* Cambridge: Cambridge University Press.

Wong Fillmore, L. (2007). English learners and mathematics learning: Language issues to consider. *Assessing Mathematical Proficiency,* 333–44.

Zwiers, J. (2008). *Building academic language.* London: Newark International Reading Association.

2

Responsive Approaches for Teaching English Learners in Secondary Science Classrooms

Foundations of the SSTELLA Framework

Jorge Solís and George C. Bunch

Overview

CHAPTER 1 ADDRESSED a new vision for secondary science education that leverages the synergistic and reciprocal relationship between language and content instruction in science classrooms. Building on research supporting an integrated approach in the teaching of language and science for English learners, chapter 2 provides relevant background on how language designations are used to describe English learners (ELs), what it means to use an integrated approach in the classroom, and how generic approaches to teaching ELs is not sufficient for promoting success for ELs in secondary school. Lastly, chapter 2 describes how new disciplinary approaches for teaching science can and should be used as opportunities for engaging in rich and varied language and literacy practices in science classrooms with all students.

Introduction: Who Are "English Learners" in Secondary Classrooms?

Nearly two decades ago, August and Hakuta (1997) argued that extending existing theories and methodologies of content-area learning and second language literacy was the highest research priority for improving the schooling for students moving across the curriculum who were still being assisted in developing English language proficiency (ELP) (often referred to as English learners, or ELs).

One reason cited was that content-area learning had been neglected in research on ELs, putting the "issue of the language instruction in the foreground and content area learning in the background" (August & Hakuta, 1997, p. 345). In the two decades since, considerable research has helped us understand how to support ELs in content-area classrooms. Nevertheless, teachers often do not get access to preparation for this form of discipline-specific and responsive teaching for ELs. If they do have some focus on ELs in teacher preparation programs or in-service professional development opportunities, they often focus on generic strategies that help ELs comprehend content but do not prepare teachers for how to support ELs in engaging in, and developing, the language and literacy practices of the disciplines.

Therefore, what *all* teachers need to know about teaching ELs remains a primary concern for new and experienced teachers working in multilingual classrooms settings across academic subjects (Bunch, 2013; Faltis et al., 2010; Flores & Smith, 2009; Goldenberg, 2013; Lee, Quinn, & Valdés, 2013; Snow & Fillmore, 2002; Téllez & Waxman, 2006; Valdés, Bunch, Snow, & Lee, 2005). Before unpacking what the research says about responsive language *and science* teaching, it is critical to know just what it means to be an "English learner."

Variability of language backgrounds, home and community experiences, and academic skills exist within the population often referred to as ELs, a term that has been used both to refer to student characteristics as well as an official designation that schools assign to students. Although ELs in secondary school have a similar potential to acquire a second language as their elementary school counterparts, these "older-school age ELs" differ in terms of their academic trajectories as language learners and the kinds of academic support needed to help them excel in school (Solís, 2009).

Older, school-age ELs are more diverse linguistically and academically, ranging from "newcomer" students who have arrived in the United States during their secondary schooling to "long-term ELs" (LT-ELs) who have attended schools in the United States since elementary school yet have not acquired the ELP to do grade-level academic work in English and so therefore still require language support services. This latter group comprises a significant proportion of the secondary EL population in the United States (Menken & Kleyn, 2010).[1]

Although many LT-ELs have acquired near grade-level oral English language fluency, they may not yet have developed the full disciplinary language and literacy required for content-area learning (e.g., in science, mathematics, and social studies). Thus, other students and even the teacher may not recognize the type of academic support needed for LT-ELs, since these students often can converse with few problems, and may even seem indistinguishable from fluent English speakers.

Finally, it is important to acknowledge that students who were once considered ELs but have since been reclassified or redesignated as "Fluent English Proficient" (often referred to as RFEP) may still be in need of support in developing aspects of the language and literacy associated with the academic disciplines, just as many of their monolingual English-speaking classmates. We consider the SSTELLA practices outlined in this book appropriate for ELs and former ELs from a range of backgrounds, although additional supports, including the use of students' home languages where possible, will be essential for newcomer students.

One way to view the language development of ELs is to consider what it is that they are able to do in more than one language thinking of them as "emergent bilinguals" rather than solely English learners (García & Kleifgen, 2010). Emergent bilingualism is a descriptor that reminds students, educators, and policy makers that ELs are not, in fact, only learners and users of English, but also have the potential to be developing linguistic resources for a wide variety of functions in their home languages. Focusing on English, the dominant and often exclusive language of content-area instruction in U.S. secondary schools, Valdés, Bunch, Snow, & Lee (2005) have compared what students at different developmental stages of English learning can do in academic settings (see table 2.1). *Incipient bilinguals* refers to ELs who may be new to U.S. schooling (i.e., newcomer ELs) and who are not usually placed in mainstream classrooms. *Ascendant bilinguals* refers to students who are on their way to acquiring English and are therefore ascendant bilinguals. Lastly, *fully functional bilinguals* are sometimes termed ELs despite being proficient in English and their native language.

The comparisons in table 2.1 serve as a reminder that, as we discuss the SSTELLA approaches and practices for "ELs" throughout this book, it is important to remember the diversity (linguistic, social, cultural, and academic) within ELs that requires different types of supports. When possible, we highlight how supports might differ for different EL groups, but the assumption is that teachers will adapt the practices based on their particular student population.

The challenge for all secondary ELs is to learn subject matter, and demonstrate their learning, through a variety of academic literacy genres (e.g., writing a lab report in science, explaining a geometric proof in mathematics, and writing a persuasive essay in language arts) (Lucas, 1997). While this literacy transition is a typical secondary school experience for all students (Abreu, Bishop, & Presmeg, 2002; Queen, 2002), secondary school ELs are often being asked to engage in these literacy tasks at grade levels beyond their demonstrated proficiency and without appropriate supports. For example,

TABLE 2.1
Characteristics of Students Known as English Language Learners

Incipient Bilinguals	Ascendant Bilinguals	Fully Functional Bilinguals
Comprehend very little oral English	Generally comprehend oral English well; may have problems understanding teacher explanations on unknown topics.	Are native-like in their comprehension of oral English
Comprehend very little written English	May have trouble comprehending written English in textbooks as well as other materials; have limitations in academic and technical vocabulary	Well-prepared students have no problems in comprehending most written English materials; have trouble reading problems and not language problems
Produce very little oral English	Produce English influenced by their first language; may sometimes be difficult to understand; may have trouble expressing statements, challenging others	Produce oral English effortlessly; can carry out presentations and work effectively in groups; can challenge, contradict, explain, and so on; traces of the first language may be detected in their pronunciation or word choice.
Produce very little written English	Written production may contain "errors" that make it difficult for teachers to focus on students' ideas. Completion of written assignments and tests takes longer.	Depending on students' previous experience with writing, written production may contain errors typical of monolingual basic writers. Dysfluencies influence may still be present.

Source: Valdés et al., 2005, p. 155.

secondary school ELs might be exposed to technical, low-frequency content-based vocabulary (e.g., *isotope, mitosis, tectonic plates*), and writing for specialized and sometimes unfamiliar purposes (e.g., writing a grant proposal for a school project, developing a model of energy consumption in their home) while still acquiring English language proficiency.

Recognizing the different academic trajectories of these students is important in designing responsive learning contexts. In this regard, integrating literacy and language instruction with content-area instruction addresses the need to teach ELs disciplinary-specific literacy tasks *without* denying them access to participating in the authentic practices at the heart of the discipline (Bunch, 2013; Janzen, 2008; Meltzer & Hamann, 2005; Short & Fitzsimmons, 2007; Schleppegrell, 2004).

EL Policy Contexts across the United States

Labels for students, such as EL, English language learner (ELL), or limited English proficient (LEP), are the varied identifiers used by local, state, and national educational agencies to describe and monitor students who are learning English in school. These labels have changed over time and as such require some articulation and acknowledgment of the social, cultural, and historical forces that have shaped them.

As Kibler, Valdés, and Walqui (2014) have pointed out, terminology to refer to students in the process of learning English at school has been "fraught with values, ideologies, and complications" (p. 436). Our use of the term *EL* is consistent with Kibler, Valdés, and Walqui's (2014) rationale for their use of the term *English language learner*, often used synonymously with *EL* in the United States, even as we agree with the limitations of these terms. There is an inherent emphasis on the learning of English neglecting both the home language and possible development of two languages that is obscured with this and other labels. Yet we reluctantly use the term EL here because it is recognized by educators and policy makers as describing the populations we are concerned with.

Terminology as described above is complicated but valuable to acknowledge for teachers. EL, ELL, and LEP are official K–12 school designations used to help monitor and support achievement of language minority students as a result of historical and persistent marginalization of these students from the mainstream curriculum. However, these terms often fail to acknowledge the varying ELP levels of different ELs as described above, and more importantly, may misconstrue or devalue the resources and language skills that students may *already* possess, both in English and in their home languages.

Furthermore, each term highlights the development of English over the development of a *bilingual* student. As opposed to EL, ELL, or LEP, referring to students learning a second language as *emergent bilingual students* highlights the "potential in developing their bilingualism" and not a limitation in comparison to those students who already speak English (Garcia, 2009, p. 322). Moreover, *emergent bilingual students* places some value on using students' range of language skills from each language they are using and learning as a resource for the other. The key point is not to be misled by a label and to understand and value the linguistic resources that students bring and know how best to support them in science classrooms.

Inconsistencies in how schools, districts, and states identify and track the progress of ELs as they transition through the K–12 system are another major challenge for secondary teachers, who usually only see their large number of students (often over one hundred and sometimes close to two hundred in number) less than one hour per day each. Recognizing the different academic trajectories of these students is important in designing appropriate educational support and teacher training.

For example, EL students are commonly tracked into permanent or long-term remedial ESL (English as a Second Language)/English immersion courses, which may provide little access to content, such as science, and by extension discipline-specific language and literacy. Valdés (1999) notes this persistent dilemma facing schools as one where students who at this stage need to acquire English but existing mainstream secondary school faculty have little exposure to ELs and limited models or guidance on how English develops as a second language.

In this regard, infusing literacy and language instruction across content-area subjects addresses the need to explicitly teach academic language tasks authentic to each academic discipline without denying access to participating in the authentic practices at the heart of the discipline (Bunch, 2013; Janzen, 2008; Meltzer & Hamann, 2005; Short & Fitzsimmons, 2007; Schleppegrell, 2004).

State and local policies can constrain how particular school systems identify, assess, and monitor ELs. ELs' ELP, usually as measured by standardized English language tests and sometimes also as scores on academic achievement tests in English language arts (ELA), is used to determine whether or not students should be considered an EL or a fluent English speaker (Heritage, Walqui, & Linquanti, 2015).

Federal guidelines for defining ELs describe students (1) who are within schooling age engaged in matriculating in elementary or secondary school, (2) whose native language is a language other than English, and finally, (3) who have difficulty speaking, reading, writing, or understanding English enough that it would deny them the ability to score as English proficient in a state's English proficiency assessment. Home language surveys are the primary way that states begin the process of determining potential ELs. Currently schools across the United States do not use common standardized and validated home language surveys. The home language survey begins the process that usually leads to newly matriculating students to get assessed to determine their ELP. State assessments are used to at least annually to assess a student's ELP.

What it means to be "English proficient" and no longer an EL, however, differs according to what state assessment is used because state assessments can conceive of and weigh language skills differently. The California English Language Development Test (CELDT), for example, weighs each of the four language domains (i.e., listening, speaking, reading, and writing) equally in arriving on a composite score for ELs in California for determining ELP.

In contrast, the Texas English Language Proficiency Assessment System (TELPAS) uses a composite score of English language skills where reading accounts for 75 percent of the composite score and writing 15 percent (Linquanti & Cook, 2013). In addition to the ELP tests used in every state to classify ELs, states can use other criteria for reclassifying ELs including content-area achievement scores, teacher evaluations, and parent or guardian input.

Reclassifying or not reclassifying ELs can have a major impact on the long-term success of ELs, especially those in secondary school who critically need access to core curriculum to improve their prospects of academic success before graduation (Estrada, 2014). ELs who are reclassified in one district quite possibly could continue as EL students in another district and therefore be long-term ELs as a result of the timing of assessments, how teacher evaluations are weighed, and varied knowledge of EL education by district administrators. In effect, state English language assessments and "exit policies" do not always adequately describe a student's language and literacy capabilities. ELs can possess varying levels of academic content knowledge and literacy levels learned in their home language not captured by state English language assessment or teacher evaluations.

Curricular programs designed to support diverse groups of ELs matriculating across the United States also represent disparate state curricular programs that in turn have varied impact on English language development and science achievement. For example, an analysis of the National Assessment of Education programs from 2000 to 2005 on the learning of science for fourth graders found significant higher science achievement for Hispanic ELs in states with stronger bilingual education programs compared to states with dominant structured English immersion programs (McEneaney, López, & Nieswandt, 2014).

ELs in fourth grade in states like Arizona and California, where most ELs received primarily English-only support, scored lower in science compared to states like Texas and New Mexico with stronger bilingual education programs. Arizona, for example, currently uses a particular type of structured English immersion that requires four hours of daily English language development instruction for all ELs apart from other subject areas like science and mathematics instruction. Recent evidence, however, indicates that this kind of language instruction is leading to greater segregation for ELs from other fluent English speakers and decreased opportunities to learn rigorous and grade-level content knowledge (Rios-Aguilar, Gonzalez Canche, & Moll, 2012). For this reason, understanding the state curricular approaches for supporting academic achievement for ELs is important.

Importantly, the need for careful designs for language and literacy support does not end once students exit the official "EL" classification. When students are exited from their EL classification, because they meet state criteria for ELP, they are often reclassified as fluent English proficient (RFEP) students and no longer ELs. EL reclassification indicates that EL students have acquired, according to state and district criteria, sufficient English language skills to engage mainstream classes.

Nevertheless, schools need to provide careful and focused support of reclassified students as they continue to matriculate through the K–12 system in classrooms where the language of instruction is English and often without sheltered language instruction. Reclassified ELs in mainstream classroom need opportunities to learn rigorous and grade-appropriate language and content knowledge. A consistent theme throughout this book is that using the SSTELLA framework has the potential to increase ELs' opportunity to receive quality academic content instruction.

An Integrated Approach to Science Learning and Language Development

Research on language development has offered useful and varied theoretical perspectives for understanding how people acquire and learn language and content (e.g., Bialystok, 2001; Fillmore, 1991; Krashen, 1981; Ochs & Schieffelin, 1989) with varying attention to the role of social context and individual traits. This section provides an overview of some key concepts for understanding how second language learners use and acquire language, and how those ideas correspond to the SSTELLA framework and secondary school contexts of science teaching and learning.

From a Cognitive to Sociocultural Perspective

In educational settings, shifts in how learning is viewed have led to shifts in classroom teaching. SSTELLA draws on sociocultural perspectives toward second language acquisition and content-area learning. While cognitivist perspectives of learning, which center on how individuals internally make sense of the external environment, typify how most teachers were prepared to teach, educational scholars are recognizing and placing a greater focus on the sociocultural contexts of learning (Johnson, 2006).

Sociocultural perspectives of language learning emerge from insights from cross-disciplinary studies in cultural psychology, anthropology, English, linguistics, and sociology. At their heart, sociocultural perspectives of language learning "view language use in real-world situations as fundamental, not ancillary, to learning" (Zuengler & Miller, 2006, p. 37). From this perspective, language learning requires practice in using language *for authentic purposes* rather than mere *exposure* to target language functions.

Through a sociocultural lens, Lantolf (2000, 2011) asks foundational questions related to second language acquisition, such as "How do humans coordinate their actions to achieve desired ends?," "How do certain contexts help or hinder learning?," and "How is language related to learning?" This "social turn" away from viewing learning, especially second language learning, as internal mental processes allows teachers to reconsider learning as *actions* and *processes* rather than objects and internal mental entities (van Lier & Walqui, 2012).

These perspectives draw principally from work by Vygotsky (1980; 1986; 1987), who proposed that thinking and speaking are interrelated and therefore not independent processes. According to Lantolf (2000) and inspired by Vygotsky, thinking and speaking (or language use) make up a dialectic unity where "publicly derived speech completes privately initiated thought" (p. 7). That is, social interaction and collaborations between more and less capable interlocutors (participants in conversation) fortify and extend individual thinking and performance.

Social Interaction and Learning

It is important to understand that language competence by itself is not a precondition for social interaction and communication. This understanding applies to all learners, including ELs. While language use is a primary tool for learning cultural knowledge, humans are predisposed to social interaction regardless of language proficiency. In fact, research by linguistic anthropologists suggests that human beings possess certain dispositions and qualities that enable face-to-face interaction regardless of formal language skills because they are equipped with a "human interaction engine" (Levinson, 2006). Human beings are able to read and respond to how conversations are unfolding, not just react through their behaviors. Comprehension happens through the construction of *mutual* knowledge shared within a community.

Communicating in any community, like classrooms or workplace settings, relies on appropriately using and interpreting cultural tools including language for specific tasks. However, being able to produce a common ideal language itself is not the only means for understanding and participating in communities. We know, for example, that people can communicate effectively and in complex ways through sign language and other visual forms of manipulating the body. Human beings have the capacity for knowing when to take on different communicative roles such as when to be a listener, when to be a speaker, and how to figure out how to include others in conversations and when conversations are over.

This capacity and predisposition for social interaction is the human interaction engine. This realization is important for classroom teachers who feel that ELs need to engage in simplified and limited interactional roles in the classroom due to their English proficiency. Simplified interactional classroom roles for ELs reduce opportunities to practice using English for a range of real-world purposes. Unfortunately, some studies of second language classrooms show that EL students can be in classrooms where they are asked to use repetitive, unauthentic, and infantilizing language more appropriate for early elementary school grades than for adolescents (Duff, 2000; Poole, 1992). Adolescent ELs can manage complex social roles in classrooms by using their "human interaction engine" (Levinson, 2006).

All students possess this fully functioning human interaction engine, with some very rare exceptions for extreme speech and language disabilities. Students are primed to take on complex social and intellectual tasks that, while requiring additional support, should not be reduced or diminished based on language proficiency levels. The human interaction engine can and should be used to engage ELs in tasks and activities that leverage these abilities for performing a wide range of typical classroom tasks and activities like taking part in observations of an experiment, being part of group presentations, and analyzing and solving problems with a partner.

Pedagogical Scaffolding

A sociocultural focus on social interaction and collaboration as a basis for learning sets the stage for the notion of *scaffolding* (Wood, Bruner, & Ross, 1976; Rogoff, 2003; Tharp & Gallimore, 1991). Vygotsy (1987) explains that "children are capable of doing much more in collective activity or under the guidance of adults" than they are by themselves (p. 88). In essence, scaffolding refers to the *temporary* assistance of others as one learns to perform more and more complex tasks, just as scaffolding on a building is meant to be temporary and taken away as more work is completed.

For learning, as one becomes more skilled at a task, less assistance is needed, resulting in the temporary nature of scaffolding. In the case of classroom contexts, while teachers are usually thought of as the "more capable other" providing assistance, students themselves may be the ones sometimes providing the valuable scaffolding to each other or even to the teacher (Walqui & van Lier, 2010). Research on a range of linguistically diverse classrooms shows that "scaffolding occurs routinely as students work together on language learning tasks" (Donato, 2004, p. 52), providing assistance like giving oral and written feedback, clarifying instructions, and solving problems. Lantolf (2000) refers to the use of tools such as language, and the surrounding social context, as evidence for how humans continuously act in the world indirectly through these social processes.

As children gain more control over tools and knowledge, the kind of assistance needed shifts. Students initially need assistance by more capable others or adults, but this assistance is needed less as learners acquire new skills. In this respect, scaffolding is dependent on a student's development of knowledge and skills over time (Tharp & Gallimore, 1991). The overarching principle of language *as a tool* for thinking and learning presents clear implications for the teaching and learning of science. This principle is especially true in multilingual classrooms, which might have multiple languages spoken, a range of proficiencies across different modalities (listening, speaking, reading, and writing) as well as countless lived experiences.

It is important to emphasize that scaffolding is different than just providing support for student learning. Teacher support or help refers to any kind of instructional move that reinforces, clarifies, or augments student comprehension of what is being taught. Scaffolding, on the other hand, is "a special kind of help that assists learner to move toward new skills, concepts, or level of understanding" (Gibbons, 2002, p. 10). That is, it does not mean merely simplifying academic tasks for ELs. Scaffolding requires assistance that is temporary and focused on a specific learning goal. The heart of scaffolding, in contrast to other forms of teacher support, is that it occurs in response to student questions and contributions. In the words of Walqui and van Lier (2010), for scaffolding to work effectively, "the teacher's role is not to control the learner but to support and encourage the learner's emergent autonomy" (p. 25).

This is not to say that the teacher's role is unimportant. The use of structured and flexible teacher scaffolding moves is critical for promoting ELs' access to science learning. The teacher can anticipate and plan for some student responses and areas for development, but teachers need to engage students in dialogue and open conversations in order to assess their actual comprehension and subsequent scaffolding needs. Providing temporary, structured, and focused support to ELs offers them more equal footing on learning science content that is naturally part of the content and language development process. That is, scaffolding is a necessary support for all learners, but in the case of ELs, scaffolding needs to address goals and objectives concerned with acquiring a second language as well as curricular content. Figure 2.1 illustrates the continuum of pedagogical scaffolding that is important to consider in working with ELs (adapted from Walqui & van Lier, 2010).

Features of Pedagogical Scaffolding (adapted from Walqui and van Lier, 2010)

More Planned	Features of Pedagogical Scaffolding	Considerations for ELs
	Continuity and Change: Class routines that change or stay the same	Provides ELs with a steady context to practice new language skills
	Supportive Environment: environment of safety and trust; experiential links and bridges	ELs can trust teacher and peers to support their new learning including miscues or unsuccessful attempts. There are safe ways for ELs to communicate ideas such formulaic expressions.
	Intersubjectivity: mutual engagement; being "in tune with each other	ELs are part of core class activities and students work together to understand each other.
	Flow: student skills and learning challenges in balance; students fully engaged	ELs are fully engaged in challenging and relevant activities.
	Contingency: tasks procedures and tasks progress dependent on actions of learners	ELs language is connected from previous interactions to new interactions.
	Emergence, or Handover/takeover: Increasing importance of learner agency	ELs become more autonomous and take on full range of language functions.

More
Improved

FIGURE 2.1
Features of Pedagogical Scaffolding (adapted from Walqui and van Lier, 2010)

The SSTELLA practices outlined in this book aspire to be consistent with pedagogical visions such as those presented by Walqui and van Lier (2010), where scaffolding for ELs is seen as part of a larger classroom learning ecology where ELs are apprenticed into engagement with disciplinary practices, and their related language and literacy components, rather than merely "helped" through a series of tasks with predetermined outcomes.

Focus on Contexts, not "Critical Periods"

Can secondary school ELs still learn English, even though they are not young children anymore? Are there certain biological or developmental impediments that prevent older, school-age ELs from acquiring a second language? These questions are sometimes heard surrounding the educational success or failure of secondary school ELs related to age of acquisition, length of residence in a new country, and ultimate attainment of the second language (Muñoz & Singleton, 2011; Samway & McKeon, 2007).

The existence of a "critical period" for second language acquisition, such as has been found to exist for young children learning their first language, has been debated by researchers for decades, with convincing evidence finding that declines in second language learning among adults are more a function of gradual declining cognitive capacity due to aging, along with environmental factors that make it difficult to learn a second language, rather than a result of attempting to learn a second language after a certain age (Hakuta, Bialystok, & Wiley, 2003). In fact, long-term English language learners in secondary school do not transition to more advanced English proficiency levels due to a variety of issues not related to the critical period hindering their development such as not being assessed properly for specific learning disabilities and being exposed to disparate literacy approaches (Menken & Kleyn, 2010).

In addition to advanced aging having a negative effect on second language acquisition, socioeconomic status, like formal education, also has an impact on the potential for learning a second language for adult ELs. For secondary ELs, therefore, much more important than a critical period for learning a second language is understanding that a supportive *learning context* is critical for ELs. While there is some research that suggests some maturational factors influence the acquisition of a second language (Birdsong & Molis, 2001), an abundance of research shows that secondary school ELs who receive appropriate support can, over time, acquire a second language successfully (Collier & Thomas, 2004; Tembe, 2008). Time is important, as some research has indicated that ELs need anywhere from five to seven years to acquire grade-level proficiency and be reclassified as no longer an English learner (Hakuta, 2011; Hakuta, Butler, & Witt, 2000).

This does not imply, however, that ELs cannot do meaningful and challenging academic work in English as they develop English; in fact, it is precisely opportunities to do such work, with proper support, that will contribute to their English language development. Additionally, the social contexts that immigrant ELs occupy and negotiate in school with teachers and peers—that is, who they have opportunities to engage with meaningfully and how they perceive their social status—have a significant impact on their language learning (Carhill, Suárez-Orozco, & Páez, 2008).

The remainder of this chapter describes varied approaches to teaching ELs, situating SSTELLA within these approaches and distinguishing it from some widely known approaches. The goal is to provide a foundational background on SSTELLA practices as they relate to ELs, including the important distinctions between mainstream teaching practices, EL-specific teaching practices, and science-specific teaching practices.

Beyond "Just Good Teaching"

A problem arises when improving teaching practices for ELs is interpreted as solely a matter of "just good teaching" that works the same for all students. As De Jong & Harper (2005) point out, teachers are often admonished to support ELs with strategies geared toward native English speakers, such as "activating prior knowledge, using cooperative learning, process writing, and graphic organizers or hands-on activities" (p. 102). These teaching strategies can be effective with a range of students, including ELs, and indeed are among those included in SSTELLA practices.

However, applying "just good teaching" strategies alone for teaching ELs in mainstream classrooms fails to recognize how linguistic and cultural contexts are linked to critical language- and content-learning factors and how learning might differ for ELs and non-ELs.

While the body of knowledge related to best teaching and learning practices for ELs is growing, most of the available research and professional development models focus on *elementary* classroom contexts or on generic approaches (regardless of the subject matter) to use in mainstream secondary classrooms with predominantly monolingual English-speaking students. There are certainly effective strategies that work for all students that are also beneficial for ELs including, but not limited to (1) engaging students in active learning environments, (2) providing individualized feedback, (3) communicating clear instructional objectives, and (4) structuring student interaction around productive activities and interactive dialogue (Tharp & Dalton, 2007). However, effective strategies for all students are not always sufficient for supporting the academic learning of ELs in mainstream and nonmainstream classrooms.

De Jong and Harper (2005) describe effective EL-specific teaching practices in mainstream classrooms for ELs as those that go beyond generic approaches, which often discount the additional knowledge and skills teachers need to support ELs in the classroom. De Jong and Harper argue that mainstream teachers must see themselves as content *and* language teachers and as brokering or facilitating new cultural understandings and meanings.

While some science teachers may see themselves as "content teachers" and not "language teachers," we argue that these are not completely separate and independent domains (Bunch, 2013). Instead of seeing language teaching as being "added on" to content, mainstream science teachers can benefit from reconceptualizing *what it means to teach their subject area* by understanding and attending to the language and literacy dimensions of that teaching. This shift means that teaching science involves scaffolding classroom activities that engage ELs in a range of cognitively challenging and socially meaningful activities that use an array of language functions and authentic interactional formats for engaging in science activities. In essence, developing students' use of language in discipline-specific contexts is part of what it means to teach a content area.

Citing the work by De Jong and Harper (2005), Faltis et al. (2010) advise secondary school teachers of ELs to apply EL-specific teaching practices that account for cultural and linguistic differences and resources:

> Secondary teachers who have English learners in their classes also need to know about the demands English learners face with social and academic language and be able to find ways to ensure that students use language in multiple ways; to understand how their students acquire oral and written English when they already know and use their primary language; to give value to their primary language for learning new material in English; to assess their learning using multiple formative measures that take language proficiency into account; to draw on and incorporate students' background knowledge and community life; and to advocate for dual-language learners when policies and practices that offer these students less than an academically challenging secondary school experience. In effect, we argue that teachers need to be aware that they are developing a rich repertoire of language skills and proficiencies with their students. (p. 322)

When considering closely the challenge of supporting EL language and literacy development in secondary school, it is also important to consider the differences between EL and non-EL (native English speaker) readers who may be having difficulty with school-based literacy. For example, applying teaching practices recommended for "struggling" readers may be necessary, but not sufficient if they do not also address EL linguistic and cultural factors related to literacy development (Bunch, Walqui, & Pearson, 2014). Short and Fitzsimmons (2007) describe critical differences between "Below Grade Level Native English Speakers" and "English learners" when developing literacy, as depicted in table 2.2.

Table 2.2 indicates that a generic approach to literacy support may not address the literacy contexts particular to ELs. ELs are more than a group of students who cannot read or write well. A review by Faltis et al. (2010) on relevant competences of secondary school teachers of ELs found key sociocultural, cognitive, linguistic, developmental, and institutional transitions affecting ELs across the K–12 system related to elementary and secondary school teacher competences:

TABLE 2.2
Literacy Development of Below-Grade-Level
Native English Speakers and English Learners

Adolescent Native English Speaker Below Grade Level	Adolescent English Language Learners
• Usually have proficient command of the spoken language, at least of conversational English • Have a wide vocabulary range • Often know meaning of words sounded out by decoding • More likely to comprehend orally presented lesson previews, vocabulary definitions, task directions, and classroom assignments	• Oral English skills will still be in development. • Decoding a word may not be sufficient to access its meaning. • Providing an oral preview of a text or assignment may not unlock its meaning unless it is accompanied by sheltered instruction techniques. • Oral language and literacy development can occur simultaneously.

Source: Short and Fitzsimmons, 2007, p. 9.

1. Understand second language acquisition as participation and identity.
2. Plan for and use theme-based content where concepts, genres, and specialized vocabulary are spiraled and used in multiple ways.
3. Build on students' background knowledge and experiences.
4. Know and advocate for legal rights of ELs.
5. Adjust instruction for variation in schooling experiences of ELs.
6. Mix English learners with native English speakers to ensure social and academic integration.

The message here is that a generic approach is insufficient for addressing the particular language and literacy contexts of ELs compared to native English speakers and that there are important instructional considerations between schooling contexts for ELs in elementary and secondary school. At the same time, secondary school science teachers can benefit from drawing from both generic and EL-specific supports when appropriate. Secondary school science teachers can also use what we know about creating safe spaces for practicing and expressing ELs' knowledge of science by carefully structuring how ELs engage classmates and academic tasks. This can include mixing small-group interactions through heterogeneous grouping strategies where ELs interact closely with native English speakers for some tasks (Bunch, 2006, 2009).

Recommended competencies for secondary school teachers emphasize the social and affective nature of learning for adolescent ELs. For older, school-age ELs, classroom contexts need to integrate students' lived experiences that can both transform the science content itself and also add personal meaning and relevance for students to fully engage in classroom topics. EL students can also benefit from teacher collaborations across subject areas (i.e., science, mathematics, language arts, and social studies) where common themes are addressed in multiple ways, providing ELs with deeper connections to academic subjects and language.

Beyond "Sheltered Instruction": Promoting Authentic Science Learning for ELs in Secondary Classrooms

Two broad approaches have typically been used for supporting ELs' content and language learning in K–12 classrooms: (1) the use of the primary language for instruction, often referred to as bilingual education, and (2) sheltered English instruction strategies, sometimes referred to as Specially Designed Academic Instruction in English (or SDAIE). The goal of both approaches is to support ELs in the content areas through rigorous academic content and language skills. Bilingual education in secondary school, however, is not a commonly used model in the United States due to a range of contentious historical debates and limitations in the U.S. secondary teaching force's linguistic capacity in students' home languages (Faltis & Ramírez-Marín, 2015).

Even without official bilingual education programs, there are a number of ways to promote the use of students' home languages as instructional supports, even by teachers who do not speak ELs' home languages. Ballot initiatives in a few states with large numbers of ELs have restricted the use of languages other than English as the predominate language of instruction, but these states vary in terms of the extent to which students' home languages can be used to support students' learning. SSTELLA practices, while designed for use even in states with the most restrictive of English-only policies, are not intended to supplant the use of students' home languages as valuable resources in students' development of disciplinary practices.

Even in states without policies curtailing bilingual education, the more commonly used sheltered instruction strategies focus on providing ELs greater access to grade-level academic content and language in English through a range of instructional *modifications*. The sheltered strategies are not meant to focus on how learning and teaching might differ across disciplines. Goldenberg (2013) lists the following eleven strategies associated with sheltered instruction (pp. 6–7):

1. Building on student experiences and familiar content (then adding on material that will broaden and deepen students' knowledge);

2. Providing students with necessary background knowledge;
3. Using graphic organizers (tables, web diagrams, Venn diagrams) to organize information and clarify concepts;
4. Making instruction and learning tasks extremely clear;
5. Using pictures, demonstrations, and real-life objects;
6. Providing hands-on, interactive learning activities;
7. Providing redundant information (gestures, visual cues);
8. Giving additional practice and time for discussion of key concepts;
9. Designating language and content objectives for each lesson;
10. Using sentence frames and models to help students talk about academic content; and
11. Providing instruction differentiated by students' ELP.

These sheltered strategies are often used in concert with some popular professional development models like Sheltered Instruction Opportunity Protocol (SIOP) and Guided Language Acquisition Design (GLAD) (Bos, Sanchez, Tseng, Rayyes, Ortiz, & Sinicrope, 2012; Short, Fidelman, & Louguit, 2012). For example the SIOP model asks teachers to adjust their teaching by "adjusting teacher speech, modeling academic tasks, and using multimodal techniques to enhance comprehension" (Echevarria, Richards-Tutor, Canges, & Francis, 2011, p. 337).

To what extent are sheltered strategies in tune with advancing ELs' scientific and engineering practices? We can think of sheltered instruction strategies as a loose collection of instructional modifications that may increase attention to English language features and content meaning by providing additional opportunities to practice academic tasks and reflect on instruction. Teachers must carefully adapt these strategies for disciplinary purposes and approaches across grade levels and content areas. For this reason, we refer to these EL strategies as "all-purpose" or "general supports" for ELs. The SIOP strategies in particular have been tested with mixed results when it comes to EL learning in middle school as teachers redesign science lessons (Echevarria et al., 2011), and they have recently come under some criticism as being based on outdated behaviorist approaches to second language acquisition (Crawford & Reyes, 2015).

Teacher moves and strategies used by both ELD and SDAIE approaches, such as those listed above, can be helpful in supporting general content comprehension by ELs in the classroom. However, what is often missing in these traditional methods for promoting language development for ELs in science is attention to students' development of specific, *authentic* disciplinary practices and the associated language practices. With the adoption of Common

Core State Standards (CCSS) in forty-three states, integrated approaches of literacy and content instruction are needed more than ever to support ELs' access to mainstream content areas like biology, chemistry, and other core and foundational science courses.

The Secondary Science Teaching with English Language and Literacy Acquisition (SSTELLA) framework suggests that teachers can best guide students by focusing on prototypical science language moves that drive the use of more authentic scientific practices. Drawing from sociocultural theories of language and literacy, we define *authentic literacy practices* as those practices where the "instructors use real-world texts for real-world purposes, not simply for the purpose of learning to read and write" (Perry, 2012, p. 62). In this way, we can view literacy as a "diverse set of contextualized practices" (Perry, 2012, p. 62) that highlight what people do with texts in authentic and real-world contexts. Within the SSTELLA framework, the scientific and engineering practices are examples of authentic science literacy practices such as asking questions and defining problems and developing and using models.

To be clear, the approach to EL learning described throughout this book calls for some of the kinds of instructional modifications and strategies that have historically been used both in mainstream settings as well as in ESL and sheltered instruction classrooms. What is at the heart of SSTELLA, however, is a focus on providing opportunities and support for ELs to engage in and develop authentic disciplinary practices—along with the associated language and literacy practices—rather than simply modifying content for comprehension or language development. A step in the right direction is to provide ELs the opportunity to experience the kind of high-quality science instruction called for by the mainstream science education community and articulated in the Next Generation Science Standards.

The SSTELLA framework begins with the premise that the best way to address the academic development of ELs in science is by primarily focusing on the language and literacy demands of the intellectual activities of scientific and engineering that students emulate while learning science. SSTELLA promotes these scientific and engineering *practices* as described in the *Framework for K–12 Science Education: Practices, Crosscutting Concepts, and Core Ideas* (National Research Council, 2012), which guided the articulation of the Next Generation Science Standards:

1. Asking questions (for science) and defining problems (for engineering),
2. Developing and using models,
3. Planning and carrying out investigations,
4. Analyzing and interpreting data,

5. Using mathematics and computational thinking,
6. Constructing explanations (for science) and designing solutions (for engineering),
7. Engaging in argument from evidence, and
8. Obtaining, evaluating, and communicating information.

The eight scientific and engineering practices are interconnected, language intensive practices that grow in complexity across the grade levels. There are significant synergies and opportunities for supporting academic development in science for ELs by addressing these eight scientific and engineering practices. Quite simply, the Next Generation Science Standards (NGSSs) revoice what we have known for a long time in the field of second language and literacy education: meaningful and deep learning relies on practicing and appropriating sociocultural and sociolinguistic tools connected to particular communities. NGSS, addressing the varied science education communities, represents a turn in how we approach science learning with a shift to the social contexts of science learning and therefore a focus on practices and not merely knowledge accumulation. Science teachers are therefore encouraged to both reframe how they teach science by using scientific and engineering practices and, also, how to interpret and use available instructional tools and knowledge for teaching science to ELs.

A shift to scientific and engineering practice called forth by the NGSS requires concomitant shifts in how we view language acquisition (Lee, Quinn, & Valdés, 2013).With a focus on disciplinary (scientific/engineering practices) language practices in science, SSTELLA recognizes that ELs need to acquire a specialized way of using language in science. As Quinn, Lee, and Valdés (2012) note, students must learn "the registers (i.e., styles of talk) used in the science classroom by teachers and students as they participate in academic tasks and activities and demonstrate their knowledge in oral or written forms" (p. 6).

Through the various registers, students attend to precise meanings that go "beyond the meaning of technical vocabulary, to the evidence and logic of connecting cause and effect, and the validity of claims or warrants" (Quinn, Lee, & Valdés, 2012, p. 6). Here it is important to note how such specialized ways of reasoning and communicating in science, or science discourse, is considered a special kind of language learning for all students and, in particular, a special kind of language learning for students acquiring a second language that involves all four language functions, not just speaking or listening. Acknowledging that ELs (and all students) need support in developing science discourse practices, beyond scaffolding of key science terms, is a significant shift in the manner in which ELs normally receive science learning support in the classroom. In this way, SSTELLA contributes to shifts away from sheltered models of language instruction and from focusing on decontextualized instruction of language vocabulary and other language skills.

Teachers therefore must learn to recognize and monitor how and when ELs are developing the language of science. An important point here is that students in science classrooms are not continually using disciplinary science language but rather use "the language of the science classroom" while involved in science classroom activities. Teachers and students shift back and forth between everyday language to more discrete language uses as needed to accomplish a range of communicative tasks that are often used in concert with the scientific/engineering practice being activated.

Therefore, science teachers need to focus on scientific sense-making as students also use a range of discourses students bring into the classroom. Again, the focus is not for science teachers to teach "language" as a separate entity, and certainly not for them to teach ELA, but rather to rethink how they teach *science*. This reorientation to teaching science involves developing teachers' *pedagogical* language knowledge to coordinate and plan activities for the development of language and literacy "through teaching the core curricular content, understandings, and activities that teachers are responsible for (and, hopefully, excited about) teaching in the first place" (Bunch, 2013, p. 298). Table 2.3 describes some features of the language of science that point to language and literacy demands for ELs.

These language features are put into action in different ways through specific scientific and engineering practices. As we will discuss in more detail in chapter 6, SSTELLA purposely focuses on authentic scientific and engineering practices to address content and language demands of the science classrooms for all students, but in particular for ELs. Table 2.4 below describes how a specific scientific and engineering practice (engaging in argument from evidence) combines both scientific sense-making and language-learning opportunities for ELs. The message here for science teachers working to support ELs is that by promoting scientific and engineering practices, particular receptive and productive language functions are activated and thus can be supported in the classroom.

As we can also see from table 2.4, using an authentic disciplinary science teaching approach to teach ELs requires a clear understanding of the language used (i.e., language functions) in the service of carrying out certain scientific practices (i.e., engaging in argument from evidence), instead of thinking about language and literacy (speaking, reading, writing, and listening) as separate or added-on teacher moves.

TABLE 2.3
Selected Features of the Language of Science

Science Discourse	• Learning the register of discourse of a discipline is a form of socialization into how members of the discipline talk, write, and participate in the knowledge construction. • Science discourse at any level requires students to attend to and argue about precise meanings. This demand for attention to precision and attention to detail goes beyond the meaning of technical vocabulary, to the evidence and logic of connecting cause and effect, and the validity of claims or warrants.
Multiple Modes of Representation	• Science information is conveyed not just through oral or textual forms but also through visual and mathematical representations, including pictures, diagrams, graphs, charts, tables, maps, and equations. • For ELLs the coordination of these multiple representations provides an additional path to language learning, as well as to science learning.
Science Texts	• Authoritativeness to "suppress" human agents behind events, concepts, and discoveries and to render the scientific discourse more objective or timeless through simple present tense, passive voice, generalized or virtual participants ("scientists," "research team members"), and hidden evaluations ("claimed," "confirmed") • Nominalization of verbs or adjectives into nouns to economically summarize sentences into one abstract noun phrase
Science Vocabulary	• Science-specific meanings that are different from or more narrowly defined than their everyday meanings (e.g., *force, energy, work, cell, space, fault*) • General academic vocabulary that is used across disciplines (e.g., *compare, infer, analyze, evaluate*; tier II words according to Beck, McKeown, & Kucan, 2002) present challenges. • Discipline-specific words invented and defined for science use (e.g., *gene, biome, proton*; tier III words according to Beck et al., 2002) are new to most students, even those with fluency in everyday English.

Source: Quinn, Lee, and Valdés, 2012, pp. 36–37.

TABLE 2.4
Language Functions of the Language of the Science Classroom

Tasks/Functions	Engage in Argument from Evidence
Analytical tasks	• Distinguish between a claim and supporting evidence or explanation. • Analyze whether evidence supports or contradicts a claim. • Analyze how well a model and evidence are aligned. • Construct an argument.
Receptive language functions (listening/reading)	• Comprehend arguments made by others orally. • Comprehend arguments made by others in writing.
Productive language functions (speaking/writing)	• Communicate (orally and in writing) ideas, concepts, and information related to the formation, defense, and critique of arguments. • Structure and order written or verbal arguments for a position. • Select and present key evidence to support or refute claims. • Question or critique arguments of others.

Source: Lee et al., 2013, p. 7.

Conclusion

In conclusion, secondary science teachers can benefit from knowing the range of EL classifications in their classrooms and which state or district assessments are used to measure ELP. ELs represent a wide range of schooling backgrounds and ELPs.

All secondary teachers should be encouraged to find out which of their students have been tested by the state EL assessment instrument (e.g., TELPAS, CELDT). If so, what does the assessment tell you about your students? Science teachers can critically reflect on familiar EL supports they may have been exposed to in their teacher education program and/or as part of professional development or mentoring (e.g., wait time; the identification of language objectives; use of realia, pictures, and visuals; graphic organizers). We can think about these generic EL teacher moves and ask ourselves how they can be used in secondary science teaching.

Throughout this chapter, we have acknowledged the usefulness of these sheltered strategies for increasing EL comprehension of science content. However, SSTELLA views these strategies as playing supporting roles in the primary activity of advancing language use in authentic scientific and engineering practices. Thus, teachers are encouraged to understand which forms of receptive and productive language functions are required for students to engage in various scientific and engineering practices, as well as how to scaffold instruction so that ELs have opportunities for practicing and becoming more proficient in these receptive and productive language functions. The next section of the book takes the foundational perspectives outlined in this chapter to detail a set of interrelated science teaching practices that provide supportive and responsive learning contexts for ELs and connect with NGSS and CCSS.

Note

1. By some estimates, over half of all adolescent ELs were born in the United States (Batalova, Fix, & Murray, 2007), meaning that a majority of all adolescent ELs have some previous exposure to English or mainstream cultural references.

References

Abreu, G., Bishop, A., & Presmeg, N. (2002). Mathematics learners in transition. In *Transitions between contexts of mathematical practices* (pp. 7–21). Dordrecht, Netherlands: Springer.

Aguirre-Muñoz, Z., & Boscardin, C. K. (2008). Opportunity to learn and English learner achievement: Is increased content exposure beneficial? *Journal of Latinos and Education, 7*(3), 186–205.

Atkinson, D. (Ed.). (2011). *Alternative approaches to second language acquisition.* London, UK; New York, NY: Routledge.

August, D., & Hakuta, K. (1997). *Improving schooling for language-minority children: A research agenda.* Washington, DC: National Academies Press.

Batalova, J., Fix, M., & Murray, J. (2007). *Measures of change: The demography and literacy of adolescent English learners: A report to the Carnegie Corporation of New York.* Washington, DC: Migration Policy Institute.

Bialystok, E. (2001). *Bilingualism in development: Language, literacy, and cognition.* Cambridge, UK; New York, NY: Cambridge University Press.

Birdsong, D., & Molis, M. (2001). On the evidence for maturational constraints in second-language acquisition. *Journal of Memory and language, 44*(2), 235–49.

Bos, J. M., Sanchez, R. C., Tseng, F., Rayyes, N., Ortiz, L., & Sinicrope, C. (2012). Evaluation of Quality Teaching for English Learners (QTEL) professional development (NCEE 2012-4005). Washington, DC: National Center for Education Evaluation and Regional Assistance, Institute of Education Sciences, U.S. Department of Education.

Bunch, G. C. (2013). Pedagogical language knowledge preparing mainstream teachers for English learners in the new standards era. *Review of Research in Education, 37*(1), 298–341.

Adger, C. T., Snow, C. E., & Christian, D. (2003). *What Teachers Need To Know about Language.* Center for Applied Linguistics, 4646 40th Street, NW, Washington, DC 20016-1859. Web site: http://www.cal.org/ncle.

August, D., & Shanahan, T. (2008). Developing literacy in second-language learners: Report of the National Literacy Panel on Language-Minority Children and Youth.

Bunch, G. C. (2009). "Going Up There": Challenges and opportunities for language minority students during a mainstream classroom speech event. *Linguistics and Education, 20*(2), 81–108.

Bunch, G.C. (2006). "Academic English" in the 7th grade: Broadening the lens, expanding access. *Journal of English for Academic Purposes, 5*(4), 284–301.

Bunch, G. C., Walqui, A., & Pearson, P. D. (2014). Complex text and new common standards in the United States: Pedagogical implications for English learners. *TESOL Quarterly, 48*(3), 533–559.

Carhill, A., Suárez-Orozco, C., & Páez, M. (2008). Explaining English language proficiency among adolescent immigrant students. *American Educational Research Journal, 45*(4), 1155–79.

Collier, V. P., & Thomas, W. P. (2004). The astounding effectiveness of dual language education for all. *NABE Journal of Research and Practice, 2*(1), 1–20.

Crawford, J., & Reyes, S. A. (2015). The trouble with SIOP®: How a behaviorist framework, flawed research, and clever marketing have come to define—and diminish—sheltered instruction. Portland: OR, Institute for Language & Education Policy.

Cummins, J. (2008). BICS and CALP: Empirical and theoretical status of the distinction. In *Encyclopedia of language and education* (pp. 487–99). New York, NY: Springer.

De Jong, E. J., & Harper, C. A. (2005). Preparing mainstream teachers for English-language learners: Is being a good teacher good enough?. *Teacher Education Quarterly, 32*(2), 101–124.

Donato, R. (2004). Aspects of collaboration in pedagogical discourse. *Annual Review of Applied Linguistics, 24*, 284–302.

Duff, P. (2000). Repetition in foreign language classroom interaction. In J. K. Hall and L. S. Verplaetse (Eds.), *Second and foreign language learning through classroom interaction* (pp. 139–59). Mahwah, NJ: Lawrence Erlbaum.

Echevarria, J., Richards-Tutor, C., Canges, R., & Francis, D. (2011). Using the SIOP model to promote the acquisition of language and science concepts with English learners. *Bilingual Research Journal, 34*(3), 334–51.

Estrada, P. (2014). English learner curricular streams in four middle schools: Triage in the trenches. *The Urban Review, 46*(4), 535–73.

Faltis, C., & Ramírez-Marín, F. (2015). Secondary bilingual education. In W. E. Wright, S. Boun, & O. García (Eds.), *The Handbook of Bilingual and Multilingual Education* (pp. 336–53). Malden, MA: Wiley-Blackwell.

Faltis, C., Arias, M. B., & Ramírez-Marín, F. (2010). Identifying relevant competencies for secondary teachers of English learners. *Bilingual Research Journal, 33*(3), 307–328.

Faltis, C. J., and Wolfe, P. (1999). *So much to say: Adolescents, bilingualism and ESL in the secondary school.* New York, NY: Teachers College.

Fillmore, L. W. (1991). When learning a second language means losing the first. *Early Childhood Research Quarterly, 6*(3), 323–46.

Flores, B. B., & Smith, H. L. (2009). Teachers' characteristics and attitudinal beliefs about linguistic and cultural diversity. *Bilingual Research Journal, 31*(1–2), 323–58.

García, O. (2009). Emergent bilinguals and TESOL: What's in a name? *TESOL Quarterly, 43*(2), 322–26.

García, O., & Kleifgen, J. A. (2010). *Educating emergent bilinguals: Policies, programs, and practices for English language learners.* New York, NY: Teachers College Press.

Gibbons, P. (2002). *Scaffolding language, scaffolding learning: Teaching second language learners in the mainstream classroom.* Portsmouth, NH: Heinemann.

Goldenberg, C. (2013). Unlocking the research on English learners: What we know—and don't yet know—about effective instruction. *American Educator, 37*(2), 4.

Hakuta, K. (2011). Educating language minority students and affirming their equal rights: Research and practical perspectives. *Educational Researcher, 40*(4), 163–74.

Hakuta, K., Bialystok, E., & Wiley, E. (2003). Critical evidence a test of the critical-period hypothesis for second-language acquisition. *Psychological Science, 14*(1), 31–38.

Hakuta, K., Butler, Y. G., & Witt, D. (2000). How long does it take English learners to attain proficiency? The University of California Linguistic Minority Research Institute Policy report 2000-1. *Adolescence, 40,* 503–12.

Harklau, L. (2011). Commentary: Adolescent L2 writing research as an emerging field. *Journal of Second Language Writing, 20,* 227–30.

Heritage, M., Walqui, A., & Linquanti, R. (2015). *English language learners and the new standards: Developing language, content knowledge, and analytical practices in the classroom.* Cambridge, MA: Harvard Education Press.

Janzen, J. (2008). Teaching English language learners in the content areas. *Review of Educational Research, 78*(4), 1010–38.

Johnson, K. E. (2006). The sociocultural turn and its challenges for second language teacher education. *TESOL Quarterly,* 235–57.

Kibler, A., Valdés, G., & Walqui, A. (2014). What does standards-based educational reform mean for English language learner populations in primary and secondary schools? *TESOL Quarterly, 48*(3), 433–53.

Krashen, S. (1981). Second language acquisition. *Second Language Learning,* 19–39.

Lantolf, J. P. (2000). *Sociocultural theory and second language learning.* Oxford, UK: Oxford University Press.

Lantolf, J. P. (2011). The sociocultural approach to second language acquisition. In D. Atkinson (Ed.), *Alternative approaches to second language acquisition* (pp. 24–47). London, UK; New York, NY: Routledge.

Lee, O., Quinn, H., & Valdés, G. (2013). Science and language for English language learners in relation to Next Generation Science Standards and with implications for Common Core State Standards for English language arts and mathematics. *Educational Researcher, 42*(4), 223–33.

Levinson, S. C. (2006). On the human "interaction engine." In N. J. Enfield & S. C. Levinson (Eds.), *Roots of human sociality: Culture, cognition and interaction* (pp. 39–69). Oxford, UK: Berg.

Linquanti, R., & Cook, H. G. (2013). Toward a "Common Definition of English Learner": A brief defining policy and technical issues and opportunities for state assessment consortia. Council of Chief State School Officers.

Lucas, T. (1997). *Into, through, and beyond secondary school: Critical transitions for immigrant youths.* Washington, DC: Delta Systems Center for Applied Linguistics.

McEneaney, E. H., López, F., & Nieswandt, M. (2014). Instructional models for the acquisition of English as bridges into school science: effects on the science achievement of US Hispanic English language learners. *Learning Environments Research, 17*(3), 305–318.

Meltzer, J., and Hamann, E. (2005). *Meeting the literacy development needs of adolescent English language learners through content-area learning.* Providence, RI: The Education Alliance at Brown University.

Menken, K., and Kleyn, T. (2010). The long-term impact of subtractive schooling in the educational experiences of secondary English language learners. *International Journal of Bilingual Education and Bilingualism, 13*(4), 399–417.

Muñoz, C., & Singleton, D. (2011). A critical review of age-related research on L2 ultimate attainment. *Language Teaching, 44*(1), 1–35.

National Research Council. (2012). *A framework for K–12 science education: Practices, crosscutting concepts, and core ideas.* Washington, DC: National Academies Press.

Ochs, E., & Schieffelin, B. (1989). Language has a heart. *Text-Interdisciplinary Journal for the Study of Discourse, 9*(1), 7–26.

Olsen, L. (2010). Reparable harm fulfilling the unkept promise of educational opportunity for California's long term English learners. Long Beach, CA: California Tomorrow.

Perry, K. H. (2012). What Is Literacy?—A Critical Overview of Sociocultural Perspectives. *Journal of Language and Literacy Education, 8*(1), 50–71.

Poole, D. (1992). Language socialization in the second language classroom. *Language Learning, 42*, 593–616.

Queen, J. A. (2002). *Student transitions from middle to high school: Improving achievement and creating a safer environment.* Larchmont, NY: Eye on Education.

Quinn, H., Lee, O., & Valdés, G. (2012). Language demands and opportunities in relation to Next Generation Science Standards for English language learners: What teachers need to know. *Commissioned Papers on Language and Literacy Issues in the Common Core State Standards and Next Generation Science Standards, 94*, 32.

Rios-Aguilar, C., Gonzalez Canche, M. S., & Moll, L. C. (2012). Implementing structured English immersion in Arizona: Benefits, challenges, and opportunities. *Teachers College Record, 114*(9), 1–18.

Rogoff, B. (2003). *The cultural nature of human development.* Oxford, UK: Oxford University Press.

Samway, K., and McKeon, D. (2007). *Myths and realities: Best practices for language minority students.* Portsmouth, NH: Heinemann.

Saunders, W. M., & Marcelletti, D. J. (2012). The gap that can't go away: The catch-22 of reclassification in monitoring the progress of English learners. *Educational Evaluation and Policy Analysis, 35*(2), 139–56.

Schleppegrell, M. J. (2004). *The language of schooling: A functional linguistics perspective.* Mahwah, NJ: Lawrence Erlbaum.

Schweingruber, H., Keller, T., & Quinn, H. (Eds.). (2012). *A framework for K–12 science education: Practices, crosscutting concepts, and core ideas.* Washington, DC: National Academies Press.

Short, D. J., Fidelman, C. G., & Louguit, M. (2012). Developing academic language in English language learners through sheltered instruction. *TESOL Quarterly, 46*(2), 334–61.

Short, D., & Fitzsimmons, S. (2007). *Double the work: Challenges and solutions to acquiring language and academic literacy for adolescent English language learners.* New York, NY: Carnegie Corporation of New York, Alliance for Excellent Education.

Slama, R. B. (2012). A longitudinal analysis of academic English proficiency outcomes for adolescent English language learners in the United States. *Journal of Educational Psychology, 104*(2), 265.

Solís, J.L., Kattan, S. & Baquedano-López, P. (2009). Socializing respect and knowledge in a racially integrated science classroom. *Linguistics & Education,* 20 (3), 273–290.

Stone, C. A. (1993). What is missing in the metaphor of scaffolding? In E. A. Forman, N. E. Minick, & C. A. Stone (Eds.), *Contexts for learning: Sociocultural dynamics in children's development* (pp. 169–83). Oxford, UK: Oxford University Press.

Téllez, K., & Waxman, H. C. (2006). Preparing quality teachers for English language learners: An overview of the critical issues. In *Preparing quality teachers for English language learners: Research, policies, and practices* (pp. 1–22). Mahwah, NJ: Lawrence Erlbaum.

Tharp, R. G., & Dalton, S. S. (2007). Orthodoxy, cultural compatibility, and universals in education. *Comparative Education, 43*(1), 53–70.

Tharp, R. G., & Gallimore, R. (1991). *Rousing minds to life: Teaching, learning, and schooling in social context.* Cambridge, UK; New York, NY: Cambridge University Press.

Valdés, G. (1999). Incipient bilingualism and the development of English language writing abilities in secondary school. In C. J. Faltis & P. Wolfe (Eds.), *So much to say: Adolescents, bilingualism and ESL in the secondary school* (pp. 138–75). New York, NY: Teachers College Press.

Valdés, G., Bunch, G. C., Snow, C. E., & Lee, C. (2005). Enhancing the development of students' language(s). In L. Darling-Hammond, J. Bransford, P. LePage, K. Hammerness, & H. Duffy (Eds.), *Preparing teachers for a changing world: What teachers should learn and be able to do* (pp. 126–68). San Francisco, CA: Jossey-Bass.

van Lier, L., & Walqui, A. (2012, January). *Language and the common core state standards.* Paper presented at the Understanding Language Conference, Stanford, CA. Retrieved from http://ell.stanford.edu/papers/language.

Vygotsky, L. S. (1978). *Mind in society.* Edited by M. Cole, V. John-Steiner, S. Scribner, & E. Souberman. Cambridge, MA: Harvard University Press.

Vygotsky, L. S. (1986). *Thought and language.* Cambridge, MA: MIT Press.

Vygotsky, L. S. (1987). *The collected works of L. S. Vygotsky: The fundamentals of defectology* (Volume 2). Edited by Robert W. Rieber and Aaron S. Carton. New York, NY: Plenum Press.

Vygotsky, L. S. (1980). *Mind in society: The development of higher psychological processes.* Harvard university press.

Walqui, A., & Van Lier, L. (2010). *Scaffolding the academic success of adolescent English language learners: A pedagogy of promise.* San Francisco, CA: WestEd.

Wood, D., Bruner, J. S., & Ross, G. (1976). The role of tutoring in problem solving. *Journal of Child Psychology and Psychiatry, 17*(2), 89–100.

Zuengler, J., & Miller, E. R. (2006). Cognitive and sociocultural perspectives: Two parallel SLA worlds? *TESOL Quarterly, 40*(1), 35–58.

II

SUPPORTIVE AND RESPONSIVE SCIENCE TEACHING PRACTICES FOR ENGLISH LEARNERS

3

The SSTELLA Framework

A Synergistic and Reciprocal Relationship between Language Development and Science Learning for Secondary Students

Sara Tolbert and Patricia Stoddart

Overview

IN THIS CHAPTER, we provide a brief overview of the Secondary Science Teaching with English Language and Literacy Acquisition (SSTELLA) framework (figure 3.1), which includes four interrelated instructional practices to guide effective secondary science teaching for ELs. Each of the four practices is detailed in subsequent chapters.

Introduction

In chapters 1 and 2, we addressed important issues in science teaching and learning—namely, the new vision of secondary science education through Next Generation Science Standards (NGSS) and Common Core State Standards (CCSS) and moving toward authentic disciplinary instruction through responsive science teaching. We now turn to a framework, SSTELLA, which provides a much-needed response in science education to the many challenges facing ELs in secondary school. SSTELLA addresses the challenges teachers (particularly new teachers) face when trying to increase EL students' opportunities to learn by advancing research-based instructional practices in the classroom.

SSTELLA is designed to prepare teachers to effectively integrate science, language, and literacy instruction for ELs by promoting the productive use of science language and literacy in authentic contexts, whereby "students are supported in

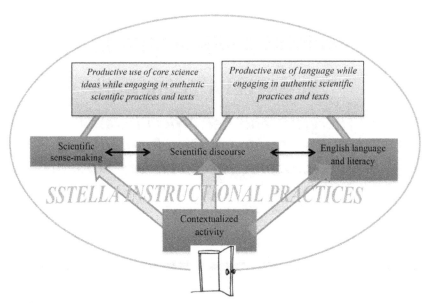

FIGURE 3.1
Secondary Science Teaching with English Language and Literacy Acquisition (SSTELLA) Framework

using multiple resources and strategies for learning science *and* developing English" (Lee, Quinn, & Valdés, 2013, p. 229). This approach aligns with the NGSS and CCSS focus on disciplinary language practices. The SSTELLA framework is represented visually in figure 3.1 to highlight the relationships among four instructional practices and two anticipated student learning outcomes.

The framework views Contextualized Science Activity (see the "doorway" in figure 3.1) as the gateway through which ELs can come to understand relationships between school science learning and their lived experiences outside of schools, and use these relationships to enhance science learning. Teachers promote scientific sense-making, scientific discourse, and English language and literacy development through these contextualized learning experiences. Science content and language then intersect as students, for example, construct oral and written explanations and engage in argument from evidence (Cheuk, 2012; Lee et al., 2013), two practices that echo CCSS for English language arts.

Thus, SSTELLA views the relationship between science learning and English language and literacy development as reciprocal and synergistic. Imagine a science classroom discussing issues of drought and water scarcity in the local community, in which students, utilizing new knowledge about the water cycle and water treatment, develop and test possible solutions and present written and oral arguments around their refined solution. Through the *contextualized* and *authentic* use of language in scientific practices, students develop and practice complex disciplinary language forms and functions. Simultaneously, through the use of language functions such as explanations and arguments in science investigations, students make sense of abstract core science ideas and enhance their conceptual understanding as well as understanding of the nature of science (Driver, Newton, & Osborne, 2000; Stoddart, Pinal, Latzke, & Canaday, 2002; Stoddart, Solís, Tolbert, & Bravo, 2010).

The four interrelated SSTELLA practices mediate two primary student learning outcomes. First, students use core science ideas (e.g., the cycle of matter and energy transfer in ecosystems) while engaging in authentic scientific practices and texts. They may be carrying out and reporting on an investigation related to ecosystems or using double-entry journals (Gomez et al., 2010) as a reading-to-learn strategy in an online article describing uses of alternative energies. Second, students will productively use language while engaging in authentic scientific practices and texts: instead of just paying attention to the science "content" while carrying out an investigation and reading an online article, the students communicate a well-structured explanation for their investigation, and identify with supporting evidence the tone and primary audience of the online article. We briefly describe each instructional practice next, which will be elaborated on in subsequent chapters.

SSTELLA Instructional Practices

Contextualized Science Activity

A key aspect of supporting ELs in learning academic content is the incorporation of their cultural and linguistic background, and lived experiences, into classroom learning experiences. Work with ELs around science concepts should be not only rigorous but also meaningful and relevant. Teachers and schools have often positioned underserved ELs as deficient and in need of remediation *prior* to engaging in rigorous content-area coursework—essentially setting students up for failure before they even step foot into a secondary science classroom (Oakes, Joseph, & Muir, 2004).

While language support is certainly necessary, and will take different forms depending on students' particular language backgrounds, teachers must understand that ELs are quite capable of grappling with authentic and contextualized real-world problems that enhance both language development and conceptual understandings, and they should provide opportunities for them to do so (Lee & Luykx, 2006; Lee et al., 2013; Moll, Amanti, Neff, & Gonzalez, 1992; Rosebery & Warren, 2008). By engaging students in science investigations and engineering design problems in authentic real-world problems, teachers can leverage students' funds of knowledge[1] from their homes and communities, the local (e.g., school building, community center, etc.) or ecological environment (local stream, watershed issues, etc.), and/or socio-scientific issues (e.g., stem cell research, sustainability science) as a way to engage ELs in meaningful and rigorous science learning experiences (Rivet & Kracjik, 2008; Rosebery & Warren, 2008).

Scientific Sense-Making through Scientific and Engineering Practices

Scientific sense-making refers to how students negotiate everyday and scientific ways of knowing while increasing awareness of the nature of science, through engagement in scientific and engineering practices. Scientific sense-making is enhanced when teachers make explicit to students what they will be learning (i.e., a "big idea"), make connections between the big idea and classroom activity and prior knowledge or experiences (August & Hakuta, 1997; Kelly, 2007; Rivet & Kracjik, 2008), and make students aware of how they will demonstrate mastery of the big idea (i.e., the learning objective) (Wiggins & McTighe, 1998).

Students can better relate to the big idea when it is situated within a puzzling question, ill-defined problem, or a partial model to test and apply (National Research Council, 2012; Passmore & Stewart, 2002; Windschitl, Thompson, Braaten, & Stroupe, 2012). Expectations and classroom rigor for ELs are maintained through deliberate and sustained scaffolding (e.g., Walqui & van Lier, 2010), which may include modeling of instruction, graphic organizers, visual representations, realia, and use of technology.

Scientific Discourse through Scientific/Engineering Practices

Developing a coherent understanding of science requires that students learn how science knowledge is constructed, presented, and shared through specialized scientific *oral and written* language forms—that is, the discourse of science (Graham & Perin, 2007; Kelly, 2007; Pearson, Moje, & Greenleaf, 2010; Snow, 2010; Veel, 1997). This can happen through students' use of scientific and engineering practices, where teachers expose students to and encourage them to engage with disciplinary specific discourses, such as communicating scientific explanations and arguments, and engineering solutions. These discourse moves promote conceptual understanding, investigative competence, and an understanding of the epistemology and social nature of science (Driver et al., 2000). Scientific discourse is, in itself, a social and collaborative practice, which can help students both make sense of science concepts and develop language (Kelly, 2007; Lemke, 1990).

English Language and Disciplinary Literacy Development

Scientific genres are typically characterized by dense clauses, technical and general academic vocabulary, and the use of the passive voice (Pearson et al., 2010; Snow, 2010). To become independent consumers and producers of science knowledge, students need to be able to both comprehend and use scientific discourses, with attention not only to technical science vocabulary but also to general academic words and English language structures commonly used in science (August, Carlo, Dressler, & Snow, 2005; Snow, 2010). In secondary schools, however, all students, but particularly ELs, face both (1) an increase in complexity of language genres and registers associated with disciplinary reading, writing, speaking, and listening (Scarcella, 2003) and (2) a decrease in authentic content learning opportunities (Bruna & Gomez, 2008). English learners can engage in authentic literacy practices that promote both content learning (e.g., core science ideas) and language and literacy development (Krajcik & Sutherland, 2010; Pearson et al., 2010).

As important as it is to understand the challenges facing English learners in comprehending and producing the linguistic and other textual features of scientific genres, it is also important to recognize that the goal is not to train ELs to reproduce these features for their own sake, outside of the sorts of sense-making and discourse practices that we have just described. Rather, the goal is to provide opportunities for ELs to become aware of—and engage with—the range of language and literacy practices used to make meaning with different audiences for different purposes across the various scientific disciplines (Darian, 2003; Duff, 2010; Lee et al., 2013; Moje, 2007). To do this, students must navigate both receptive and productive language in a number of different interactive "modes" (e.g. listening to the teacher lecture to the entire class, engaging in a whole-class discussion, participating in a partner or small group activity; reading a text alone and writing a response) (Lee et al., 2013), while engaging with oral and written texts of various types. Thus, we focus on creating opportunities—and providing support—for ELs to interact with others in a wide variety of language-rich science activities; to use and develop key science vocabulary in the context of that interaction; and to engage in authentic literacy tasks as they make sense of science and communicate their understandings with others.

To summarize, the four interrelated instructional practices just described highlight the reciprocal and synergistic relationship between science learning and English language and literacy development. The challenge remains for secondary science teachers to infuse these practices into their classroom teaching. In the next four chapters, we unpack each SSTELLA practice and provide guidance as to how each practice can be implemented in ways that support science learning for ELs.

Note

1. "Funds of knowledge" are the historically marginalized life experiences and household/community practices of minoritized students and families that can be leveraged as meaningful intellectual resources in formal classroom and school settings (Gonzalez, Moll, & Amanti, 2005). (See chapter 4 for more on funds of knowledge in SSTELLA.)

References

Achieve. (2013). *Next generation science standards*. Washington, DC: Author.

August, D., & Hakuta, K. (1997). *Improving schooling for language-minority children: A research agenda*. Washington, DC: National Academies Press.

Bruna, K. R., & Gomez, K. (Eds.). (2008). *The work of language in multicultural classrooms: Talking science, writing science*. New York, NY: Routledge.

Cheuk, T. (2012). *Relationships and convergences found in the Common Core State Standards in Mathematics (practices), Common Core State Standards in ELA/ Literacy (student portraits), and a Framework for K–12 Science Education (science & engineering practices)*. Unpublished manuscript. Stanford, CA: Stanford University, Understanding Language Initiative.

Common Core State Standards Initiative. (2010). Retrieved from www.corestandards .org

Darian, S. (2003). *Understanding the language of science*. Austin, TX: University of Texas Press.

Driver, R., Newton, P., & Osborne, J. (2000). Establishing the norms of scientific argumentation in classrooms. *Science Education, 84*(3), 287–312.

Duff, P. (2000). Repetition in foreign language classroom interaction. In J. K. Hall and L. S. Verplaetse (Eds.), *Second and foreign language learning through classroom interaction* (pp. 139–59). Mahwah, NJ: Lawrence Erlbaum.

Echevarría, J., Vogt, M., & Short, D. J. (2012). *Making content comprehensible for English learners: The SIOP model* (4th ed.). Boston, MA: Pearson.

Kelly, G. (2007). Discourse in science classrooms. In S. K. Abell & N. G. Lederman (Eds.), *Handbook of research on science education* (2nd ed., pp. 443–70). Mahwah, NJ: Lawrence Erlbaum Associates.

Krajcik, J. S., & Sutherland, L. M. (2010). Supporting students in developing literacy in science. *Science, 328*(5977), 456–59.

Lee, O., & Luykx, A. (2006). *Science education and student diversity: Synthesis and research agenda*. New York, NY: Cambridge University Press.

Lee, O., Quinn, H., & Valdés, G. (2013). Science and language for English language learners in relation to Next Generation Science Standards and with implications for Common Core State Standards for English language arts and mathematics. *Educational Researcher, 42*(4), 223–33.

Lemke, J. (1990). *Talking science: Language, learning, and values*. Norwood, NJ: Ablex.

Moje, E. B. (2007). Developing socially just subject-matter instruction: A review of the literature on disciplinary literacy teaching. *Review of Research in Education, 31*(1), 1–44.

Moll, L., Amanti, C., Neff, D., & Gonzalez, N. (1992). Funds of knowledge: A qualitative approach to developing strategic connection between homes and classrooms. *Theory Into Practice, 31*, 132–41.

National Research Council. (2012). *A framework for K–12 science education: Practices, crosscutting concepts, and core ideas.* Washington, DC: National Academies Press.

Oakes, J., Joseph, R., & Muir, K. (2004). Access and achievement in mathematics and science: Inequalities that endure and change. In J. Banks & C. Banks (Eds.), *Handbook of research on multicultural education* (2nd ed., pp. 69–90). San Francisco, CA: Jossey Bass.

Passmore, C., & Stewart, J. (2002). A modeling approach to teaching evolutionary biology in high schools. *Journal of Research in Science Teaching, 39*(3), 185–204.

Pearson, P. D., Moje, E., & Greenleaf, C. (2010). Literacy and science: Each in the service of the other. *Science, 328*(5977), 459–63.

Rivet, A., & Krajcik, J. (2008). Contextualizing instruction: Leveraging students' prior knowledge and experiences to foster understanding of middle school science. *Journal of Research in Science Teaching, 45*, 79–100.

Rosebery, A. S., & Warren, B. (2008). *Teaching science to English language learners.* Alexandria, VA: National Science Teachers Association.

Scarcella, R. (2003). *Academic English: A conceptual framework* (The University of California Linguistic Minority Research Institute Technical Report 2003-1). Retrieved from http://escholarship.org/uc/item/6pd082d4#page-2

Snow, C. E. (2010). Academic language and the challenge of reading for learning about science. *Science, 328*, 450–52.

Stoddart, T., Pinal, A., Latzke, M., & Canaday, D. (2002). Integrating inquiry science and language development for English language learners. *Journal of Research in Science Teaching, 39*(8), 664–87.

Stoddart, T., Solís, J., Tolbert, S., & Bravo, M. (2010). A framework for the effective science teaching of English Language Learners in elementary schools. In D. Sunal, C. Sunal, & E. Wright (Eds.), *Teaching science with Hispanic ELLs in K–16 Classrooms* (pp. 151–81). Charlotte, NC: Information Age.

Veel, R. (1997). Learning how to mean—scientifically speaking: Apprenticeship into scientific discourse in the secondary school. In F. Christie & J. R. Martin (Eds.), *Genre and institutions: Social processes in the workplace and school* (pp. 160–95). London, UK: Cassell.

Walqui, A., & van Lier, L. (2010). *Scaffolding the academic success of adolescent English language learners.* San Francisco, CA: WestEd.

Wiggins, G., & McTighe, J. (1998). *Understanding by design.* Alexandria, VA: Association for Supervision and Curriculum Development.

Windschitl, M., Thompson, J., Braaten, M., & Stroupe, D. (2012). Proposing a core set of instructional practices and tools for teachers of science. *Science Education, 96*(5), 878–903.

4

Contextualizing Science Activity

Sara Tolbert

Overview

IN THIS CHAPTER, we introduce and contrast two classroom scenarios to analyze how teachers can more authentically engage students in investigations of "real-world" science problems. We then provide a rationale and theoretical basis for the Secondary Science Teaching with English Language and Literacy Acquision (SSTELLA) instructional practice, Contextualizing Science Activity. Next, we outline connections between Contextualizing Science Activity and the Next Generation Science Standards (NGSS) and Common Core State Standards (CCSS). Finally, we walk teachers through the process of designing meaningful and relevant science lessons, drawing on Contextualized Science Activity as a guiding principle during both lesson planning and implementation.

Introduction: Exploring Contextualized Science Activity

Below are interactions from two high school chemistry classrooms: Ms. M's and Ms. R's. Both teachers have tenth- and eleventh-grade students, including English-dominant students; current, long-term English leaners (ELs) with intermediate to advanced English language proficiency (ELP); redesignated ELs; and a few newcomers.

Textbox 4.1 has some questions to consider about the interactions.

Textbox 4.1

1. What do you notice about how each teacher makes the lesson comprehensible for students?
2. Does Ms. M's lesson help EL students develop a broader understanding of the role of science in their local community? In society at large? Why or why not? What about Ms. R?
3. What strategies does Ms. R use to make the water decomposition lesson more engaging and relevant for EL students? Are there other ways that you could modify the lesson to increase its relevance for EL students in secondary classrooms?

Interaction 1

Ms. M, a high school chemistry teacher, introduces decomposition of water by asking students to consider the driving question: Can we split water into its components: hydrogen and oxygen? She explains that, in order to better explore this question, students will first need to recall what they remember about the molecular structure of water. She asks students to jot down a few notes regarding what they remember about water molecules, and then compare their notes with a partner. After reviewing the bell work activity, Ms. M asks students to draw a model or representation of how a water molecule might be split into its components: hydrogen and oxygen. Ms. M organizes students into small groups and facilitates small-group discussions around a central question: What would need to happen in order for a water molecule to split into hydrogen and oxygen? Some groups determine that energy would be required to break the bonds between atoms in order to separate the hydrogen and oxygen in a water molecule. They also decide that there would need to be two water molecules for this reaction to occur, and that products would be hydrogen gas (H_2) and oxygen gas (O_2). Many students represent this process as an equation: $2H_2O \rightarrow 2H_2 + O_2$. Others draw Lewis dot structures (representing the configuration of electrons in an element).

Ms. M then explains that tomorrow in class students will be decomposing water in a lab using Epsom salts and electrical energy. She asks students to consider in small groups what other materials they might need to conduct this lab, and how they might design an experiment in which they could use these materials to decompose water. She reminds them that they must include a procedure for testing that their experiment was successful (i.e., that both hydrogen and oxygen gas were produced during the experiment). She explains that in post-lab, students will revisit the driving question—Can we split water into its components: hydrogen and oxygen?—and revise their initial ideas according to the new information they learned from the lab.

Interaction 2

Ms. R, a high school chemistry teacher, had asked her students during the previous day's lesson to go home and talk to a family member about their experiences with air pollution. During today's lesson, she asks students in her chemistry class to share with a partner what they learned from their family interviews about air pollution. She then asks them to discuss in pairs their experiences with public transportation (e.g., riding buses, taking the subway, etc.), and to consider the relationships between using public transportation and air quality.

Next, she introduces decomposition of water by asking students to consider the driving question: How could we create usable hydrogen energy from a water molecule? She explains that they will be investigating how hydrogen energy has been explored as a potential alternative fuel source in public bus systems both nationally and globally. She remarks that, in order to better explore this question, students will first need to recall what they remember about the molecular structure of water. She asks students to jot down a few notes regarding what they remember about water molecules, and then compare their notes with a partner. She then asks students to consider why scientists and policy makers would be interested in exploring hydrogen gas as an energy source. Students have a few minutes to discuss their ideas in small groups. Presenters in each group take turns paraphrasing the discussion that occurred in their small group. Ms. R then gives a brief overview of how nearby cities have incorporated sustainable fuel technologies into public transit systems. Students explore some of these projects on the American Public Transportation Association Website (www.apta.com).

Ms. R asks students to think about how hydrogen energy could be extracted from a water molecule. Students determine that it would have to be separated into its various components: hydrogen and oxygen. Ms. R distributes foam balls to represent atoms in water molecules: red for oxygen, blue for hydrogen, and toothpicks to represent chemical bonds. She then asks them to use the foam balls and toothpicks to explore how a water molecule might be split into hydrogen and oxygen gas while discussing the following question in small groups: What would need to happen in order for a water molecule to split into hydrogen and oxygen? Some groups determine that energy would be required to break the bonds between atoms in order to separate the hydrogen and oxygen in a water molecule. They also decide that there would need to be two water molecules for this reaction to occur, and that products would be hydrogen gas (H_2) and oxygen gas (O_2). Many students represent this process as an equation: $2H_2O \rightarrow 2H_2 + O_2$. Others draw the Lewis structures to represent this process.

Ms. R then explains that tomorrow in class students will be decomposing water in a lab using Epsom salts and electrical energy. She asks students to consider in small groups what other materials they might need to conduct this lab, and how they might design an experiment in which they could use these materials to decompose water. She reminds them that they must include a procedure for testing that their experiment was successful (i.e., that both hydrogen and oxygen gas were produced during the experiment). She explains that after conducting the lab, they will return to the original driving question, revisiting how usable hydrogen energy is created from a water molecule. Students will record how their initial ideas changed according to the new information they learned from the lab.

After completing and sharing their results from the lab, Ms. R invites a couple of her chemistry students' parents who work for the local public transit system to come speak with her classes about the use of alternative energy in public transportation. Ms. R then asks students to work in groups to evaluate the feasibility of extracting on a large scale hydrogen gas from water via electrolysis. Students use Internet resources to pursue this question, such as Alternative Energy (www.altenergy.org/renewables/hydrogen_and_fuel_cells.html), National Renewable Energy Laboratory's site for Hydrogen and Full Cell Research (www.nrel.gov/hydrogen/), and hydrogen fuel cell bus projects in the United States and worldwide (www.nrel.gov/hydrogen/proj_fc_bus_eval.html).

Finally, students analyze the challenges and affordances of hydrogen energy as a sustainable alternative energy source, including what the most viable sources of hydrogen energy could be. They will construct an argument from the evidence to determine whether or not their city should explore the use of hydrogen as a fuel source in public transportation, and write letters to their local city councilmembers to communicate their arguments.

Throughout this chapter, we will discuss the multiple approaches to Contextualizing Science Activity that teachers can use to *better support and promote EL students' engagement and participation in complex classroom science learning tasks.*

What Is Contextualized Science Activity, and Why Is It Important?

We draw on sociocultural approaches to informal and formal science education, with a focus on ELs, to provide a theoretically informed rationale for the SSTELLA practice, Contextualizing Science Activity. At the heart of the rationale for contextually authentic instruction is the idea that instruction should be meaningful to students (e.g., Buxton, 2006; King, 2012; Rivet & Kracjik, 2008;

Stoll Dalton, 1998). *Meaningfulness* from a sociocultural perspective is achieved when instruction is connected to students' everyday experiences, home and community knowledge, local environment, and/or real-world issues.

In other words, science activity is "contextualized" when teachers facilitate authentic connections between classroom learning and issues, contexts, problems, and/or experiences that extend beyond the science classroom. The contextualized approach to instruction contrasts with decontextualized approaches observed in most science classrooms, whereby even if/when students are engaged in constructivist inquiry learning activities, they may still not be contextually authentic (see Ms. M vs. Ms R, for example) (Aikenhead, 2006; Buxton, 2006).

We recognize that inquiry movements in science education have encouraged science teachers to move away from an approach to science as memorization and recall, and toward engaging students in science and engineering practices to explore scientific phenomena or develop engineering solutions. In other words, instead of being asked to memorize scientific facts, laws, and theories, students are now often being asked to explore scientific facts, laws, and theories by engaging in scientifically authentic practices, which mimic what scientists do in the real world, that is, "scientists' science" (Chinn & Maholtra, 2002).

We see in interaction 1 that even Ms. M engages students in rich sense-making and argumentation practices as they explore how a water molecule could be separated into its components. Indeed, SSTELLA builds on this conception of scientific authenticity via attention to scientific and engineering practices outlined in the framework (National Research Council, 2012; see also chapter 5). However, we also argue that authenticity must not only be understood as that which is authentic to science, but also include that which is authentic to students, communities, and real-world contexts beyond the science classroom or scientific and engineering laboratories (Buxton, 2006). This approach to authenticity creates multiple entry points, so that all students are more meaningfully engaged as knowledge producers, equitably contributing to the dialogic[1] sense-making activity of the secondary science classroom.

Contextualized Science Activity in SSTELLA is seen as the "doorway" to secondary science learning: when teachers design science activities that are relevant and meaningful beyond the science classroom, students are more likely to "see themselves" in school science, and therefore more likely to engage with classroom science learning tasks (Elmesky, 2005; Buxton, 2006; Rosebery, Warren, & Conant, 1992).

When teachers present science concepts, void of connections to relevant contexts, problems, or experiences, a student's source of motivation for learn-

ing those concepts must stem from either (1) an overall desire to be successful in school or school science or (2) an interest in school science learning for the sake of school science learning alone—in other words, a unique interest in the concept and its abstractions. We know from the research that few students are motivated by these two factors alone (Aikenhead, 2006; Costa, 1995).

On the other hand, teachers can create multiple entry points for student engagement when science activities are embedded within larger societal problems, local issues, or students' own experiences outside of the science classroom. When teachers frame the science learning goals within a larger contextualizing socio-scientific problem or scenario and build on students' out-of-school experiences and contributions, they provide EL students with more meaningful opportunities to learn science.

Scaffolding Language and Literacy Development

In a typical secondary science class, there are often more new vocabulary and technical science terms presented than there are in a foreign language class (Groves, 1995). Science teachers typically have presented scientific vocabulary and concepts via decontextualized lectures and/or "cookbook"-style labs. Students are expected to memorize terms and engage in teacher-directed lab activities without a coherent understanding of the epistemic or conceptual learning goals, or how and why we come to develop science concepts via science and engineering practices (Duschl, 2008; National Research Council, 2007).

Research in science education has indicated that this approach not only impedes conceptual understanding, but is also inauthentic to science and engineering disciplines and how we employ science and engineering in the service of understanding and solving complex real world problems (American Association for the Advancement of Science, 1993; Next Generation Science Standards, 2013; National Research Council, 1996, 2000, 2007, 2012). In chapter 5, we discuss how EL students can develop scientific understandings through opportunities for scientific sense-making or engineering design that are organized around a "big idea." In chapter 7, we also explain how the physical contextualization of language via such moves as the manipulation of physical objects is integral to facilitating both language development and conceptual understandings in science.

In this chapter, we outline how teachers can create richer and more meaningful opportunities for language by drawing on EL students' out-of-school experiences, home and community knowledge, and everyday sense-making resources in the service of science learning. In Contextualized Science Activities, EL students draw on scientific and engineering practices as well as their

own sense-making resources to explore relationships between complex science ideas and real-world applications of those ideas.

Leveraging Students' Everyday Interests and Experiences

We view EL students' everyday experiences as "critical but often misunderstood and undervalued intellectual resource[s] in science learning and teaching" (Rosebery & Warren, 2008, p. 48). However, students' experiences with science outside of the classroom setting are often understood by teachers as limited to trips to museums, hiking or camping, reading books about science at home, and so on. This restricted perspective does not acknowledge that such experiences may or may not be shared by students from nondominant backgrounds, and that nondominant forms of participation in science activity are frequently unrecognized by teachers.

By taking time to find out about students' interests, teachers can make more meaningful connections between students' experiences and school science. For example, teachers might create a student questionnaire in the beginning of the year to explore the types of hobbies (e.g., film production, music, sports, arts and crafts, dance, gardening), domestic activities (e.g., caring for younger brothers and sisters), music, or extracurricular programs in which their students are involved or interested. Teachers can also take advantage of opportunities to get to know students outside of the classroom if/when possible, by attending school extracurricular events, talking with students during lunch duty, and so on. The teacher can then call on student experts to share their experiences when studying related science topics (e.g., force/motion, human growth/development, sound).

We also recognize that students' interests and experiences within the school setting can be leveraged as resources for engaging in scientific practices. Rosebery, Warren, and Conant (1992) took advantage of bilingual students' observations about which water fountains in their school had the "best" water.

Students designed an investigation of water fountains on several different floors of the school, learning new information at each stage of the investigation, which led to designing subsequent investigations incorporating new measures of quality and retesting their original hypotheses. They discovered that their preferences were likely related to the cooler temperature of the preferred water fountain, but results indicated that the preferred water fountain may have in fact been of poorer quality than the less preferred fountains. Teachers can become investigators of students' school-related concerns and experiences, and take advantage of the local physical school environment as a rich context for exploring and learning about science in more contextually authentic ways, while preparing all students for more active and informed participation in local and global science-related issues.

Connecting to Home-Community Funds of Knowledge

Effective science teachers of EL students explore how students' funds of knowledge from their homes and communities can be connected to school science instruction. Moll, Amanti, Neff, and Gonzalez (1992) define *funds of knowledge* as the "knowledge and skills found in local households" (p. 133). They articulate several categories of funds of knowledge infrequently recognized as resources by classroom teachers. Some of these include ranching and farming, mining, construction, repair (e.g., automobile, house maintenance), medicine, folk medicine, and household management. Gonzalez, Moll, and Amanti (2005) outline how teachers can make strategic connections between the cultural and intellectual practices of minoritized students, families, and classroom practices.

Since the publication of the original "funds of knowledge" study in 1992 researchers have used the funds of knowledge framework for exploring how the cultural, linguistic, and intellectual resources of nondominant students (e.g., low-income students, EL students, students of color) can be engaged in classroom learning across the curriculum. Science education researchers have demonstrated that using a funds-of-knowledge approach to science instruction with nondominant students promotes student participation, agency, and voice in science learning (Basu & Barton, 2007; Barton & Tan, 2009), increases science achievement (Rivet & Kracjik, 2008), and facilitates science language and literacy development (Moje, Collazo, Carrillo, & Marx, 2001; Moje et al., 2004).

Elizabeth Moje and colleagues (2004) investigated how students' funds of knowledge and language practices can be integrated with the discourses (i.e., official ways of talking, communicating, and interacting that characterize particular communities, such as scientific communities; see Gee, 1996) and knowledge they encounter within formal institutions, such as secondary science classrooms. They explored how the funds of knowledge of bilingual Latino students in a predominantly working-class community of Detroit might impact classroom science teaching and learning. In one example, the teacher, who was Latino and had a strong chemistry background, engaged students in a study of air and water quality.

Students' own experiences and funds of knowledge around these issues, however, were rarely acknowledged during the unit. Though Juan, a student in the class, left his home in Mexico City because his asthma became so extreme that his family decided to move in order to improve Juan's respiratory health, his experiences were not elicited during the lessons. However, he revealed in interviews with researchers that he identified strongly with environmental science, given his personal experiences with air pollution. Moje and colleagues (2004) elaborate on these missed opportunities:

> As these youth were reading and writing classroom texts about water cycles and molecular structures of pollutants, their parents' work lives—and the economic and scientific conditions of their work—were absent from the conversations. Bringing these knowledges into classroom conversations would not only build bridges between students' out-of-school experiences and the target content knowledges but also expand the target content knowledges to encompass a wider range of implications for scientific concepts. (pp. 52–53)

> Students might also, for example, raise questions about how the EPA averages [for air quality] of such a sprawling city [Detroit] are calculated, wondering whether the clean air in one neighborhood—one with fewer factories and more green spaces—averages out the pollutant levels in more industrial neighborhoods. (p. 55)

Moje et al. (2004) identified examples of funds of knowledge that are useful for science teaching and learning. These include family knowledge and experience (e.g. work inside and outside of the home), community knowledge and experience (a commitment to social and community activism or a strong ethnic identity), popular culture (music and television), peer activities (riding bicycles or skateboards, fashion, sports, using cell phones), and talents and interests (art, debate, blogging, poetry).

They illustrate, for example, how students can share their funds of knowledge that then become resources in the science classroom: (1) sharing home knowledge about chilies sweating their skins in a plastic bag to explore condensation/evaporation, (2) noticing brown/black spots on tortillas that form while being heated on the pan to discuss chemical reactions (black carbon formation), or (3) sharing stories about riding bikes to investigate the physics of wearing a helmet. They explained how these and other funds of knowledge, though by-and-large overlooked in most science classrooms, could create meaningful contexts for science learning.

Moje et al. (2004) affirm that teachers can leverage these rich funds of knowledge to create space in the science classroom where diverse forms of knowledge and discourses are valued. They argue that teachers can facilitate "third spaces" in science classrooms, where students' funds of knowledge and language practices converge with official school science discourses and scientific practices: "In third space, then, what seem to be oppositional categories can actually work together to generate new knowledges, new Discourses, and new forms of literacy" (p. 42). In other words, rather than viewing students' out-of-school knowledge and language practices as oppositional to academic content and literacy development, teachers can facilitate opportunities to leverage both classroom and community knowledge and literacies to create a hybrid learning space in which all students contribute their expertise and experiences.

Studying the Local Environment

Using the local ecological environment is another way that science instruction can be made both more meaningful and accessible. Scientific investigations in the local environment can help students explore abstract science concepts within tangible, relevant contexts. Rosebery, Warren, and Conant (1992) describe how bilingual students in a high school English as a Second Language/Basic Skills class investigated the ecology of a pond located near the school.

The teacher explained that students would be creating a field guide based on their observations of the pond. Students observed that the pond was quite polluted, noting that it had oil on the surface and was littered with trash. They were particularly concerned about the state of the pond because it was located about five hundred feet from the municipal drinking water reservoir. Students collectively decided that their field guide would encompass a comprehensive study of the health of the pond. They came up with a list of questions to explore and divided into small groups so that each group could investigate a subset of the questions:

> One group designed and built tools that they used to measure the depth, length, and width of the pond. A second group created a profile of the air and water temperatures at the pond. After much discussion, they decided to obtain temperature readings at different locations and depths within the pond in an effort to correlate temperature and forms of microscopic life. A third group analyzed the pond's chemistry, measuring its pH, turbidity, and salinity. A fourth catalogued the plant and animal life they observed. . . . In the end, the students used their data to produce the field guide. (Rosebery et al., 1992, p. 73)

Both before and after completing this activity, researchers asked students to think aloud about how they might investigate and explain two ill-defined real-world science problems. One of these problems was a "near transfer" problem, that is, an analysis of water contamination, similar to what the students had investigated in school; the other was a "far transfer" problem, that is, an investigation as to what might be causing children to become suddenly ill. Rosebery, Warren, and Conant (1992) found that students moved from literal comprehension in the preliminary think-aloud to inferential reasoning at the conclusion of the school science investigations:

> In the September interviews students showed almost no evidence that they understood what it means to reason scientifically and, specifically, to put forward hypotheses having deductive consequences that can be evaluated through experimentation. . . . The June interviews indicate how the students began to take control of scientific discourses. . . . The students were beginning to reason in terms of a larger explanatory framework. They knew more about water pollution and aquatic ecosystems than they did in September, and they used that knowledge to generate explanations and hypotheses. (p. 85)

In this case, the teacher made use of the local environment (the pond) as well as students' interests and concerns about the pollution of the pond to create a more meaningful and relevant context for scientific learning. The pond investigation had observable impacts on students' scientific reasoning and argumentation skills as well as conceptual understandings that were transferable to novel contexts.

Promoting Awareness of Social and Global Science-Related Issues

Contextualized Science Activity is also designed to engage EL students, who are often denied access to rigorous learning experiences, in complex thinking around local and global socio-scientific issues (SSI). In such instances, EL students are provided with a meaningful context for using language to communicate the relationship between science content and broader social and environmental challenges. This also plays an important role for all students, who must become better prepared to actively grapple with real-world science-related issues, particularly as communities around the world consider scientific innovations and technological solutions to societal problems (Achieve, 2013; National Science Teachers Association, 2010; Zeidler, Sadler, Simmons, & Howes, 2005).

We draw on SSI as a framework for thinking about how to embed science learning within larger social and global problems and contexts (Zeidler et al., 2005). We recognize that the SSI approach is grounded within a perspective that all students should have opportunities to develop a "functional" scientific literacy—where *functional* is understood as related to the ability to not only apply scientific and engineering concepts to real-world issues, but also understand the moral, ethical, and socioemotional dimensions of those issues, and that cultural knowledge, discourses, power, and nature of science issues shape the development of functional scientific literacies in SSI instruction.

Zoellner, Chant, and Wood (2014) describe how researchers and teachers in science and social studies education collaborated on a high school chemistry unit to facilitate student investigations of the relatively few diesel-powered cars in the Unites States when compared with countries in Europe. Before the unit was introduced, students were asked to take photographs of cars they saw in their communities, such as in the parking lots of schools and local businesses. In class, students compiled and analyzed the photographs, noting the very few numbers of hybrid vehicles and the complete absence of diesel-powered vehicles.

Using a graphic organizer, students were asked to articulate and provide evidence for their initial ideas about why there were so few diesel-powered cars in the United States, given that the majority of personal vehicles in Europe were powered by diesel fuel. In the process of searching for evidence to support their claims, students reevaluated their original ideas and accommodated new information about diesel-powered cars, bringing "high-level chemistry concepts to bear when discussing the usage of diesel fuel in cars" (Zoellner et al., 2014, p. 502). Students explored how U.S. residents appear more reticent toward the use of diesel fuel and discussed how some of those concerns are tied to persistent misconceptions, or issues of affect, rather than scientific evidence. Through exploring SSI, students can analyze the scientific, affective (i.e., emotional), political, and economic dimensions of individual and community-based decision making related to societal issues in science.

Connecting Contextualized Science Activity to Next Generation Science Standards and Common Core State Standards

The Next Generation Science Standards explicitly acknowledge that, while visionary for the time in which they were released, past national standards reform movements have not given enough attention to issues of diversity and equity. In particular, the science contributions from other cultures (e.g., indigenous, early Egyptian, Chinese, Arabic) were overlooked, presenting a "limited or distorted view of science" (Achieve, 2013, p. 4, appendix J) and recommendations for improving the performance and participation of underserved students were not explicit. Though NGSS still falls far short of offering a consistent and coherent focus on equity and diversity (see Rodriguez, 2015), it is an improvement from past national science standards in terms of the increased focus on disciplinary language and literacy development (e.g., through scientific and engineering practices).

The NGSSs draw attention to strengthening connections between EL students' experiences from home and school science via more authentic engagement with community science issues, students' funds of knowledge, parents as experts (regardless of their formal science background), multicultural contributions to science, and SSI. The increased focus on engineering and technology classroom learning through a social problem-solving approach can help facilitate these connections: "By solving problems through engineering in local contexts (e.g., gardening, improving air quality, or cleaning water pollution in the community), students gain knowledge of science content, view science as relevant to their lives and future, and engage in science in socially relevant and transformative ways" (Achieve, 2013, p. 5, appendix J).

Research shows that when science instruction is contextually authentic (e.g., physically contextualized through hands-on science investigations that leverage students' funds of knowledge, social/global issues, local places, and community concerns), the science achievement and participation of underserved students, including ELLs, significantly improves (e.g., Buxton, 2006, 2010; Barton & Tan, 2009; Rivet & Kracjik, 2008; Sadler, Barab, & Scott, 2007).

According to the National Science Teachers Association (2010) position statement, "We have yet to ensure all students have the ability to use what they have learned [in science] when making decisions about what is appropriate in personal, societal, and global situations involving science and technology, and to value these endeavors" (p. 1). Both CCSS and NGSSs are designed to provide students with more rigorous learning experiences that prepare them to solve real-world problems. Contextualized science instruction, then, engages students in rigorous hands-on science learning activities that prepare them for success in postsecondary science courses, degree programs, and future careers in science, and to use science knowledge to make more informed personal and public decisions about the role of science and technology in the efforts to create a more sustainable future (Duschl, 2008).

The SSTELLA vision of contextualized science teaching and learning is consistent with two core ideas identified by the NGSS (2013): *the interdependence of science, engineering, and technology*, and *the influence of science, engineering, and technology on society and the natural world*. Science, technology, and engineering are becoming increasingly interconnected disciplines as we take on the global challenges of pursuing both sustainable development and technological advancement. These complex issues require that students in secondary classrooms engage with equally complex "real-world" science investigations and engineering design problems. Not only does this type of problem-based science and engineering instruction prepare students to be better situated for grappling with the science and engineering challenges of the future, but it also strengthens connections between students' experiences outside of school, including informal science learning experiences, with school science learning.

Guided Practice: Contextualizing Science Activity in the Classroom

Many science teachers would generally agree that science instruction should be meaningful and relevant for all students. One perceived impediment is lack of time—there is too much material to cover, and therefore not enough time to make the curriculum more relevant for students. Another barrier that science teachers face is that they have often received very little training or professional development concerning how to make authentic connections to relevant contexts, particularly when standards and curriculum are typically very decontextualized. In the sections that follow, we address these concerns, providing explicit instruction as to how lessons can be designed in ways that are more meaningful for all students, including EL students.

Before we begin to provide guidelines and suggestions for Contextualizing Science Activity, we will address the issue of time mentioned above. We argue that, when science instruction is decontextualized, that is, a transmission of canonical ideas and content in science, students will neither develop in-depth conceptual understandings about the content nor understand how what they learn in school science applies to issues and problems beyond the science classroom. As we stated at the beginning of this chapter, Contextualizing Science Activity is the doorway, or entry point, for engagement by all students, including ELs, with scientific sense-making, scientific and engineering practices, scientific discourse, and disciplinary literacy and language development.

We also argue that a key goal of the NGSS is to provide opportunities for in-depth investigation of fewer concepts. This is a shift from previous state and national standards movements in science, which have focused on breadth over depth. We recognize that interaction 2 described in the introduction reflects a high level of contextualization, but we argue that Contextualizing Science Activity is a practice that is accessible to both novice and experienced teachers. The detail and depth of contextualization will vary, depending on a variety of factors, including the content to be addressed, as well as teachers' experience and comfort levels. In the following sections, and in order to address the second concern related to the question of "How do I contextualize a decontextualized curriculum or standard?," we delineate how teachers at varying levels of experience and comfort can find ways to increase the meaningfulness and relevancy of science instruction for EL students.

Framing: Developing Science Lessons That Are Meaningful and Relevant

A key challenge in Contextualizing Science Activity is designing questions that are well connected to relevant sociocultural contexts *and* the science learning goals. In this regard, teachers must think carefully about how to *frame the unit or lesson* with an overarching driving question to create a motivational context for learning while connecting to relevant science concepts and practices. Unit planning generally requires that teachers think about the "big ideas" of the unit, as well as the driving questions or problems that will guide student exploration of those big ideas (see chapter 5 for a detailed explanation of "big ideas" in science; see also Wiggins & McTighe, 2005).

Reflecting on how classroom concepts connect to broader contexts both within the discipline and beyond the classroom is a key component of identifying big ideas. When thinking about Contextualizing Science Activity while *framing a new unit or lesson*, teachers can reflect on how the driving questions within the unit might connect to local, ecological, home, community, social/global issues, multicultural science, or other relevant sociocultural contexts. For example, imagine a teacher in the southwestern United States is drawing the big idea from the NGSS "Ecosystem Dynamics, Function, and Resilience: Anthropogenic Changes Can Disrupt an Ecosystem and Threaten the Survival of Some Species" (HS-LS2-7). She can consider how the core idea connects to local ecological concerns and environmental movements in the community. In the city where her school is located, a proposed copper mine in one of the nearby mountain ranges has been the subject of public debate for several years. At issue is the impact on alpine ecosystems, including two federally protected riparian ecosystems. Therefore, one driving question for the lesson might be the following: What is the relationship between the proposed copper mine and its potential impact on surrounding ecosystems? The core idea will be explored through a locally relevant and highly debated issue.

While it might appear to be easier to connect some core ideas (e.g., ecology) to relevant contexts than others (electrochemistry), there are multiple ways to Contextualize Science Activity. Using local ecological contexts is only one of many ways. As demonstrated in interaction 2 at the beginning of this chapter, teachers can create driving questions that facilitate student interaction with complex ideas in science (*How could we create usable hydrogen energy from a water molecule?*), and extend the learning beyond mere understanding to its real-world application.

Teachers can draw on the multiple funds of knowledge and everyday interests and experiences of students as resources for Contextualizing Science Activity (see Tolbert & Knox, 2016). In a unit or lesson on vertebrate phylogeny, students could trace the phylogenetic history of a pet. Similarly, when studying genetics, students could investigate how and why there are so many different breeds of dogs, or explore force vectors through playing soccer. Current events or "front page science" can also create relevant contexts for science learning, and can help students learn to comprehend and communicate science concepts for different purposes and different audiences (Saul, Kohnen, Newman, & Pearce, 2012). Using case studies or "science stories" can help students understand how the core ideas in science are applied in real-world contexts (Herreid, Schiller, & Herreid, 2012). The National Center for Case Study Teaching in Science (NCCSTS) provides a growing collection of case studies in science, organized by type (e.g., clicker case, role play, laboratory activity), content area, and grade level, and case studies can be downloaded and used in classrooms, free of charge (see http://sciencecases.lib.buffalo.edu/cs).

Another challenge to Contextualizing Science Activity is that, while science teachers may attempt to include relevant topics or activities in instruction, teacher-selected topics and activities can often appear more relevant to teachers than students. It is absolutely crucial that teachers take time to get to know about students' interests, experiences, concerns, communities, and families, via means such as individual interviews, informal conversations, and periodic questionnaires. Teachers can and should build in opportunities to get to know more about students during their lessons, which leads us into the next section on student contributions.

Adapting and Applying: Providing Opportunities for Students to Contribute Their Experiences

In Contextualized Science Activities, students are asked to contribute their own lived experiences and funds of knowledge, as well as build on and respond to peer contributions. The teacher adapts and applies student contributions to science activities during the lesson by helping students see connections between their contributions and the learning goals, but also by encouraging students to explore connections between the learning goals and family, community, and local and global contexts.

Teachers can combine English language development (ELD) strategies (see chapter 7) to create opportunities for collaboration and dialogue in small groups, pairs, and whole-class settings in which students are prompted to share experiences from out of school. For example, in interaction 2, Ms. Rivera encourages students to share stories with a partner about their experiences with public transit. Later in the lesson, she facilitates connections between public transportation and hydrogen as fuel, inviting parents as experts on the topic. Furthermore, she generates small-group discussions throughout the lesson around open-ended versus closed-ended questions (e.g., Can hydrogen gas be from water via electrolysis on a large scale? Is hydrogen gas a viable source of alternative energy?), for which the purpose is not to come up with a "correct" answer, but rather to evaluate the available evidence, explore multiple viewpoints, and come up with an informed recommendation on the topic. These types of open-ended discussions encourage divergent perspectives, allowing students to build on their out-of-school experiences and classroom science learning to construct arguments from evidence.

Facilitating student contributions throughout the lesson means that teachers also take time to acknowledge when students contribute their personal experiences during a lecture or whole-class discussion. Often, student contributions are overlooked or even dismissed. This may be connected to teachers' anxieties about not being able to cover the content. However, teachers can incorporate classroom protocols or strategies to ensure that they make time to honor student contributions during class and still address the learning goals. One of these strategies is to have a Questions box or "I wonder . . ." board in the classroom, where students can come up and write down their questions, concerns, or ideas as they arise. These could then be assigned as extra-credit investigations or science fair topics, or teachers could devote some class time one day per week to exploring students' experiences and interests.

Another protocol that teachers can adopt is to make it a "rule" that any student who raises his/her hand to contribute a related experience or question must be called on before moving on to the next activity. Classroom protocols such as these help ensure that the classroom culture is one where all students' ideas and experiences are valued, and all students are producers of knowledge. This is particularly important for EL students, who must feel that the classroom environment is safe and supportive, creating an atmosphere of risk-taking that is a prerequisite for language and science learning.

Conclusion

To summarize our key points in this chapter:

1. Even "inquiry-based" lessons can lack meaning and relevance for students.

2. Contextualizing Science Activities can more meaningfully engage all students in school science learning experiences, while increasing EL students' access to classroom science learning.

3. Teachers should attend to both *framing* (i.e., creating relevant lesson contexts for science learning by drawing on local or global issues in science, local ecological contexts, home/community knowledge, etc.) and *adapting and applying* (i.e., eliciting students' lived experiences and facilitating connections between students' experiences and science learning).

Notes

1. From Klages (2012): "Dialogic is a term associated primarily with the works of Mikhail Bakhtin, a literary and linguistic theorist. . . . Dialogic speech . . . always involves a multiplicity of speakers and a variety of perspectives; truth becomes something negotiated and debated, rather than something pronounced from on high."

References

Achieve. (2013). *Next generation science standards.* Washington, DC: Author.

Aikenhead, G. (2006). *Science education for everyday life: Evidence-based practice.* New York, NY: Teachers College Press.

American Association for the Advancement of Science. (1993). *Benchmarks for science literacy.* Retrieved from www.project2061.org/publications/bsl

Barton, A. C., & Tan, E. (2009). Funds of knowledge and discourses and hybrid space. *Journal of Research in Science Teaching, 46*(1), 50–73.

Basu, S. J., & Barton, A. C. (2007). Developing a sustained interest in science among urban minority youth. *Journal of Research in Science Teaching, 44*(3), 466–89.

Buxton, C. A. (2006). Creating contextually authentic science in a "low-performing" urban elementary school. *Journal of Research in Science Teaching, 43*(7), 695–721.

Buxton, C. A. (2010). Social problem solving through science: An approach to critical, place-based teaching and learning. *Equity & Excellence in Education, 43*(1), 120–35.

Chinn, C. A., & Malhotra, B. A. (2002). Epistemologically authentic inquiry in schools: A theoretical framework for evaluating inquiry tasks. *Science Education, 86*(2), 175–218.

Costa, V. B. (1995). When science is "another world": Relationships between worlds of family, friends, school, and science. *Science Education, 79,* 313–33.

Duschl, R. (2008). Science education in three-part harmony: Balancing conceptual, epistemic, and social learning goals. *Review of Research in Education, 32*(1), 268–91.

Elmesky, R. (2005). "I am science and the world is mine": Embodied practices as resources for empowerment. *School Science and Mathematics, 105*(7), 335–42.

Gee, J. P. (1996). *Social linguistics and literacies: Ideology in discourses* (2nd ed.). London, UK: Falmer.

Gonzalez, N., Moll, L., & Amanti, C. (2005). *Funds of knowledge: Theorizing practices in households, communities and classrooms.* Mahwah, NJ: Erlbaum.

Groves, F. H. (1995). Science vocabulary load of selected secondary science textbooks. *School Science and Mathematics, 95*(5), 231–35.

Herreid, C. F., Schiller, N., & Herreid, K. (2012). *Science stories: Using case studies to teach critical thinking.* Arlington, VA: NSTA Press.

King, D. (2012). New perspectives on context-based chemistry education: Using a dialectical sociocultural approach to view teaching and learning. *Studies in Science Education, 48*(1), 51–87.

Klajes, Mary. (2012). Key terms in literary theory. New York, NY: Continuum.

Moje, E. B., Ciechanowski, K. M., Kramer, K., Ellis, L., Carrillo, R., & Collazo, T. (2004). Working toward third space in content area literacy: An examination of everyday funds of knowledge and discourse. *Reading Research Quarterly, 39*(1), 38–70.

Moje, E. B., Collazo, T., Carrillo, R., & Marx, R. W. (2001). "Maestro, what is 'quality'?": Language, literacy, and discourse in project-based science. *Journal of Research in Science Teaching, 38*(4), 469–98.

Moll, L., Amanti, C., Neff, D., & Gonzalez, N. (1992). Funds of knowledge: A qualitative approach to developing strategic connection between homes and classrooms. *Theory Into Practice, 31*, 132–41.

National Renewable Energy Laboratory. (2014). *Hydrogen & fuel cell research.* Retrieved from www.nrel.gov/hydrogen

National Research Council. (1996). *National science education standards.* Washington, DC: National Academy Press.

National Research Council. (2000). *The digital dilemma: Intellectual property in the information age.* Washington, DC: National Academy Press.

National Research Council. (2007). *Taking science to school: Learning and teaching science in grades K–8.* Washington, DC: National Academy Press.

National Research Council. (2012). *A framework for K–12 science education: Practices, crosscutting concepts, and core ideas.* Washington, DC: National Academies Press.

National Science Teachers Association. (2010). NSTA position statement: Teaching science and technology in the context of societal and personal issues. Retrieved from www.nsta.org/about/positions/societalpersonalissues.aspx

Next Generation Science Standards. (2013). *A science framework for K–12 science education.* Developed by the National Research Council. Washington, DC: National Academies Press.

Rivet, A., & Krajcik, J. (2008). Contextualizing instruction: Leveraging students' prior knowledge and experiences to foster understanding of middle school science. *Journal of Research in Science Teaching, 45*, 79–100.

Rodriguez, A. J. (2015). What about a dimension of engagement, equity, and diversity practices? A critique of the next generation science standards. *Journal of Research in Science Teaching, 52*(7), 1031–51.

Rosebery, A. S., & Warren, B. (2008). *Teaching science to English language learners.* Alexandria, VA: National Science Teachers Association.

Rosebery, A. S., Warren, B., & Conant, F. R. (1992). Appropriating scientific discourse: Findings from language minority classrooms. *Journal of the Learning Sciences, 21,* 61–94.

Sadler, T. D., Barab, S. A., & Scott, B. (2007). What do students gain by engaging in socioscientific inquiry? *Research in Science Education, 37*(4), 371–91.

Saul, W., Kohnen, A., Newman, A., & Pearce, L. (2012). *Front page science: Engaging teens in science literacy.* Arlington, VA: NSTA Press.

Stoll Dalton, S. (January 1, 1998). *Pedagogy matters: Standards for effective teaching practice.* Research report. Center for Research on Education, Diversity, & Excellence (CREDE). University of California–Santa Cruz, Santa Cruz, CA.

Tolbert, S. & Knox, C. (under revision). "They might know a lot of things that I don't know": Investigating differences in preservice teachers' ideas about contextualizing science instruction in multilingual classrooms. *International Journal of Science Education.*

Wiggins, G., & McTighe, J. (2005). *Understanding by design.* Alexandria, VA: ASCD.

Zeidler, D. L., Sadler, T. D., Simmons, M. L., & Howes, E. V. (2005). Beyond STS: A research-based framework for socioscientific issues education. *Science Education, 89*(3), 357–77.

Zoellner, B. P., Chant, R. H., & Wood, K. (2014). "But aren't diesel engines just for big, smelly trucks?" An interdisciplinary curriculum project for high school chemistry students. *Journal of Chemical Education, 91*(4), 497–504.

5

Scientific Sense-Making through Scientific and Engineering Practices

Edward G. Lyon and Sara Tolbert

Overview

A PRIORITY IN science education is for students to make sense of core ideas in science while they come to understand and emulate the intellectual activities in which scientists and engineers routinely engage (i.e., scientific/engineering practices). This chapter describes different approaches to promoting students' sense-making in science and argues for an approach where "big ideas," as opposed to fragmented concepts, are communicated while students develop, test, and refine scientific models to ultimately explain natural phenomena. Engaging in scientific and engineering practices allows opportunities for English learners (ELs) to learn discipline-specific language practices, while employing their own linguistic practices as important sense-making resources. Moreover, scientific and engineering practices can provide a meaningful and tangible context for building science understandings. However, careful supports should be considered to move students toward deeper sense-making of science ideas.

Introduction: Exploring Scientific Sense-Making

Two high school chemistry teachers at the same school are in the middle of a unit on thermochemistry. In particular, they are focusing on the relationship between energy and phase changes so that students can eventually solve energy calculations using the mathematical equation $q = mc\Delta T$. Both teachers have tenth and eleventh grade students, including English-only students; current, long-term ELs with intermediate to advanced EL proficiency; and redesignated ELs.

Textbox 5.1

Questions to consider as you read the two interactions:

1. How does each teacher communicate what students are to be learning?
2. What opportunities are there in each interaction for students to make sense of phase changes? What appears to be the students' role (or job) in making sense of the science in each interaction? What about the teachers' role (or job)?
3. What supports are available to help English learners to make sense of phase changes in each of the interactions?

Interaction 1

Ms. A uses a PowerPoint presentation titled with today's topic, "Phase Changes," followed by a learning objective: "Students will understand the relationship between energy and phase changes of water." She proceeds to remind students of property difference among solid, liquid, and gaseous substances, using water as an example. Ms. A then displays a heating curve representing changes in a substance's state (i.e., solid, liquid, gas) at varying temperatures. Her heating curve is depicted in figure 5.1.

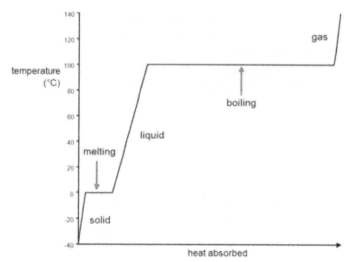

FIGURE 5.1
Ms. A's Heating Curve

Ms. A instructs students to copy the curve in their notes, while she defines and explains each phase change in relation to energy: "The heat added to ice begins increasing the speed of molecules, thus raising the average temperature of the molecules. However, at a certain point, the heat is not moving water molecules, but rather breaking hydrogen bonds freeing water molecules from each other until they are in the liquid state. During this time, the temperature does not rise, because the heat is breaking bonds, not increasing movement of molecules."

The next day, Ms. A gives students a worksheet titled "Graphing the Phase Changes of Water." The worksheet includes a list of procedures, prompting students to submerge ice in a beaker with some water over a hot plate. The worksheet includes a data table to record the temperature every three minutes with a thermometer (assuming the heat plate provides a constant source of heat). Students record the temperature as the ice turns to liquid water and eventually boils to produce steam. Using the graphing paper provided with labeled axes (time [representing heat absorbed] on the x axis and temperature on the y axis), students graph their data, which looks like the same heating curve they encountered the previous day. At the bottom of the worksheet is space for students to then describe what happened to the temperature as heat was added to the ice.

Interaction 2[1]

Ms. C knows that an important scientific practice for her students to master is to "develop and use a model based on evidence to illustrate the relationships between components of a system" (National Research Council, 2012). She also recognizes that a core idea in chemistry is the energy transfer between objects and systems—in this case the phase change of water, which is accounted for by the "motions of particles or energy associated with the configuration of particles" (NGSS HS-PS3-2). Ms. C begins class using a document camera displaying the following heading: "Vapor, Liquid Water, and Ice: Thermodynamics in the Home."

She allows an electric kettle to heat up, giving off steam. With the heated water, she steeps some mate, a caffeinated Argentinean beverage, which she knows some of her students' parents drink. She then reviews with students the three phases of water—vapor (gas), liquid water, and ice (solid)—and asks students to share with a partner their observations of water changing phases in home/daily life. After discussing in pairs, students are then called on to share some of their experiences with the whole class. Students offer examples such as "hanging clothes on the line," "cooking vegetables," "ironing," "making ice cream," and "steam cleaning the carpet."

While recording these examples on the board, Ms. C asks students to talk to their partners again and identify the phase change that would be observed in each of these examples. After calling on students to share their ideas with the whole class, she asks them whether or not any single example represents all three phases of water, that is, gas, liquid, and solid. The students note that none of the examples represent how water transitions through all three phases. Ms. C. then shows students a container of ice cubes: "Let's say I need some steam to clean my carpet, but all I have is this ice. How could I turn this into steam?" Students offer: "heat it" and "put it in a pot of boiling water." Ms. C probes further: "How long would it take?" and "What factors might I need to consider?" She then displays the big idea, explaining that all of these questions relate to a larger one, "How is energy transferred and conserved during phase changes?"

Ms. C refines the problem: "What we really want to know is the *relationship* between energy and temperature in these phase changes." Students take out their daily objective worksheet and record today's objective: "Explain the relationship between energy and phase changes for water." Ms. C writes up a set of axes (heat vs. temperature) as students collectively hypothesize what might be happening to the temperature as ice is changed into steam. Ms. C gives students a sentence frame: As energy is applied to ice, the temperature (increases/ decreases) at a (linear rate/nonlinear rate)." The purpose of the sentence frame is to give students within groups of four some language to begin formulating a hypothesis related to the model they will refine.

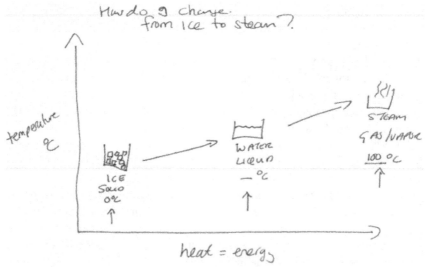

FIGURE 5.2
Ms. C's Student Generated Initial Heating Curve

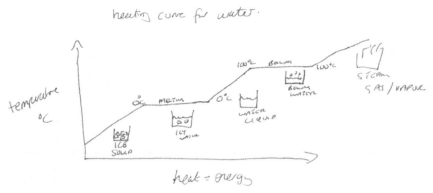

FIGURE 5.3
Ms. C's Student Generated Final Heating Curve

The lesson continues the next day with Ms. C displaying various materials that students can then use to seek evidence in support of their hypothesized model: water, ice, a hot plate, and a thermometer. As done in previous investigations, students are to develop a set of procedures to test the hypothesis, including the use of any appropriate data tables, and then to check their plan with Ms. C. After Ms. C provides students with feedback on their plan and probes for the reasoning behind initial models, students begin collecting data. Some students observe their ice at a temperature lower than 0°C. While walking around the class, Ms. C encourages students in one group to think about what this means for the visual model they have created.

The students recognize the need to relocate the position of the first beaker in the diagram. Additional observations lead students to notice that their thermometer stays at 0°C while the ice melts; Ms. C probes them to diagram what is happening at the particle level. At the end of the activity, students make a revised model on large whiteboards based on the data they have collected. Ms. C displays optional phrases that she encourages students to use to practice explaining their model in their groups: "I claim that the diagram should really look like . . . because. . . ." She also reminds students that the job of scientists is to explain and represent natural phenomena in a way that best fits the evidence they have—until new evidence comes along to refine (or change) their explanation. As a whole class, each group explains their revised model, with Ms. C asking questions that help build on their ideas and deepen their understanding of energy conservation in this system.

In this chapter, we take the position that science should be presented as more than a "body of knowledge" that is transmitted from teacher to student. Instead, we emphasize the role of helping students make sense of, instead of knowing facts about, natural phenomena by engaging them in the intellectual activities that scientists and engineers routinely do to explanation natural phenomena or propose solutions to real-world problems. We refer to these intellectual activities as scientific/engineering *practices,* currently being promoted in Next Generation Science Standards (NGSS).

Through the process of constructing meaning, ELs not only deepen their understanding of science (both core ideas and the nature of science), but also use a variety of language functions as they ask questions or pose problems, collect and interpret data, develop models, and formulate solutions and explanations. Moreover, student engagement in scientific and engineering practices broadens ELs' access to authentic and rigorous science learning, thereby increasing opportunities to learn science through more "hands-on" and "minds-on" secondary school science experiences. We will explain (1) how scientific sense-making looks through a sociocultural framing and (2) the role that scientific and engineering practices play as students make sense of science ideas. We will also compare different instructional approaches (as seen in the interactions at the beginning of this chapter) to understand how they may enhance or hinder sense-making opportunities, particularly for ELs.

What Is "Scientific Sense-Making"?

There are various perspectives on how individuals make meaning of the world around them and the discipline-specific concepts learned in school settings. One perspective assumes that individuals are essentially "blank slates" and that an authoritative source (e.g., a teacher speaking or a textbook) transmits information to the student. Another perspective argues that individuals construct meaning as they interact with the environment around them—either fitting in experiences with their preestablished beliefs or shifting their individual beliefs to accommodate the conflicting experiences.

Yet another perspective acknowledges that meaning is constructed through social interactions, where individuals mutually appropriate the norms and language of the community and where learning happens through this participation in a community of practice (Lave & Wenger, 1991; Lemke, 1990). A related perspective affirms that individuals bring diverse cultural practices and intellectual resources to bear when constructing meaning from experience. As depicted in the previous chapter on contextualization, multiple and even conflicting discourses (ways of talking and knowing) among individuals in a learning community can be productive tools for mediating learning in hybrid discourse environments (Gutiérrez, Baquedano-López, & Tejeda, 1999), and everyday discourses are, in many ways, scientific in their own right (Warren,

Bollenger, Ogonowski, Rosebery, Hudicourt-Barnes, 2001). Secondary Science Teaching with English Language and Literacy Acquisition (SSTELLA) draws heavily on these latter two perspectives; thus scientific sense-making becomes a process of students leveraging multiple ways of knowing to make sense of complex ideas in science.

The Importance of Involving English Learners in Complex Science Ideas and Scientific and Engineering Practices

All four SSTELLA practices relate to science learning and the development of language and literacy, but here we focus on the role of scientific and engineering practices to leverage sense-making. We argue that student engagement in scientific and engineering practices provides ELs with access to a multitude of ways of using language—more varied and complex than can be accomplished by merely listening to or reading about scientific facts and explanations. Moreover, sense-making through scientific and engineering practices becomes a contextualized use of language that helps ELs understand complex science ideas by exploring ideas and connecting to real-world uses and everyday experiences and thinking.

We have previously made the argument that ELs, more so than their English-only counterparts, are often denied opportunities to engage in rigorous subject matter, perhaps due to perceptions that limited English proficiency inhibits them from learning such rigorous content. However, research demonstrates that ELs do improve in science achievement when given instruction that is meaningfully contextualized and inquiry-based (Lee & Luykx, 2006).

Furthermore, contextualized, content-based instruction in students' second language can enhance the language proficiency of ELs while also supporting academic learning (Lee & Luykx, 2006; Met, 1994; Shaw, Lyon, Stoddart, Mosqueda, & Menon, 2014; Thomas & Collier, 2012). We should note that even though studies have looked at EL learning with a range of English proficiency levels, beginning ELs usually need additional supports to improve learning, such as providing home language instruction in core content areas. The subject matter content provides a meaningful context for the learning of language structure and functions, and the language processes provide the medium for analysis and communication of subject-matter knowledge. Inquiry science, therefore, is an excellent context for learning language and literacy. In particular, inquiry via the development and use of scientific models allows for even greater use of language to comprehend conceptual ideas, represent them (e.g., visually, mathematically, or in writing), and explain them to others.

In the sections that follow, we communicate how teachers can facilitate ELs' sense-making by attending to big ideas in science and engaging students in scientific and engineering practices to understand those big ideas.

Shifting from "Science Topics" to "Big Ideas in Science"

Imagine yourself planning a unit of instruction, like Ms. A and Ms. C in the introduction. You have various curricular resources to draw on: standards, a textbook, a description of an investigation found online, and of course your own content expertise. Where do you start? What is at the core of this unit that everything will be centered around? Wiggins and McTighe (1998) proposed a model for planning instruction referred to as backwards design (see figure 5.4 below). In backwards design, we can take a topic—for example, chemical reactions—and categorize science ideas (e.g., terms, processes, theories) into (1) what students need to at least be familiar with, (2) what students need to understand as important to know and do, and then (3) that one idea that explains the central phenomenon of interest. This latter idea is what we refer to as "the big idea" of a science unit.

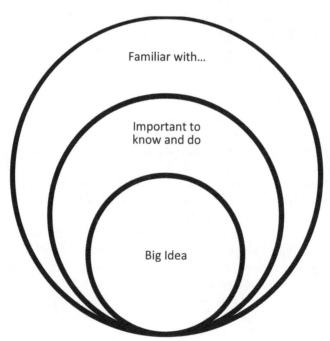

FIGURE 5.4
Backwards Design Model

Big ideas are more than just *really* important concepts, such as conservation of matter. In a series of tools developed for novice science teachers, the Ambitious Science Teaching project (2014) proposed that big ideas refer to the relationship between some natural phenomenon and a causal explanation that helps us understand that phenomenon. For instance, if the natural phenomenon is about metal rusting (such as on a bike), the big idea might be "chemical processes can cause a change in the chemical and physical property of substances." This can also be stated as an essential question: "What chemical processes are occurring to rust metal?"

By focusing on an actual process, model, or theory, the science learning moves beyond a body of knowledge alone. Learning becomes about *explaining* natural phenomena through the core knowledge-building activities of science: developing initial models to explain ideas, collecting evidence to support models, and then defending explanations. All these activities require language to be used in meaningful and purposeful ways. Furthermore, big ideas allow the teacher to focus on particular contexts (a local or global issue, a phenomenon experienced by students) that once again make learning purposeful, meaningful, and relevant, as described in chapter 4.

To further contextualize the big idea described above, we might rephrase the essential questions: "Why does my bicycle rust when I leave it outside? What chemical processes cause this to happen?" For ELs, a process- or theory-focused big idea increases their access to more rigorous and authentic science, and allows them to use language in multiple ways as they make sense of this phenomenon of study. Put simply, shifting the focus from topics to big ideas shifts what is communicated to students about science and how they will eventually learn science.

Ways to Communicate the Big Idea and Learning Goals

Clear expectations for learning are positively linked to improved student learning (Hattie, 2009). Consequences of not being clear in what students are supposed to learn or how to demonstrate what they have learned include potential student misunderstandings about the purpose of an activity (is the activity's purpose to arrive at some expected "result" or understand the concept being investigated?). In some cases, the teacher himself might not have a clear idea about what students should be taking away from the lesson, which would make it challenging to bridge multiple lessons together that help to deepen student understanding around focused science ideas.

Sometimes a big idea is *implicit* in the lesson, meaning that students have limited opportunity to think about, discuss, or apply the big idea while learning science than if that idea was presented explicitly. For instance, the teacher may state an idea at the start of class—"Today, we are interested in . . ."—or title a lab activity or other artifacts with a big idea or objective. Alternatively, the teacher may explain the big idea while delivering content, but never really draw students' attention to it as *the* take-home message that ties together all activities and concepts or come back to the big idea at the end of the lesson.

Instead, when the teacher continuously draws students' attention to the big idea and connects big ideas to prior and ongoing activities (i.e., *explicit communication*), teachers' instruction and assessment are more focused. Students' initial ideas are a springboard for moving toward understanding deeper, bigger ideas as they seek to explain a phenomenon of interest or contemplate solutions to a real-world problem. For example, the teacher might display a video or actual bike with rust while noting that today they will be finding out: "Why does my bicycle rust when I leave it outside? What chemical processes cause this to happen?" She then can ask students (orally or through a quick write), "What have we already learned about chemical reactions that might help us answer this?" and explain the activity that will be explored to answer the question. At the end of class, the teacher can focus a science talk (see chapter 6 on discourse) around evidence collected that can help students make sense of the big idea. Remember that big ideas become even more meaningful when framed around phenomena, models, or problems relevant to students' lived experiences.

Sense-making is also enhanced when teachers make it clear how students will make progress toward understanding the big idea (i.e., a learning objective) and what is expected in their talk and work (i.e., expectations for success). These connections between the big idea, classroom activity, prior knowledge, and lived experiences are critical for learners, particularly ELs (August & Hakuta, 1997; Kelly, 2007; Rivet & Krajcik, 2008). Table 5.1 below displays a graphic organizer that students might complete throughout a unit to keep a record of the daily learning objectives, what activities were associated with that objective, and any reflective notes on their learning (was there a concept they still didn't get? Some connection to events in daily life? Connection to prior activities/concepts?).

Learning Objective Outline[2]

The last column in table 5.1 allows students to become more aware of their own learning progress. Other strategies to promote self-regulated learners include (1) completion of a (Think I) Know-Want to Know-Learned (KWL) charts, (2) exit tickets that ask students "3 things I learned today," or (3) writing goals (related to science understanding) for the upcoming unit. Rubrics

TABLE 5.1
Learning Objective Outline

"Big Idea": How does density influence the impact of motor oil in our environment?		
Learning Objective	Associated Activity	Reflection Notes
Using a foldable, determine the relationship between mass, volume, and density.	Jigsaw foldable from textbook (measurement, density, volume, mass)	*Density is a measurement of how much stuff [or mass] there is for a certain size, or volume.*
Explain, using density, how you can tell if mystery cubes will sink or float in the storm drain.	Determine density of mystery cubes, graph density, and predict if they will float in a storm drain: https://phet.colorado.edu/ en/simulation/density	*Density of water = 1 g/ml* *Cube A (motor oil) is less dense than water (will float).* *Cube B is more dense than water (will sink).* *What happens to cube that has the same density as water?*
Explain, using density, the impact motor oil will have on our environment.	Density lab (to collective evidence) Write explanation	*Density of motor oil = .95 g/ml* *Density of mud = 1.33 g/ml* *Motor oil will float on water and then can enter storm drains.* *Is there anything else besides density that I should know about motor oil?*

Source: Adapted from instructional activities developed by Emily Carrasco, a middle school science teacher in Mesa, Arizona.

can also be an effective way for students to self-assess their own learning. Furthermore, teachers can help students see how their learning has *changed* over time. For instance, at the start of a unit or lesson the students might depict an initial model of what causes the seasons, and then by the end of the lesson (or lessons) they may revisit and revise their models—explaining what revisions they made and why.

Referring back to the two interactions at the beginning of the chapter, we observe differences in both the nature of the learning goals and how they were communicated to students. While the *topic* of the two lessons is nearly identical, Ms. A communicated the learning objective as knowledge to be acquired ("Students will understand the relationship between energy and phase changes of water"). Furthermore, "understanding" as a learning outcome can be assessed many different ways, making it more challenging for students to know how they will eventually demonstrate the learning goal.

Ms. C, on the other hand, communicated the learning objective as a specific intellectual activity embedded within a scientific and engineering practice (constructing claims from evidence) for which there is a measurable outcome ("Explain the relationship between energy and phase changes for water"). Ms. C related the objective within the larger context of the big idea, communicated as an essential question for the unit: "How is energy transferred and conserved?" To contextualize the big idea, Ms. C elicits from students their experiences observing phase changes of water outside of school. She ensures that multiple students have opportunities to discuss these examples in a variety of formats (pairs, whole class) before connecting their experiences (e.g., "Let's say I need some steam to clean my carpet, but all I have is this ice. How could I turn this into steam?") to the driving question for the day: "What we really want to know is the relationship between energy and temperature in these phase changes [for water]."

Scientific Sense-Making through the Core Knowledge-Building Activities of Scientists

Referring back to the introductory interactions, Ms. A positions herself as the authority, providing information to her students. Although she does engage students in an investigation, she is the one who decides what is being investigated and how students will collect and interpret data. Thus, the students' role is to receive, memorize, and recall knowledge and procedures. In addition to hindering students' deep conceptual understanding of science, students are not engaged in constructing knowledge, as "student scientists," or in seeing the connection with their own lived experiences (as described in chapter 4).

According to a sociocultural perspective, an approach resembling interaction 1 is limited in helping students, particularly ELs, make sense of complex science ideas. For one, a sociocultural perspective posits that learning is a social phenomenon and multidirectional. Individuals do not just take in information; instead they construct their own meaning of it, which is shaped by many factors—social and cultural. It is the process of thinking and investigating the natural world that allows students to interpret and productively use discipline-specific language, which in turn has been shown to help ELs acquire second language proficiency.

This emphasis on student questioning and investigating the natural world is generally referred to as an "inquiry-based" approach to teaching science. However, the term *inquiry* has been interpreted in very different ways across a range of communities (including scientists, science educators, and science education researchers). One problem that arose was that inquiry sometimes became synonymous with "hands-on" learning, where students are merely manipulating various materials (e.g., using a pH strip to identify the pH of a substance), without any real opportunity to develop an understanding of how to plan and conduct an investigation, connect investigative experiences with the science they are supposed to be learning, communicate and share findings, and explore how scientists use data to develop models and theories about the natural world.

As a response to the many faces of inquiry, Windschitl (2008) categorized common science classroom activities in "families" that elucidate what is—and, perhaps more importantly, what is not—in the spirit of inquiry. Windschitl began by arguing that a central goal of scientists is to "develop defensible explanations of the way the natural world works." His focus on "defensible explanations" differs greatly from many science classroom activities where the goal is to "get a result" (e.g., What happens when an enzyme catalase is mixed with the substrate hydrogen peroxide?). Windschitl does not suggest that the role of science classrooms is to actually make empirical breakthroughs—but rather that the science activities should approximate the actual core knowledge-building practices of scientists. He described four interrelated "conversations" that can lead to defensible explanations:

- Organizing what we know and what we'd like to know
- Generating a model
- Seeking evidence
- Constructing an argument

Note that these conversations do not explicitly mention "making predictions," "designing controlled experiments," or other processes typically associated with "the scientific method." There are many ways to seek and interpret evidence, but the commonality is that evidence is what we use to support (via an argument) how a particular model (or representation) best explains a phenomenon. It is also important to note Windschitl's use of the word *conversation*. Consistent with a sociocultural approach, scientists (and students learning science) engage in talk throughout the various knowledge-building activities. Furthermore, the various activities (e.g., generating a model and seeking evidence) happen reciprocally, not linearly. Scientists, working within scientific communities, continuously go back and revise models and seek new evidence to better explain the natural world.

So if inquiry means engaging in the four conversations listed above, with the ultimate goal being defensible explanations, how do other commonly observed science classroom activities hold up? Windschitl proposed another family of activities that support the inquiry process. These activities include conducting background library/Internet research, watching teacher-led demonstrations, performing lab-practicals, completing exercises to "make something happen" (e.g., convection currents in an aquarium, an acid-base reaction), or learning the use of equipment or lab procedures.

At some point the skills of conducting literature reviews and knowing how to carry out the procedure to seek your evidence will be useful (or even necessary) to engage in actual inquiry. However, if left on their own, they do not represent "doing inquiry." Finally, a family of activities such as investigating arbitrary questions (effect of rock and roll on bean plants), "cookbook" investigations (where the teacher gives all instruction and information needed to carry out an investigation), and performing process skills in isolation (making a prediction or observations) should be reconsidered given that they may actually supplant making meaningful sense of science and lead to confusion about the nature processes of doing science.

From Inquiry to Scientific and Engineering Practices: Connection to NGSS and CCSS

The National Research Council's *A Framework for K–12 Science Education: Practices, Crosscutting Concepts, and Core Ideas* (2012) shifted the focus from the nebulous construct of "inquiry" to a clearly articulated set of eight scientific and engineering "practices" listed below.

1. Asking questions and defining problems
2. Developing and using models
3. Planning and carrying out investigations
4. Mathematical and computational thinking
5. Analyzing and interpreting data
6. Constructing explanations and designing solutions
7. Engaging in argument from evidence
8. Obtaining, evaluating, and communicating information

This set of practices directly informed the NGSS and the intellectual resources that SSTELLA promotes to help students make sense of complex science ideas. A major rationale for this shift coincided with Windschitl's (2008) main argument: that scientists do much more than just "investigate" the natural world; they also evaluate evidence collected by arguing, critiquing, and analyzing in order to develop theories and models that explain how the natural world works (see figure 5.4).

Engineers engage in some similar activities, but often for a different purpose: to design solutions for identified problems under certain constraints (e.g., resources, priorities, margin of error). According to Osborne (2014), the purpose of involving students in scientific practices is to help them better understand what we know about the natural world and how we know it, in addition to developing a deeper understanding of science concepts generated from investigations of the natural world. For example, the development of scientific models allows students to connect scientific processes to representations that have predictive and explanatory power, thus coordinating knowledge and skills.

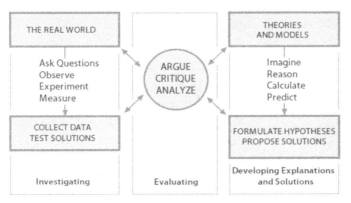

FIGURE 5.5
Source: **National Research Council (2012).**

Scientific and engineering practices also call on students to use language in a variety of ways that are discipline-specific and reflect many of the same expectations called on in Common Core State Standards (CCSS) for English language arts and disciplinary literacy. Like the framework, the CCSS call for students to engage with argumentative (arguing from evidence) and informative/explanatory texts (constructing explanations) in writing and reading. However, additional practices also relate to CCSS. For example, the CCSS call for students to "integrate and evaluate multiple sources of information presented in diverse formats and media (e.g., quantitative data, video, multimedia) in order to address a question or solve a problem"—which includes the interpretation and analysis of data.

Furthermore, students are called on to "Follow precisely a complex multi-step procedure when carrying out experiments, taking measurements, or performing technical tasks; analyze the specific results based on explanations in the text" (9-10.RST.3), which is done while planning and carrying out investigations. Thus, even scientific and engineering practices engage students in using language—which then provides challenges and opportunities for ELs.

Focusing on the Development and Use of Scientific Models

We have discussed the limited opportunities for students, particularly ELs, to make sense of phase changes in interaction 1 at the beginning of this chapter. Interaction 2 differs particularly in the role of Ms. C and her students during instruction. Ms. C also engages students in scientific and engineering practices. However, the purpose of the practices is to give students a way to construct meaning, not confirm what they have already been told. Ms. C also gives priority to student development and use of scientific models.

Scientific models are essentially representations of some natural phenomenon. These representations could be physical (diagrams of processes), mathematical (gas laws), or even explanatory (sets of ideas, such as Darwin's inferences about the theory of natural selection). The scientific practice of developing and using models requires much more than asking students to replicate a food web or a diagram depicting convection currents. We want students to develop their own initial models of some phenomenon, test and revise the models, and then use them to explain what is happening. Through this process, students have multiple opportunities to make sense of the core science ideas by constructing them as scientists would, *while engaging in multiple analytic tasks and language functions.* We outline a way to sequence scientific modeling as done by other science education scholars (e.g., Passmore & Stewart, 2002).

Framing the Unit. Chapter 4 discussed the importance of instructional framing to make learning meaningful and relevant for students. Framing not only relates science concepts to students' lives outside of school, but also helps students see themselves in/through science and understand how science is used in society by exploring partial scientific models, puzzling phenomenon, or an ill-defined problem. Table 5.2 contains some examples.

Since the process of developing and using models takes time, the introduction of a puzzling phenomenon, partial model, or ill-defined problem would most likely occur at the start of an instructional unit and thus be a thread running through the whole unit. You might see how this framing works together with a big idea. The big idea helps communicate the explanation students will eventually arrive at to account for the observable phenomenon or model, or the solution to the problem. In interaction 2, Ms. C presents the phenomenon of how ice can be turned into steam—which

TABLE 5.2
Unit Framing Examples

Framing Example	How Scientific Sense-Making Is Promoted
Puzzling phenomenon: Teacher places an ice cube in a beaker with water and another ice cube in a beaker with rubbing alcohol (they appear identical to students). "Why does one sink and one float?"	Students are encountering a phenomenon that conflicts with everyday experiences. They must draw on scientific principles to make sense of the situation. Experience anchors future exploration into density.
Partial model: Teacher shows a time-lapse video of a moon cycling through each of its phases.	This is a partial model since it is not apparent how the relative position of the earth, moon, and sun explain and predict the moon phases. Students can then use materials to explain what they see and develop the complete model.
Ill-defined problem: "How do we best reduce the number of plastic bottles used in our school?"	Students are challenged to consider constraints and affordances (using scientific principles) in addition to differing values and priorities.

was an example that she elicited from students' everyday experiences. Thus, framing is enhanced when students engage in scientific practices that are connected to their lives outsides of school.

Developing an Initial Model. Either as part of the initial framing, or shortly afterward, students would develop their own initial models to represent what is happening. Referring back to interaction 2, Ms. C facilitated a class discussion in which the students collectively came up with an initial model—one that explained the relationship between phase changes and energy input as a linear relationship.

Testing the Model. Ms. C used the students' partial model as the hypothesis to now test—instead of giving them a predetermined question to answer. Students used what they knew, and available materials, to come up with a plan to provide evidence of the model. The teacher's role here was to facilitate—by eliciting and probing for student thinking.

Revising the Model. Students could then evaluate their models based on the data collected and make needed revisions. In Ms. C's classroom, the whole class discussion resulted in students changing the linear graph to one that reflected a stable temperature during the periods of melting and boiling—even though heat was continuously added. Thus, through the revision students could represent (either graphically, mathematically, or by using other means of representation) what was really happening, again with facilitation by the teacher. This revision step is critical to help students make sense of the core science ideas through engagement of multiple science and engineering practices, such as analyzing data and communication information. In the next chapter, we will discuss how teachers can facilitate productive student talk that would serve to elicit student ideas and deepen their understanding during model revision, all while giving multiple opportunities to use and develop language.

Applying the Model. Finally, the student-constructed model can be used to explain with evidence the original phenomenon of interest as well as use the model to predict outcomes for new phenomenon, or see possible limitations of the model. For instance, would the heating/cooling curve be the same for a different substance? How is a heating/cooling curve used in real-life applications?

To summarize, a key difference between the two examples is that in interaction 2, *students* are doing the sense-making—developing initial ideas, figuring out how to support their ideas, and then revising based on evidence *they* have uncovered. Students are figuring out relationships and using chemical principles (e.g., particulate nature of matter) to explain a natural phenomenon. In essence, authority for knowledge generated has been redistributed to students. However, the teacher plays a pivotal role in facilitating activities and discussions to make content and language accessible to all students, including ELs, so that they can be supported in sense-making.

Supporting ELs' Scientific Sense-Making

Engaging ELs in scientific and engineering practices does not in itself lead to scientific sense-making. Each scientific or engineering practice requires students to navigate multiple analytical tasks (*or the intellectual activities associated with disciplinary practices*) and language functions (*various communicative acts [saying, writing, doing, and being] used while transmitting ideas in a socially mediated context*). Table 5.3 outlines analytical tasks and language functions for one particular practice: developing and using models.

Even when tasks are student-centered, research shows that ELs benefit from supports to access academic tasks (Echevarria, Vogt, & Short, 2012). Table 5.4 describes various types of teacher moves that can be supportive. For instance, in interaction 2, Ms. C uses real examples (realia) of two water phases (steam and ice) to ensure that students at varying levels of English proficiency are provided with concrete representations of the lesson activities. These instructional moves in the context of communicating the learning goals, using realia, and eliciting connections to students' lived experiences are essential to supporting EL students' access to the big idea of the lesson.

TABLE 5.3
Analytical Tasks and Language Functions When Developing and Using Models

Analytical tasks (intellectual activities associated with disciplinary practices)	• Develop and represent an explicit model of a phenomenon or system. • Use a model to support an explanation of a phenomenon or system. • Make revisions to a model based on either suggestions of others or conflicts between a model and observation.
Receptive language functions (communicative acts to interpret ideas)	• Comprehend others' oral and written descriptions, discussions, and justifications of models of phenomena or systems. • Interpret the meaning of models presented in texts and diagrams.
Productive language functions (communicative acts to produce ideas)	• Communicate (orally and in writing) ideas, concepts, and information related to a phenomenon or system using a model developed for this purpose. • Label diagrams of a model and make lists of parts. • Describe a model using oral and/or written language as well as illustrations. • Describe how a model relates to a phenomenon or system. • Discuss limitations of a model. • Ask questions about others' models.

Source: Lee et al., 2013.

A sociocultural perspective moves beyond *momentary* supports and emphasizes the role of *scaffolding* instruction—that is, determining what individuals can do on their own versus what they can do with support (from some tool, including a more capable peer), and then gradually taking away (or fading) the support once students are successful (Walqui & van Lier, 2010). To move beyond momentary supports, consider (1) what students need to eventually be able to do (a culminating learning objective), (2) conceptual checkpoints along the way, and (3) how some of the moves from table 5.4 can be *adjusted* as students meet the checkpoints. These adjustments may differ among students, particularly depending on a student's EL proficiency in various modalities (speaking, listening, reading, and writing).

As an example of scaffolding sense-making for ELs, a teacher teaching density to eighth grade students wanted her students to apply knowledge of the relationship between mass, volume, and density to explain how the interaction of oil and water (different densities) accounts for the impact of motor oil in the environment (via storm drains). The teacher knew that one key checkpoint is for students to understand that an object's mass does *not*

TABLE 5.4
Sense-Making Supports

Support	Description	Example (for developing and using models)
(Teacher) modeling	The teacher provides examples or demonstrates how students are to perform a task.	The teacher displays a model developed by a student on a white board (e.g., particle diagram of a reaction), and talks through how to evaluate and make revisions to the model based on observations from an investigation.
Graphic organizers	Organizes information to better make sense of relationships, such as Venn diagrams, word webs, concepts maps, etc.	A graphic organizer could include boxes for "inputs" and "outputs" of photosynthesis and cellular respiration—later refined as students understand how energy is transferred.
Visual representations	Could be in the form of pictures, charts, diagrams, videos	Teacher shows a time lapse video of the moon as it cycles through its phases— students then try to replicate what is happening with Styrofoam balls and a light source.
Realia	Actual objects that students can experience or manipulate	Students may test their model of a chemical equation by reacting various reactants.
Use of technology	Can range from technology used to present information (webquests, weeblies) to collect or analyze data, to products produced by students	Students enter data from the phase change experiment on an Excel spreadsheet and then use the graphing function to produce a digital representation of their results.

determine whether it will sink or float in a liquid (such as water). Throughout a week of instruction, the teacher scaffolded sense-making of density through several key instructional moves.

First, at the onset of the unit, she used an online simulation with a smart board in which cubes of various sizes could be manipulated and dropped into water to see if they would "sink" or "float." Students typically made predictions based on apparent volume only (larger- vs. smaller-sized cubes). This use of technology initially helped students visualize and understand that size or "volume" alone does not explain sinking or floating, with the process being modeled by the teacher. To clarify, the teacher in this case does not address other contributing factors nor the notion of buoyancy, which could deepen student understanding. The technology in itself was a tool for assisting sense-making. Later in the unit, students calculated actual densities of the various objects, and used those predictions to determine whether each substance would sink or float in water. The teacher stressed to students that after they have figured out how to calculate densities of objects, they would not even need the visual cues from the simulation.

To better understand this important relationship, groups of four "jigsaw" information from a textbook—one taking mass, one volume, one density, and one measurement. They record notes on a piece of paper divided into four quadrants, and then together come up with a consensus summary statement written in the middle of the paper. This summary ends up being the relation among the various concepts. For some groups, their summary *was* the constructed equation to find "a measurement of how much stuff [or mass] there is for a certain size, or volume."

Later in the unit, students utilized their summaries to calculate the same cubes in the simulation. With facilitation by the teacher, students graphed and used the density calculations to determine whether objects would sink or float. Finally, all activities were recorded in students' interactive notebook, which they could refer to throughout the week. Thus, three primary tools were used (an online simulation, a jigsaw page of notes, and an interactive notebook). The teacher guided the first use of technology, which in itself was a guide, but then the teacher reduced herself and the technology as the authority and instead let students rely on their own expertise to make sense of the cubes. By the end of the unit, students needed neither the notes nor the technology to explain the phenomenon of interest.

The key difference between momentary supports that increase access to content and supports that truly scaffold sense-making is that in the latter case, the teacher has a clear sense of the big idea she wants her students to eventually understand, as well as clear learning objectives and expectations throughout to help students make progress toward that big idea. Moreover, supports can help draw on students' prior engagement in intellectual activities, such as constructing an equation and justifying predictions as resources for later activities. Thus, students gain a deeper connection between prior and ongoing activities. As a final note, students themselves serve as supports for scaffolding through purpose collaborative groups, as will be discussed further in chapter 7.

Summary

Our driving question throughout this chapter was "How do I help ELs best make sense of complex scientific concepts and develop competencies with the practices of scientists and engineers?"

To summarize our key points in this chapter:

1. Scientific sense-making is a process by which students bring to bear multiple ways of knowing to make sense of complex ideas in science.
2. Involving students in scientific and engineering practices facilitates this transition by allowing them to construct meaning *through* various analytical tasks and language functions.
3. Scientific and engineering practices also communicate how science is more than just a "body of knowledge" and even more than just observing, predicting, and engaging in "hands-on" activities.
4. ELs benefit when instruction is scaffolded through sense-making supports that are well connected to the big idea and clear objectives (e.g., teacher modeling, graphic organizers, visual representations, realia, and use of technology).

Notes

1. This vignette was adapted from one developed by Joanne Couling, a doctoral student in the Education Department at the University of California, Santa Cruz.

2. Adapted from instructional activities developed by Emily Carrasco, a middle school science teacher in Mesa, Arizona.

References

August, D., & Hakuta, K. (1997). *Improving schooling for language-minority children: A research agenda.* Washington, DC: National Academies Press.

Echevarría, J., Vogt, M., & Short, D. J. (2012). *Making content comprehensible for English learners: The SIOP model* (4th ed.). Boston, MA: Pearson.

Gutiérrez, K. D., Baquedano-López, P., & Tejeda, C. (1999). Rethinking diversity: Hybridity and hybrid language practices in the third space. *Mind, Culture, and Activity, 6*(4), 286–303.

Hattie, J. (2009). *Visible learning.* New York, NY: Routledge.

Kelly, G. (2007). Discourse in science classrooms. In S. K. Abell & N. G. Lederman (Eds.), *Handbook of research on science education* (2nd ed., pp. 443–70). Mahwah, NJ: Lawrence Erlbaum Associates.

Lave, J., & Wenger, E. (1991). *Situated learning: Legitimate peripheral participation.* Cambridge, UK; New York, NY: Cambridge University Press.

Lee, O., & Luykx, A. (2006). *Science education and student diversity: Synthesis and research agenda.* New York, NY: Cambridge University Press.

Lemke, J. (1990). *Talking science: Language, learning, and values.* Norwood, NJ: Ablex.

Met, M. (1994). Teaching content through a second language. In F. Genesee (Ed.), *Educating second language children: The whole child, the whole curriculum, the whole community* (pp. 159–82). Cambridge, UK: Cambridge University Press.

National Research Council. (2012). *A framework for K–12 science education: Practices, crosscutting concepts, and core ideas.* Washington, DC: National Academies Press.

Osborne, J. (2014). Teaching scientific practices: Meeting the challenge of change. *Journal of Science Teacher Education, 25*(2), 177–96.

Passmore, C., & Stewart, J. (2002). A modeling approach to teaching evolutionary biology in high schools. *Journal of Research in Science Teaching, 39*(3), 185–204.

Rivet, A., & Krajcik, J. (2008). Contextualizing instruction: Leveraging students' prior knowledge and experiences to foster understanding of middle school science. *Journal of Research in Science Teaching, 45,* 79–100.

Shaw, J., Lyon, E. G., Stoddart, T., Mosqueda, E., & Menon, P. (2014). Improving science and literacy learning for English language learners: Evidence from a preservice teacher preparation intervention. *Journal of Science Teacher Education, 25*(5), 621–43.

Thomas, W. P., & Collier, V. P. (2012). *Dual language education for a transformed world.* Albuquerque, NM: Fuente Press.

Walqui, A., & van Lier, L. (2010). *Scaffolding the academic success of adolescent English language learners: A pedagogy of promise.* San Francisco, CA: WestEd.

Warren, B., Ballenger, C., Ogonowski, M., Rosebery, A., & Hudicourt-Barnes, J. (2001). Rethinking diversity in learning science: The logic of everyday sense making. *Journal of Research in Science Teaching, 38,* 529–52.

Wiggins, G., & McTighe, J. (1998). *Understanding by design.* Alexandria, VA: Association for Supervision and Curriculum Development.

Windschitl, M. (2008). What is inquiry? A framework for thinking about authentic scientific practice in the classroom. In J. Luft, R. L. Bell, & J. Gess-Newsome (Eds.), *Science as inquiry in the secondary setting* (pp. 1–20). Arlington, VA: National Science Teacers Association Press.

6

Scientific Discourse through Scientific and Engineering Practices

Edward G. Lyon and Jorge Solís

Overview

IN ADDITION TO making sense of core science ideas, a goal of secondary science education is for students to develop the communication practices that are central for individual and collective reasoning about science ideas (collectively referred to as scientific discourse). Discipline-specific forms of communication both deepen students' understanding of content and enrich opportunities for productive use of language. Because learning science and using the language of science are intertwined, we emphasize productive use of language through discourse-focused scientific and engineering practices (arguing from evidence and constructing scientific explanations) and science *talk* as a way to elicit students' ideas, draw on their funds of knowledge, and also deepen their understanding of science.

Introduction: Exploring Scientific Discourse

We start with dialogues from two different high school conceptual physics classrooms (Ambitious Science Teaching, 2015).[1] Both teachers have a similar classroom context to the interactions described in chapters 4 and 5, namely a combination of intermediate-level English learners (ELs), former ELs, and English-only students. Both classrooms also have two newly arrived ELs who have each taken general physics as part of their middle school curriculum.

Textbox 6.1

Questions to consider about each dialogue:

1. What do you notice about . . . ?
2. *Who* is talking to *whom*? How frequently?
3. How does the teacher react to student responses?
4. What opportunities are there for students to . . . ?
5. Make sense of science ideas?
6. Support ideas with evidence?

Dialogue 1

Ms. D: So we measure mass in _____? (with rising intonation in the voice)

Paul [an English Only student]: Weight?

Ms. D: Noooo . . . (again the rising intonation of voice)

George [an EO student]: Pounds?

Ms. D: Almost . . . can anyone help?

Sandra [an EO student]: Newtons?

Ms. D: That's right.

Dialogue 2

Just preceding the dialogue, Ms. E hangs a mass from a spring-scale at the front of the classroom. The scale reads "1 kilogram." She then produces a large bell jar, which she places over the entire scale and attaches the jar to a vacuum pump.

After asking, "Can anyone share their thinking about what the scale might read if I pump all the air out? Let's take a minute to generate some hypotheses," students think quietly and then offer a few thoughts.

Jaden [an EO student]: I'd say it would weigh less.

Ms. E: Can you say more about that?

Jaden: Because before you put the jar on top, the air is pushing down on it—the air weighs something, so it's the weight of the thing plus the weight of air.

Ms. E: And when you pull the air out?

Jaden: It's not pushing down anymore so it weighs just a little bit less.

Ms. E: Mm-hmm. [Waits in silence]. Okay groups, put your heads together. Do you agree or disagree with Jaden? And justify your thoughts!

Students are used to the routine of discussing within their group of four, who each has a number. Ms. E will call on one number to continue the conversation. Ms. E is well aware of who her ELs are when choosing which number.

Ms. E: Okay, how about #2 from Table "Curie" [tables are named after important physicists].

Immaculeta [newly arrived EL from Nigeria]: Well, air weighs something, but air I think pushes on all sides of the thing, not just top.

Jaden [other students are invited to respond as part of class norms]: Like water, if you're under water in a pool.

Immaculeta: Yeah.

Ms. E: Wait, Jaden are you changing your mind? How is your pool example like Immaculeta's claim?

Jaden: So if you are under water, maybe you can feel pressure from all sides?

Yessica [intermediate-level EL]: So it's like a submarine—it can get crushed if it goes too deep, crushed on all sides, so that's evidence—I can look it up.

Ms. E: Evidence of what, Yessica?

Yessica: Water . . . the air is like an ocean, pushing on all sides, so we get that pressure on all sides all the time.

Ms. E: Okay, Yessica, so it sounds like you've claimed that air has the same effect that water does: it exerts pressure on all sides. Does that mean the mass would weigh the same without air in the bell jar? More? Less?

Yessica: The same? Now I'm not sure.

The Secondary Science Teaching with English Language and Literacy Acquisitions (SSTELLA) instructional practice, "Promoting Scientific Discourse through Scientific and Engineering Practices" (henceforth referred to as "Scientific Discourse") centers on promoting (1) scientific argumentation and explanation and (2) productive student talk. Throughout this chapter, we will discuss the nature of scientific discourse in secondary science classrooms so that *teachers can better support all students and in particular ELs as they learn to communicate the range and particular forms of language used in scientific practices and expressed in science texts.*

Although science classroom activities do not function to emulate the full range of intellectual work of scientists or engineers, teachers' and students' *approximation* of real-world disciplinary activities, including how scientists and engineers communicate, allow for richer learning opportunities than a classroom-only focused student recall of factual knowledge. A classroom in which teachers and students are developing scientific discourse connects with what Langer (2011) refers to as the two major components of academic learning in science: (1) learning science content and (2) learning the ways of knowing and doing "appropriate and necessary for participating in a particular scientific field" (p. 77). As described in chapter 5, SSTELLA encourages science classroom activities that integrate science content learning with the "doing" of science via scientific and engineering practices. This chapter addresses the integrated learning process by focusing on how students learn to communicate scientific knowledge for particular purposes.

Scientific Discourse: The "Specialized Language" of Science and Why This Is Important

Science is not carried out individually, but rather as a community. Although we tend to associate some important scientific "discoveries" with individuals—Darwin and natural selection, Einstein and $E = mc^2$—these accomplishments would not have happened without reading and understanding what others have done before them, communicating their ideas to fellow experts in the field, drawing on their own everyday experiences, and then representing the findings (in writing, orally, and often graphically) to be critiqued and supported through more research. Over time, scientists, similar to professionals in other communities (actors, professional baseball players, teachers), have developed their own specialized vocabulary (*rehearse a scene, home run, think-pair-share*), as well as larger discourse practices (such as presenting a research poster or constructing a graph) to communicate to each other.

This specialized language is much more than a collection of vocabulary terms,[2] such as *photosynthesis* and *stoichiometry*. Instead, this specialized language is organized in particular ways, serving its intended audience and purpose (Pearson, Moje, & Greenleaf, 2010; Snow, 2010; Veel, 1997). Take a typical article in a journal to report new empirical scientific research. The organization of the article often follows a consistent pattern, including an introduction to the problem/issue, background literature, research questions, method of data collection and analysis, and results and conclusion. Look closer at the content of the article, and common uses of language may appear, such as in the seminal article in science presented below.

> We wish to suggest a structure for the salt of deoxyribose nucleic acid (D.N.A.). This structure has novel features which are of considerable biological interest. . . .
>   We wish to put forward a radically different structure for the salt of deoxyribose nucleic acid. This structure has two helical chains each coiled round the

same axis (see diagram). We have made the usual chemical assumptions, namely, that each chain consists of phosphate diester groups joining beta-D-deoxyribo-furanose residues with 3',5' linkages. The two chains (but not their bases) are related by a dyad perpendicular to the fiber axis. Both chains follow right-handed helices, but owing to the dyad the sequences of the atoms in the two chains run in opposite directions. Each chain loosely resembles Furberg's[2] model No. 1; that is, the bases are on the inside of the helix and the phosphates on the outside. The configuration of the sugar and the atoms near it is close to Furberg's "standard configuration," the sugar being roughly perpendicular to the attached base. There is a residue on each 3.4 A. in the z-direction. We have assumed an angle of 36° between adjacent residues in the same chain, so that the structure repeats after 10 residues on each chain, that is, after 34 A. The distance of a phosphorus atom from the fiber axis is 10 A. As the phosphates are on the outside, cations have easy access to them.

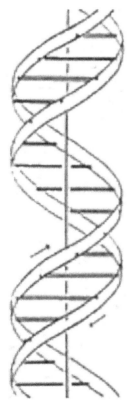

FIGURE 6.1
This figure is purely diagrammatic. The two ribbons symbolize the two phosphate-sugar chains, and the horizonal rods, the pair of bases holding the chains together. The vertical line marks the fiber axis.

The structure is an open one, and its water content is rather high. At lower water contents we would expect the bases to tilt so that the structure could become more compact.

The novel feature of the structure is the manner in which the two chains are held together by the purine and pyrimidine bases. The planes of the bases are perpendicular to the fiber axis. They are joined together in pairs, a single base from one chain being hydroden-bonded to a single base from the other chain, so that the two lie side by side with identical z-coordinates. One of the pair must be a purine and the other a pyrimidine for bonding to occur. The hydrogen bonds are made as follows: purine position 1 to pyrimidine position 1; purine position 6 to pyrimidine position 6.

If it is assumed that the bases only occur in the structure in the most plausible tautomeric forms (that is, with the keto rather than the enol configurations) it is found that only specific pairs of bases can bond together. These pairs are: adenine (purine) with thymine (pyrimidine), and guanine (purine) with cytosine (pyrimidine).[3]

Some features that can appear across science journal articles include (1) use of first or third person, which can switch rapidly between the two ("We wish to suggest. . . . This structure has novel features"), (2) dense, multiclause sentences ("If it is assumed that the bases only occur in the structure in the most plausible tautomeric forms . . ."), (3) domain-specific vocabulary that is not defined ("phosphate diester groups joining beta-D-deoxyribofuranose residues with 3',5' linkages"), and (4) hegemonic, rather than absolute, language such as *suggest*, *assume*, and *plausible*. This text structure serves a particular purpose—to communicate, as economically as possible, important findings to advance a particular field of research.

The structure and content of scientific texts differ in part by the function the text serves. For example, a laboratory *protocol* looks very different from a *report* since it serves to explicate exactly how one is to replicate a technique or investigation, rather than account for what happened. Thus, sentences often take the command form (e.g., "Using a 100–1,000 μL micropipette with sterile tip, transfer 250 μL of LB nutrient broth to the '+ plasmid' tube") and may be numbered rather than in narrative form for clarity.

The individual scientific and engineering fields (and subfields) vary in their use of language conventions and standards for the function of effective communication in the particular fields. In a similar vein, discourse in science classrooms will look different from the work of scientists and engineers, since the focus is primarily on learning science, including its discourse. Classrooms have their own (albeit overlapping) set of texts, procedures, and ways of communicating.

For instance, lab reports used in science classrooms may include response to pre-lab and analysis questions, as well as student reflection that aims to prepare students for the science being carried out and demonstrating what they have learned. Regardless of context, *we refer to these particular oral and written forms of language central for individual and collective reasoning about and communication of scientific ideas as "scientific discourse." Scientific discourse involves certain communicative practices, classroom routines, as well as learning tools/artifacts in the classroom.*

Connecting Scientific Discourse to Next Generation Science Standards and Common Core State Standards

Scientific discourse is valued in the Next Generation Science Standards (NGSS) for two fundamental reasons, both of which are described in the *Framework for Science Education* ("the framework"). First, "The argumentation and analysis that relate evidence and theory are also essential features of science; scientists need to be able to examine, review, and evaluate their own knowledge and ideas and critique those of others" (National Research Council, 2012, p. 27). For students, our goal is to help them understand core ideas in science by *approximating* the same dialogic activities that scientists use—giving priority to evidence, considering alternative explanations and counterevidence, and using data to develop models explaining natural phenomena.

The focus on discourse in NGSS positions scientific inquiry as much more than collecting and recording data; as described in chapter 5, the central goal is to develop defensible explanations of the way the natural world works. This goal entails being able to construct an argument from evidence. Second, the framework acknowledges that "science is fundamentally a social enterprise, and scientific knowledge advances through collaboration and in the context of a social system with well-developed norms" (National Research Council, 2012, p. 27). For example, in a study by Sampson and Clark (2009), when secondary students were given this opportunity to form collaborative arguments in groups, they demonstrated higher mastery of argumentation in transfer tasks compared to students who were instructed to construct arguments individually.

The framework explicitly embeds scientific discourse in two particular scientific practices: constructing explanations and engaging in argument from evidence. However, all scientific/engineering practices support each other so that students have something to explain and argue about. Furthermore, as discussed earlier, all NGSS integrate a scientific or engineering practice with a crosscutting concept and a core science idea. Therefore, what is important is not just teaching students the science discourse *skills* (e.g., how to explain or argue), nor getting them to use specialized scientific vocabulary or language conventions for their own sake, but rather involving them in explaining or arguing *about* core science ideas.

The Common Core State Standards (CCSS) for literacy in social studies, sciences, and technical subjects also emphasize informative/explanatory texts and arguments, as indicated below:

- Delineate and evaluate the argument and specific claims in a text, including the validity of the reasoning as well as the relevance and sufficiency of the evidence.
- Write arguments to support claims in an analysis of substantive topics or texts using valid reasoning and relevant and sufficient evidence.
- Write informative/explanatory texts to examine and convey complex ideas and information clearly and accurately through the effective selection, organization, and analysis of content.

However, once again, the standards do not promote decontextualized explaining and arguing, but rather explaining and arguing about something (e.g., "substantive topics" and "complex ideas and information"). In essence, science content and language *intersect* as students construct oral and written explanations and engage in argument from evidence (Cheuk, 2012; Lee, Quinn, & Valdés, 2013). Learning the discourse of science is enhanced when students can use language productively through other scientific and engineering practices. By asking questions, planning investigations, developing and using models, interpreting data, and communicating information, *students are exposed to more complex ways to use language and given a context in which to talk or write about science.*

Supporting Students' Scientific Discourse through Argumentation and Explanation

A primary goal for SSTELLA is to promote student use of disciplinary-specific language as they make sense of core science ideas and emulate the intellectual activities of scientists and engineers. Engaging students in constructing explanations and arguing with evidence are two key ways to promote disciplinary language and scientific/engineering practices. Moreover, Windschitl (2008) argues that defending explanations of the natural world is a central goal of scientists. However, middle school and high students rarely have opportunities to explain or argue about natural phenomena (Osborne, 2010). All too often, science is either taught as discrete facts (e.g., there are prokaryotic and eukaryotic cells) or the teacher provides all of the explanations for students (e.g., the process of osmosis occurs when there is a difference in solute concentration across a semipermeable membrane).

Yet science education scholars argue that for students to develop a coherent understanding of science, they must learn *how* science knowledge is constructed, presented, and shared. Argumentation and explanation assist students in unpacking knowledge construction in science. In turn, argumentation and explanation promote conceptual understanding, investigative competence, and understanding the epistemology and social nature of science (Driver, Newton, & Osborne, 2000). These competencies extend outside of the school setting and a career in science; they allow individuals to be critical consumers of knowledge and participate in a democratic society.

Explanation and argumentation also connect important features of the science language used in the classroom with authentic scientific practices in real-world scenarios. They involve all four language modalities (listening and reading [receptive], and speaking and writing [productive]), as opposed to just oral language production as often associated with "discourse." A focus on only talking science discounts how reading, writing, and listening can allow students to more effectively engage in science talk, just as talking science enhances student reading and writing in science. Furthermore, explanation and argumentation involve a complex set of analytical tasks and language functions—that is, what students *do* with language (see table 6.1), as we have noted for other scientific practices (see chapter 5).

Even if teachers expect secondary science students to explain and argue, students (especially ELs) are not guaranteed to receive assistance appropriate for their linguistic background. The various ways to support student

TABLE 6.1
Analytical Tasks and Language Functions When Arguing from Evidence

Analytical tasks	• Distinguish between a claim and supporting evidence or explanation.
	• Analyze whether evidence supports or contradicts a claim.
	• Analyze how well a model and evidence are aligned.
	• Construct an argument.
Receptive language functions (listening, reading)	• Comprehend arguments made by others orally.
	• Comprehend arguments made by others in writing.
Productive language functions (speaking, writing)	• Communicate (orally and in writing) ideas, concepts, and information related to the formation, defense, and critique of arguments.
	• Structure and order written or verbal arguments for a position.
	• Select and present key evidence to support or refute claims.
	• Question or critique arguments of others.

Source: Adapted from Lee et al., 2013.

competency with scientific explanation and argument described next better allow ELs to leverage scientific discourse as a way for deeper scientific sense-making, opportunities for English language development, and connections to real-world science.

Understanding the Structure and Function of Explanations and Arguments

Scientific arguments tend to possess common and predictable elements. Consider the following student written response:

> From the data I have received, I have determined that region C is at the greatest risk of a [malaria] epidemic in the next twenty years. Region C has the highest rate of increase in urbanization and agricultural development, both of which provide breeding groups for mosquitoes. Also, examining its current TRE [measure of climate] trend, I could see that in the next twenty years region C will be at its best to support *Anopheles arabiensi*s, one of the parasites-carried by mosquitoes.

You may not know exactly (a) the context of the response (this was part of a paper-and-pencil assessment in which students were presented with data related to risk factors for malaria epidemics in African regions), (b) the data given to students, or even (c) whether the statements made by students are accurate or relevant. However, you may still be able to determine that the student is making an *argument*. But what makes it an argument? Many science education researchers have drawn on a model by Toulmin (1958) that looks at structural elements: Is there an identifiable assertion, or *claim*? What *evidence* is used to support the claim? Usually most difficult for individuals of all ages, are their statements that *justify* how the data support the claim? Sampson and Clark (2008) constructed the model below to describe the relationships among those three components: *claim, evidence, and justification.*

In the student example, the claim is "I have determined that region C is at the greatest risk of an epidemic in the next twenty years." The student uses evidence in the form of actual trends in the data: "It has the highest rate at increase in urbanization and agricultural development" and "Also, examining its current TRE [measure of climate] trend, I could see that in the next twenty years region C will be at its best to support *Anopheles arabiensi*s." Finally, the student justifies how the evidence supports the claim: "both of which provide breeding groups for mosquitoes" and "one of the parasite-carrying mosquitoes."

Another common scientific discourse move, a scientific explanation, is related but subtly different. According to Osborne and Patterson (2011),

A Scientific Argument

The Claim
A conjecture, conclusion, explanation, generalizable principle or some other answer to a research question

Fits with... Supports...

The Evidence
Data (measurements and observations) or findings from other studies that have been collected, analyzed, and then interpreted by the researchers

Supported by... Explains

A Justification of the Evidence
A statement that explains the importance *and* the relevance of the evidence by linking it to a specific concept, principle, or underlying assumption

FIGURE 6.2
Source: Sampson and Clark (2008)

explanations "should make sense of a phenomenon based on other scientific facts . . . [a] defining feature of an explanation is that the phenomenon to be explained is not in doubt" (p. 629). You may ask students to explain "how individuals bitten by a mosquito may eventually die of malaria." There is a well-grounded and supported chain of events related to malaria-induced death of which very few scientists would disagree. However, the example used previously responds to an *ill-defined* problem.

There are multiple factors that may lead a particular geographic region to becoming or being more susceptible to malaria epidemics. In addition, how an individual makes sense of the multiple pieces of data will have implications for how the individual constructs their argument. Thus, an argument attempts to justify conclusions that are uncertain with a claim that is supported by the data. Of course, the distinction is never completely transparent. Science is founded on the idea of tentativeness—there are often multiple explanations for given observations. Arguments are a way to reach consensus about which explanation best fits the data. In fact, convincing arguments often consider those alternative explanations and provide justifications for how they do or do not fit the given data.

Teachers can help students understand the structure and quality of explanations and arguments by providing explicit models of them to deconstruct and compare. To caution, teachers frequently explain natural phenomenon in the course of their teaching—answering a student's question about "why the moon looks so big at times" or while giving a lecture on how changes in the DNA sequence may lead to alternated proteins and eventually altered phenotypes. Although this may seem like modeling itself, students do not have opportunities to understand that science presses for explanations (*how/why* something happens) not just the fact that something happens. Further, students certainly would not have opportunity to understand what makes an effective explanation. Therefore, teachers should promote student analysis of varying ways to explain and argue, including for *whom* the argument was written and for what reason (i.e., attending to audience and purpose).

Learning Goals and Expectations

In chapter 4, we emphasized establishing big "ideas" and specific learning objectives. We have also discussed in this chapter how scientific discourse (e.g., arguing from evidence) is a scientific practice that can be used in classrooms to communicate and make sense of core science ideas. Thus, promoting student use of scientific discourse is not a separate learning goal from content, but rather an integrated one, as exemplified in the following NGSS:

Make and defend a claim based on evidence that inheritable genetic variations may result from: (1) new genetic combinations through meiosis, (2) viable errors occurring during replication, and/or (3) mutations caused by environmental factors.

Throughout an entire unit on genetics, teachers may be teaching different aspects of genetic variation. Some lessons may involve teaching students the function of meiosis, and how events such as *independent assortment* and *crossing over* lead to new combinations of genetic material in the gametes. Other lessons may focus on various types of mutations and how they arise. As stipulated in the standard, the ultimate learning goal is not to just "understand" these sources of genetic variation, but to actually defend a claim about the sources of variation. Therefore, students need to demonstrate understanding *through* scientific discourse—specifically making a claim, providing evidence, and justifying that evidence.

Teachers can use the "analytical tasks" identified by Lee et al. (2013) to sequence learning objectives in a way that scaffolds students' argumentation, as outlined in figure 6.3. Note that the learning progression simultaneously (not independently) engages students in learning the big idea of genetic variation and developing competency with arguing from evidence. Thus, analytical tasks (e.g., analyze whether evidence supports or contradicts a claim) are not "add-ons" to the curriculum, but rather seamlessly integrated with learning the core idea. Put another way, students are learning about genetic variation through the defending of claims. They are *not* learning about genetic variation, and then applying it to the practice of arguing from evidence.

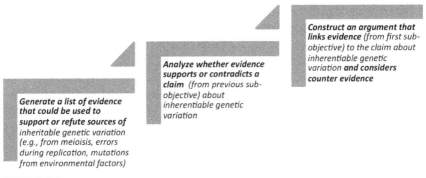

FIGURE 6.3
Progression for defending claims about genetic variation

From learning goals, a teacher can derive specific expectations that allow her to interpret student progress toward meeting competencies associated with arguing and explaining in a specific science topic context. Drawing on the same basic model of an argument, McNeill, Lizotte, Krajcik, and Marx (2006) developed rubrics for a middle school science curriculum to interpret students' *explanations* via three components: claim, evidence, and reasoning. McNeill and colleagues tailored the rubric for the specific science units through scientific principles (e.g., ideal gas laws, evolution by natural selection) they would expect students to utilize while "reasoning."

Furthermore, teachers can tailor the rubric to specific activities and investigations. As an example, researchers developed a rubric for the malaria epidemic problem discussed earlier to allow high school science teachers to interpret the extent to which students (1) included appropriate evidence (e.g., rate of urbanization in the regions, climate index), (2) appropriately transformed data (using historical data to extrapolate to the future), and (3) reasoned about relationships between factors (increased urbanization leads to increased risk of malaria epidemics).

Activities That Promote Scientific Explanation or Argumentation

Researchers have explored many types of science classroom activities that effectively promote argumentation and explanation. We present some examples that depict four common categories of activities: constructing individual arguments, critiquing individual arguments, debating socio-scientific issues (SSI), and engaging in argument-based inquiry.

Constructing Individual Explanations and Arguments. Students may individually construct explanations and arguments in a variety of ways: after analyzing data from an investigation, taking a position on a controversial issue in science (e.g., stem cell use), or responding to a prompt that elicits the student's initial conceptions about a natural phenomenon (e.g., light refraction). This does not mean students individually engage in all activities associated with the explanation or argumentation. For instance, students may work collaboratively to seek evidence that will eventually support the individual argument or collaboratively discuss arguments individually written by their peers. SSTELLA recognizes that there are advantages for ELs to collaborate with peers as well as to have time to process and produce ideas in oral or written form.

Page Keeley, Lynn Farrin, and Francis Eberle (2005) have produced entire books with carefully designed prompts that allow science teachers to probe student concepts about particular scientific phenomena. Here is one example probe, from the book *Uncovering Student Ideas in Science: Another 25 Formative Assessment Probes* (Kelley, Farrin, & Eberle, 2005, p. 51):

> Adrienne placed a small mirror flat against a wall. Standing close to the mirror, Adrienne could see her face from her eyebrows to her chin. Adrienne backed up five steps away from the mirror. Adrienne is now farther away from the mirror. How much of her face will Adrienne see in the mirror this time?

A: She will see more of her face.
B: She will see less of her face.
C: She will see the same amount of her face.

The probe intends to uncover how students use ideas about light to make sense of what they see in a mirror. The selected-response component (A, B, or C) alone might provide some whole-class patterns that can guide classroom discussion and instructional planning. However, the real probing comes by the statement following the list of potential claims: "Explain your thinking. Describe your reasoning or any experiences you have had with mirrors that helped you decide what Adrienne would see."

The key is to elicit more than just "Does a student understand a concept or not?" but to understand the student's reasoning process, which could illuminate *why* the student does or does not understand a concept (as being taught in class), and possible ways of knowing and cultural worldviews that the teacher can draw on to deeper student learning. With the added statement, teachers can use the student "arguments" to elicit students' reasoning about mirrors and reflections, students' lived experiences and interests, and as a way for students themselves to reflect on what they know and need to know. More pertinent to discourse, it can be used as a way to discuss what it means to explain and "describe reasoning." After learning about mirrors and reflection, students can revisit the same scenario to revise their arguments.

Several productive language functions are involved when students individually construct arguments, such as to depict what Adrienne would see: identifying key evidence (or experiences) to support the claim, communicating in writing ideas and information related to the formation of an argument, and properly structuring the written or oral arguments. Students need to be supported in each language function, which will allow them to more effectively argue from evidence, and thereby develop competency with scientific discourse.

Graphic organizers can be used to help students categorize explanations and argument features (i.e., claim, evidence, reasoning/justification) and visualize the relationship among these features. Graphic organizers can then be used to develop more sophisticated explanations and arguments, either orally or in writing. In a study on teachers' use of such supports, McNeill, Lizotte, Krajcik, and Marx (2006) found that students write higher-quality explanations when the support is used more in the early stages of students' explanation development, rather than always providing the support to students. Thus, teachers should be careful not to *over*scaffold (more support than what is always needed), just as they should be careful about not providing any support.

Individually Critiquing Explanations or Arguments. Instead of construct-ing an argument or explanation, teachers many present students with one to critique. While the science education community has emphasized student construction of explanations and arguments, less attention has been given to critiquing them (Ford, 2008). For example, in an activity described by Samp-son and Schleigh (2013) in their book *Scientific Argumentation in Biology: 30 Classroom Activities*, students would learn about the Body Mass Index (BMI) and four methods (or explanations) for decreasing your BMI over a twelve-month period. They would engage in an online simulation in which they collect evidence, evaluate the potential methods using this evidence, and finally construct an individual argument discussing their evaluation. Cri-tiquing arguments calls on students to engage in yet another set of language functions, including (1) comprehending arguments made by others orally or in writing and the productive language function of this, (2) communicating ideas related to the critique of arguments, and (3) questioning or critiquing arguments of others.

Debating Socio-Scientific Issues. The descriptions and example above represent explanations and arguments as individual activities. As a teacher, you may want students to individually write an argument or critique one already written. However, to promote science and science learning as fun-damentally social activities, students can also engage in argumentation as they discuss opposing viewpoints, attempting to convince another student and ultimately reach consensus. It is the community (of scientists) or the classroom participations that set the goals, norms, and expectation for what counts as quality arguments.

There are many social issues that involve science or technological aspects—use of stem cells, climate change, and genetically modified food are just a few examples. These SSIs are complex; not only do they involve scientific principles and applications, but they also tend to include moral, ethical, and economical values. Thus, they can be a rich context for engaging students in argumentation. They can also make classroom science more relevant and meaningful for students, as described in chapter 4.

For example, the teacher can assign students two grade-level-appropriate articles related to a particular SSI, such as genetically modified organisms (or GMOs).[4] While reading the articles, students can construct a "T" chart to identify at least three pieces of evidence that support the development and use of GMOs and at least three pieces of evidence *against* their development and use. Next, students can write a draft argument using evidence placed in the "T" chart to state their position on the use of GMOs. Alternatively, teach-ers can assign students a position, which could be particularly beneficial for students who may be arguing against their current position.

The written argument would (1) state the evidence in support of their position, (2) state the evidence contrary to their position, and (3) defend why the evidence in support of their position outweighs the contradicting evidence. After peer and teacher feedback, students with similar positions will compare their arguments and come up with (1) an initial argument and (2) possible responses to rebuttal against the opposing position. Then students can engage in a class debate about GMOs (pro vs. con).

Argument-Based Inquiry. In chapter 5, we discussed models as a way to drive inquiry in the classroom and thus promote scientific sense-making through scientific and engineering practices. Ideally, students also engage in written and dialogic argumentation while making sense of science. As part of a research study, Sampson, Grooms, and Walker (2011) embedded argumentation into inquiry-based investigations. Students were presented with a research question and instructed to plan and carry out an experiment to address the question. Groups then developed a tentative argument to share with other groups (on a white board or poster) and wrote individual reports that included the argument.

After constructing arguments, students critiqued arguments from other groups and used feedback from their peers to revise arguments. The session concluded through a whole-class discussion in which students reflect on what they learned about both the science content and the nature of science. The entire process simulated how scientists construct and critique arguments in the community—consistently sharing findings and receiving feedback that can be used to refine the argument. The whole-class discussion allows for more explicit modeling of why scientists engage in argumentation—since students can relate back to their investigation. Students engaged in the process improve in both understanding of core science ideas and argumentative writing over time.

This latter example emphasizes the collaborative nature of constructing and critiquing scientific arguments and explanations, which allows English learners to hear a variety of discourse forms and practice interpersonal communication (i.e., communication between people).

The contrasting dialogues at the onset of the chapter highlight what a classroom looks like that focuses on understanding science through factual information versus one that promotes explanation and argumentation. Both dialogues relate to mass and weight. However, from the perspective of SSTELLA what they are talking about differs greatly. In dialogue 1, it is arguable whether students are making sense about anything. Loosely, the conversation is around a single piece of knowledge—mass is measured in Newtons. In dialogue 2, students are attempting to explain a phenomenon using their own ideas about science and language. The teacher takes Jaden's initial ideas as a claim that all students are then given opportunities to examine and build on. The teacher also points out particular features of an explanation: "How is your pool example like Immaculeta's claim?," not just a fact. They are explaining talking about their own thinking, which may not be exactly right, but stimulates the class discussion, which collectively leads to reasoning about relationships among concepts—mass, weight, pressure, and so on. Furthermore, they are talking about claims and evidence for their ideas—being pressed to defend claims and evaluate the arguments of others.

Promoting Discourse through Productive Student Talk

SSTELLA also promotes *productive student talk*, which often embeds elements of argumentation or explanation, as a way for students to engage in scientific discourse. We draw from the work on fostering productive disciplinary engagement within classroom learning communities (Engle & Conant, 2002), which addresses student participation in classrooms through a set of guiding principles, outlined in table 6.2.

TABLE 6.2
Four Guiding Principles

1. *Problematizing*:	Students are encouraged to take on *intellectual* problems.
2. *Authority*:	Students are given *authority* in addressing such problems.
3. *Accountability*:	Students' intellectual work is *made accountable to others* and to disciplinary norms.
4. *Resources*:	Students are provided with *sufficient resources* to do all of the above.

Source: Engle and Conant, 2002, pp. 400–401.

Engagement and Productive Student Talk

Productive student talk involves *engaging* a wide range of students in scientific discourse. As teachers, we must ask ourselves the following questions related to student engagement during focal activities:

- *Who* is participating? Who is not participating? (i.e., ELs, students of color, girls, shy students, etc.)
- *How* are students participating in focal activities?
- Are students engaging *other students* or *other contributions*?
- Are students *connecting ideas* over time—from previous lessons to current lessons?

Engle and Conant (2002) suggest that students are more engaged in classroom learning during instances when: (1) more students in a group attempt and make "substantive contributions," (2) student contributions are coordinated with other student contributions (teachers might ask groups to compare findings from an investigation), (3) few students are perceived as being "off-task," (4) students are actively listening to each other, and (5) students continue to engage over extended periods of time.

Engagement becomes *disciplinary* engagement when student participation interacts with the issues and practices of a discipline's discourse—for instance, when students are participating by arguing from evidence about a SSI. Finally, disciplinary engagement becomes *productive disciplinary* engagement when students are making some intellectual growth, such as deepening their understanding of a concept to help meet the learning objective. Students take on (problematizing) and discuss (authority) intellectual problems, utilizing scientific discourse norms (arguing *with evidence*—accountability).

Resources are provided (prior instruction, texts, and classroom spaces) for students to engage in this work. Thus, productive disciplinary engagement can be seen as a *series of activities with increasing complex use of scientific explanations and argumentation.* Through interaction with the content and peers in the classroom, "learning is a simultaneously cognitive and social process" (Engle and Conant, p. 403). By attending to the production and structure of student science talk, teachers allow individual and collective thinking and reasoning around science concepts to be public in the classroom, thus valuing *student* voice, not just the teacher's.

For SSTELLA, productive student talk happens when the teacher *facilitates and fosters sustained student discussions about science concepts through the use of productive disciplinary principles (i.e., problematizing, authority, accountability, and resources) and a range of dialogic strategies (e.g., revoicing, reporting, restating, quoting, questioning, etc.).*

Facilitating Productive Science Talk: Instructional Conversations Engaged in Science (or ICES)

One particular type of student talk has been shown to foster disciplinary engagement and learning, referred to as *instructional conversations.* Researchers have studied instructional conversations across a range of classroom age groups, cultural communities, and subjects. At the heart of *instructional conversation* engaged in science (or ICES) is a discursive exchange both between teacher and student and among students (*conversation*) in order to promote engagement with and understanding of scientific topics (*instruction*). While these exchanges can occur in multiple participant structures (e.g., lab work, small groups, whole class), they share similar processes and functions. The ultimate goal of an instructional conversation is to scaffold students' scientific discourse to a more sophisticated form in which the students use scientific reasoning to sustain discussion and explain scientific topics.

As an example of ICES in action, Gallas (1995) showed that the ideas arising from her elementary students' "science talks" reflect theories about the importance of students self-reflecting on *what* they believed in and then *analyzing* the basis on which they anchor those beliefs (e.g., Is it bad for the local environment to buy bottled water?). Through the process of discussing scientific (and relevant) topics, students had meaningful opportunities to deepen their understanding of science ideas, articulate a legitimate line of reasoning, and bridge everyday language with the language of science (including vocabulary) learned in class (Ballenger, 1997; Brown & Ryoo, 2008).

Distributing Authority in ICES. Successfully promoting scientific argumentation in the classrooms requires that teachers view authority (or knowledge production) as shared among the teacher, students, texts, and community resources. Instead of merely explaining concepts to students, teachers encourage students to work together (e.g., in small groups) on the critical construction and deconstruction of possible explanations of scientific phenomena and/or SSI. Instructional conversations engaged in science provide a useful context to promote the discourse of science with a focus on argumentation and explanation. Another way to distribute knowledge production is to provide students with assigned roles that emulate ways that scientists communicate with each other.

For example, in a study by Herrenkohl and Guerra (1998), as student groups presented findings to the whole class, student audience members were given specific types of questions to ask the presenters relating to prediction (e.g., Do you think your prediction was right?), theory (e.g., What was your theory?), results (e.g., What helped you find your results?), and relating predictions, theories, and findings (e.g., Did what you think was going to happen really happen?). This process engaged the whole class (not just the presenters) in reflecting and revising theories—thus promoting discourse. More informally, the teacher can continuously remind students of how "scientists" construct and critique arguments.

Establishing Norms for ICES. Engaging in discussions about abstract science concepts is typically not a familiar or intuitive process for students. Like other aspects of teaching, it is important to set, communicate, and model clear norms and expectations for students, as well as continuously remind students of the norms (e.g., keep them displayed on the wall). It is also important to note that such norms could be unfamiliar to some students. Ideally, these norms are co-constructed and negotiated between the teacher and students, which can allow teachers to understand the variety of ways students may have learned to engage in discourse, as well as further value the cultural and linguistic resources that a diverse group of students brings. Here are just a few examples of norms:

- Turn taking (the goal is for students to be taking turns on their own, without the teacher directing turn taking)
  - Just speak up (instead of raising hand)
  - Throwing a ball to the next student

- Responding to peers: follow up on the previous talker by identifying his/ her idea and then
  - (a) expanding/revising the idea,
  - (b) supporting the idea, or
  - (c) asking a clarifying question about the idea

- Sharing the floor
  - If you are talking frequently, give generous wait time before chiming in. In you are talking infrequently, take a risk and share your ideas with the group.

- Respecting diverse experiences and perspectives (and explain *why* this is important!)

Configuring ICES. Teachers can engage students in productive student talk through a combination of classroom activities (e.g., anticipatory question, demonstration, student-led investigation, discussion after an investigation) and teacher-student talk formats (whole class, small group, pairs, etc.). Within each configuration, there are particular ways to promote student talk with each other. Imagine a classroom arrangement in which students are seated in rows and columns. The teacher is standing at the front of the class and begins the science talk with a guiding question.

If you were a student in the class, where would your attention be? Would you feel like you have any control of the conversation? Although logistically difficult with thirty-plus students, configuring the classroom for a productive discussion can tremendously improve the discussion. The teacher can arrange seats so that students see and face each other (to encourage talking to *each other*, not the teacher!). One strategy is a "fish bowl" discussion where a group of students (four to eight) are arranged in the center with the rest of the class seated on the outside. This allows for more focused participation by students (who could be chosen to represent varying EL proficiencies, perspectives on a science idea from earlier discussions/activities, etc.). The remainder of the class has the task of taking notes and reflecting on the talk.

Many activities lend themselves to students working in small groups or in pairs; however, that is not the only rationale for small-group work. Small groups, for one, maximize interaction among ELs, so that ELs can communicate using both English and their native language (if students speak a similar native language). Teachers should find out about student characteristics (native language, EL proficiency [read/write/speak/listen], academic background) to help form purposeful groups. During these activities, the key is again for students to have clear guidelines, roles, and opportunities to talk to each other.

Questioning and Responding during ICES. The ICES process should begin by the teacher initiating a conversation that elicits student dialogue. Teachers can initiate though a demonstration (refer back to dialogue 2 in the introduction), asking a well-structured *question*, or responding to student input from a previous dialogue or activity. The nature of this initiation should be open-ended enough to stimulate various responses and student thought. For instance, instead of the closed-ended "What happens when I throw this ball up in the air?" the teacher can ask, "Why, when we throw a ball up in the air, does it come back down?" It is not easy to come up, in the moment, with effective open-ended questions. Therefore, teachers can carefully design open-ended guiding questions that will elicit the type of critical thinking we desire from our students.

Questioning, perhaps unsurprisingly, is a key element of *sustaining* ICES. Students often only receive opportunities to respond to known-answer, factual questions, such as "What is gravity?" or, even more closed-ended, "What force keeps us from floating off the ground?" These types of questions do have their place in discussions, but only if they eventually lead to more open-ended questions that probe for student thinking about science ideas. Gallas (1995) suggests, especially for older grades, discussing as a class how to ask questions that better promote dialogue. "Asking questions" is a scientific practice depicted in the framework, and ICES provides a useful context to promote this practice. To clarify, the scientific practice of asking questions refers to exploring how to ask explainable/testable questions, such as "What is the relationship between pressure and volume of a gas?" It does not mean that anytime a student asks questions they are engaging in the scientific practice.

Gallas (1995), among others, stresses the importance of structuring conversations in ways that build on students' knowledge and experiences (especially linguistic knowledge and experience) to *scaffold* discourse (see chapter 2 for more details on how we approach scaffolding throughout the book). The teacher should not expect all students to initially converse exclusively with technical language or sophisticated reasoning. However, the teacher should recognize the reasoning present in student responses and provide opportunities to scaffold student learning to more sophisticated reasoning and to incorporate learned or new vocabulary into the conversation. Employing instructional conversations successfully should be inclusive and a beneficial support for ELs. This use of scaffolding should acknowledge the language proficiency ELs come in with (both English and native, across modalities, such as listening, speaking, reading, and writing) as a resource and encourage students to engage in various discursive genres (e.g., writing a science report vs. writing a blog) when communicating about science.

Effective scaffolding during a lesson and over time requires considerable attention to *follow-up* questioning.[5] Michaels and O'Conner (2012) describe nine different talk moves as part of the Talk Science project, divided into four goals that can facilitate follow-up questioning.

- *Help Individual Students Share, Expand, and Clarify Their Own Thinking*

  ◦ Examples: Time to think (wait time/partner talk/writing as think time), "Say more," "So, are you saying . . . ?"

- *Help Students Listen Carefully to One Another*

  ◦ "Who can rephrase or repeat?"

- *Help Students Deepen Their Reasoning*

  ◦ Asking for evidence or reasoning
  ◦ Challenging or offering a counterexample

- *Help Students Think with Others*

  ◦ Agree/disagree and why
  ◦ "Who can add on?"
  ◦ Explain what someone else means

Involving More Students during ICES. Another important aspect of the ICES process is to eventually include more students in the conversation (particularly ELs) and have students talk to each other, with the teacher facilitating the conversation. In small groups, conversations among all students may arise spontaneously, but the teacher must still engage students in using dialogue to advance the collective understanding and explanations. In whole-group conversations, the teacher should explicitly *recast* student responses by restating them for others to respond. The recast should be kept as close as possible to the original language while still maintaining the meaning of the response.

As a final remark on facilitating ICES, students will bring a variety of values, beliefs, and ways of knowing and thinking that shape how they engage in scientific discourse in the classroom. Studying science learning in classrooms with Haitian Creole students, Warren and colleagues (2001) found many instances of student talk that differed greatly from the typical forms of discourse teachers might expect or promote, but nevertheless, students' nondominant argumentation practices were also important forms of scientific reasoning in their own right. Like Warren and colleagues, the SSTELLA framework operates from a similar premise that students' everyday discourses are intellectually legitimate resources for constructing scientific arguments.

Now, reread the contrasting dialogues at the beginning of the chapter. In light of our key points, reconsider (using the language you have learned in this chapter) differences between the two interactions, including who is talking and responding, and opportunities for making sense of science ideas and using language.

Who is talking to whom? In dialogue 1, the teacher *i*nitiates, a student *r*esponds, and the teacher *e*valuates (or I-R-E pattern). In dialogue 2, the teacher does initiate through the demo and the open-ended question "Can anyone share their thinking about what the scale might read if I pump all the air out?" However, the teacher also calls on students to respond to their peers, and eventually students talk to each other without the teacher responding in between. Finally, what does the teacher do to deepen student understanding (of both the content and scientific discourse)? In dialogue 2, the focus is on distributing knowledge construction—the teacher most likely knows the answer to the question posed, but allows the students to think about and discuss it. The teacher's probing questions "Can you say more about that?" and "And when you pull the air out?" allow students to venture beyond what they comfortably know. The teacher also presses students to use evidence and consider where they really stand: "Wait, Jaden are you changing your mind? How is your pool example like Helena's claim?"

Overall, the teacher in dialogue 2 has facilitated productive student talk that helps them deepen their understanding of science concepts and engage in scientific discourse by arguing with evidence. For ELs, these are fruitful opportunities to use language in the context of doing science. In the next chapter we also focus more on productive use of language, but emphasize how students, particularly ELs, develop disciplinary literacy and English language development through authentic scientific tasks and texts.

Summary

Our driving question throughout the chapter was: *How do I help my ELs communicate the complex forms of language needed to learn science?*

To summarize our key points in this chapter:

- *Scientific discourse* refers to the particular oral and written forms of language needed to communicate scientific ideas.
- Scientific explanations and arguments involve a range of analytical tasks and language functions that allow students, including ELs, to understand the nature of science and develop English language and literacy while they communicate scientific ideas.
- Facilitating productive science talking involves strategic planning of how to distribute knowledge production, establish norms, configure, question and respond, and involve more students during ICES.

Notes

1. Adapted from tools developed by Windschitl and colleagues for the Ambitious Science Teaching project (see http://ambitiousscienceteaching.org).

2. The focus on science vocabulary will be addressed further in chapter 7. It is especially problematic to consider vocabulary as the main focus of language scaffolding for students acquiring English.

3. From Watson and Crick (1953).

4. We acknowledge Dr. Barry Roth for his contribution to this exemplar.

5. Follow-up appears as a particularly significant and productive element in the classroom that can transform productive student science talk. See Wells (1999, 2002).

References

Ambitious Science Teaching (2015). A discourse primer for science teachers (2015). Retrieved from http://ambitiousscienceteaching.org/wp-content/uploads/2014/09/Discourse-Primer.pdf.

Ballenger, C. (1997). Social identities, moral narratives, scientific argumentation: Science talk in a bilingual classroom. *Language and Education, 11*(1), 1–14.

Brown, B. A., & Ryoo, K. (2008). Teaching science as a language: A "content-first" approach to science teaching. *Journal of Research in Science Teaching, 45*(5), 529–53.

Cheuk, T. (2012). *Relationships and convergences found in the Common Core State Standards in mathematics (practices), Common Core State Standards in ELA/literacy (student portraits), and a framework for K–12 science education (science & engineering practices)*. Unpublished manuscript. Stanford, CA: Stanford University, Understanding Language Initiative.

Common Core State Standards Initiative (2010). Retrieved from www.corestandards.org.

Driver, R., Newton, P., & Osborne, J. (2000). Establishing the norms of scientific argumentation in classrooms. *Science Education, 84*(3), 287–312.

Engle, R. A., & Conant, F. R. (2002). Guiding principles for fostering productive disciplinary engagement: Explaining an emergent argument in a community of learners classroom. *Cognition and Instruction, 20*(4), 399–483.

Ford, M. (2008). Disciplinary authority and accountability in scientific practice and learning. *Science Education, 92*(3), 404–23.

Gallas, K. (1995). *Talking their way into science: Hearing children's questions and theories, responding with curricula.* New York, NY: Teachers College Press.

Herrenkohl, L. R., & Guerra, M. R. (1998). Participant structures, scientific discourse, and student engagement in fourth grade. *Cognition and instruction, 16*(4), 431–73.

Keeley, P., Erbele, F., & Farrin, L. (2005). *Uncovering student ideas in science: 25 formative assessment probes.* Arlington, VA: NSTA Press.

Langer, J. A. (2011). *Envisioning knowledge: Building literacy in the academic disciplines.* New York, NY: Teachers College Press.

Lee, O., Quinn, H., & Valdés, G. (2013). Science and language for English language learners in relation to Next Generation Science Standards and with implications for Common Core State Standards for English language arts and mathematics. *Educational Researcher, 42*(4), 223–33.

McNeill, K. L., Lizotte, D. J., Krajcik, J., & Marx, R. W. (2006). Supporting students' construction of scientific explanations by fading scaffolds in instructional materials. *The Journal of the Learning Sciences, 15*(2), 153–191.

Michaels, S., & O'Connor, C. (2012). *Talk science primer.* Cambridge, MA: TERC.

National Research Council. (2012). *A framework for K–12 science education: Practices, crosscutting concepts, and core ideas.* Washington, DC: National Academies Press.

Osborne, J. (2010). Arguing to learn in science: The role of collaborative, critical discourse. *Science, 328*(5977), 463–466.

Osborne, J. F., & Patterson, A. (2011). Scientific argument and explanation: A necessary distinction? *Science Education, 95*(4), 627–38.

Ovando, C. J., & Combs, M. C. (2012). Bilingual and ESL classrooms (5th ed.). Boston, MA: McGraw-Hill.

Pearson, P. D., Moje, E., & Greenleaf, C. (2010). Literacy and science: Each in the service of the other. *Science, 328*(5977), 459–63.

Sampson, V., & Clark, D. B. (2008). Assessment of the ways students generate arguments in science education: Current perspectives and recommendations for future directions. *Science Education, 92*(3), 447–72.

Sampson, V., & Clark, D. (2009). The impact of collaboration on the outcomes of scientific argumentation. *Science Education, 93*(3), 448–84.

Sampson, V., Grooms, J., & Walker, J. P. (2011). Argument-driven inquiry as a way to help students learn how to participate in scientific argumentation and craft written arguments: An exploratory study. *Science Education, 95*(2), 217–57.

Sampson, V., & Schleigh, S. (2013). *Scientific argumentation in biology: 30 classroom activities.* Arlington, VA: NSTA Press.

Snow, C. E. (2010). Academic language and the challenge of reading for learning about science. *Science, 328*, 450–52.

Toulmin, S. E. (1958). The uses of argument. Cambridge, UK: Cambridge University Press.

Veel, R. (1997). Learning how to mean—scientifically speaking: Apprenticeship into scientific discourse in the secondary school. In F. Christie & J. R. Martin (Eds.), *Genre and institutions: Social processes in the workplace and school* (pp. 160–95). London, UK: Cassell.

Warren, B., Ballenger, C., Ogonowski, M., Rosebery, A., & Hudicourt-Barnes, J. (2001). Rethinking diversity in learning science: The logic of everyday sense making. *Journal of Research in Science Teaching, 38,* 529–52.

Watson, J. D., & Crick, F. (April 25, 1953). The structure for Deoxyribose Nucleic Acid. *Nature, 171*(4356).

Wells, G. (1999). *Dialogic inquiry: Towards a socio-cultural practice and theory of education.* Cambridge, UK: Cambridge University Press.

Wells, G. (2002). The role of dialogue in activity theory. *Mind, culture, and activity, 9*(1), 43–66.

Windschitl, M. (2008). What is inquiry? A framework for thinking about authentic scientific practice in the classroom. In J. Luft, R. L. Bell, & J. Gess-Newsome (Eds.), *Science as inquiry in the secondary setting* (pp. 1–20). Arlington, VA: NSTA Press.

7

English Language and Disciplinary Literacy Development in Science

Jorge Solís

Overview

CHAPTER 6 ON scientific discourse practices addresses important issues and provides examples surrounding oral and written language functions to express scientific arguments and explanations. Chapter 7 furthers our attention on how language and literacy tasks are inherently part of particular disciplinary ways of reading, writing, speaking, and listening in secondary school science contexts (Shanahan & Shanahan, 2008). Historians, mathematicians, and scientists alike use language and literacy in particular ways. Moreover, chapter 7 will offer explanations and examples of how instructional attention to language and literacy in science provides English learners (ELs) greater access to science content and language comprehension and learning. These two ideas (i.e., that science uses language and literacy in particular ways and that ELs benefit from this approach) are different and at the same time mutually supportive instructional goals.

Introduction

Student engagement in scientific and engineering practices without question involves the use of language for speaking, listening, reading, and writing. Some have even suggested that learning the language of science is like learning a new language. However, Lemke (1990) goes a step further in suggesting that learning the language of science is much different and perhaps more difficult than learning a foreign language; in the case of a new language, speakers tend to build from a grammatical foundation, while in science, new users of the language of science need to learn how to express their conceptions of unfamiliar thematic patterns (e.g., erosion patterns, forest succession) potentially not previously mastered in any language. This chapter highlights the ways that language and literacy activities in science serve to move forward complex and authentic understandings of scientific concepts and practices, and how science activity can simultaneously serve as an environment for language and literacy development.

As discussed in chapter 6, scientific language functions involve both receptive and productive skills. The chapter also draws attention to examples that illustrate how language tasks can support the development of particular lesson objectives as well as ways that slight lesson modifications of language and literacy activities could improve student engagement for all students, especially ELs. The Secondary Science Teaching with English Language and Literacy Acquisition (SSTELLA) framework addresses three specific instructional practices related directly to English language and disciplinary language and literacy development, namely (1) widespread student interaction, (2) sub-opportunities for the use and development of key science vocabulary, and (3) engaging in authentic literacy tasks. While these three instructional practices explicitly address both science and language development, it should be noted that the SSTELLA framework represents an integrated approach to teaching science to diverse learners, where contextualized scientific sense-making and discourse also rely on and are made possible through a range of language and literacy functions. In other words, the four SSTELLA practices are overlapping and mutually supportive of each other.

Instructional Practices under English Language and Disciplinary Literacy Development

Chapter 7 focuses on three instructional practices within SSTELLA's English language and disciplinary literacy development approach. The first instructional practice concentrates on *promoting opportunities for English language development for ELs through student interaction*. This practice builds from previous research that demonstrates that all learners, but especially second language learners, greatly benefit from classroom activities where students are able to interact with each other (Tharp & Gallimore, 1991).

Widespread student interaction means that students are able to interact with each other through a variety of classroom activities such as class discussions, oral presentations, partner talk, and small-group interactions. When this practice is well supported, all students have multiple and widespread opportunities for interaction and participation where students are monitored and supported through a range of teacher strategies like modeling effective interactions, using heterogeneous grouping structures, use of clear ground rules and expectations for group work, and ensuring equitable participation of all students especially ELs.

The second instructional practice, under SSTELLA's English language and disciplinary literacy development approach, refers to *promoting opportunities for English language development for ELs through vocabulary support*. This instructional practice acknowledges the varied role that scientific and technical terms and other forms of academic language can have in learning science. This instructional practice addresses science vocabulary and other related terms within the context of supporting scientific and engineering practices and not as a separate learning goal.

When this instructional practice is not followed, students are either not exposed at all to science terms (where the teacher may even avoid key science terms) or science terms may be shared with students, but with little to no support provided in using key terms themselves or comprehending scientific terms. When this practice is well implemented, the teacher provides several types of support so that students can gain access to the language and content of a lesson including the use of visual or graphical representation of key terms, using the context of the learning activity to help make sense of a term, to help students learn new vocabulary. Many strategies can be used to promote greater comprehension of content and key terms including some often referred to as Specially Designed Academic Instruction in English (SDAIE) strategies.[1]

Teachers can leverage relevant Spanish-English cognates for example by asking students about familiar words related to focal science activities (e.g. *observación* for observation, *mitosis* for mitosis, *modelo* for model, etc.)

The third instructional practice, under SSTELLA's English language and disciplinary literacy development approach, refers to *pressing for authentic science literacy tasks*. This view considers the social and cultural aspects of literacy development as a process of ongoing negotiation of knowledge between individuals and their communities (i.e., classroom, home, peer group, etc.) (Goldenberg, Rueda, & August, 2006; Perry, 2012). Texts used for reading and writing are therefore always the focus of specific social purposes to accomplish a range of actions or goals.

Texts here refers to visual representations that have specialized meanings and that requires visual decoding of those meanings like units of measurement, line graphs, written observations, symbolic/material models, and so on. From this perspective, texts in science classrooms fulfill scientific sense-making purposes to address a range of communities or audiences where certain genres and text features are expected. When this instructional practice is not present, the teacher does not provide opportunities for students to read, write, and/or discuss texts during a lesson nor is there any assistance in reading and/or writing of science texts.

While difficult to fathom, these kinds of science lessons have the teacher doing most if not all of the reading and writing of texts shared in a lesson with little to no direct student manipulation or production of texts. When this instructional practice is addressed well, the teacher provides ample opportunities for students to read, write, and discuss texts used for scientific and engineering practices like using and making models or recording and explaining data. Moreover, the teacher can support student engagement of texts by monitoring their use, providing feedback when appropriate, and even modeling how certain science texts are read and written for different audiences.

Background on Language and Literacy in Science Classrooms

Previous chapters introducing the SSTELLA framework (introduction) as well as the chapter on responsive approaches to ELs (chapter 2) make the case for understanding how language works in science, recognizing the challenges and opportunities that language presents for ELs and all students. There are numerous approaches to promoting literacy for ELs in secondary school settings.

For example, a recent study by Olson et al. (2012) shows that mainstreamed ELs' writing in secondary school can be enhanced when taught by teachers using the cognitive strategies promoted by the Pathways Project. These strategies include tapping prior knowledge about a topic before writing, asking questions and generating predictions, revising drafts, evaluating and reviewing writing, and constructing preliminary ideas or organizing information. The issue here is that how literacy is used differs across subject areas. These strategies are the type of generic EL modifications and supports that are not sufficient for enhancing EL success in science referred to in chapter 2.

Language and literacy development in science can be referred to as *science language, scientific discourse*, or *science literacy*. The term *disciplinary literacy* has been used to focus variably on cognition and learning, on the cultural practices of the disciplines (i.e., the culture of science), and the cultural practices of the learners (Moje, 2007). Developing disciplinary literacy involves teaching ways of thinking and of using linguistic processes within disciplinary communities as well as ways of bridging knowledge between disciplines. Duff (2000) describes the intersection of language and academic content as "forms of oral and written language and communication—genres, registers, graphics, linguistic structures, interactional patterns" (p. 175) that are expected, scaffolded, and evaluated in educational and professional contexts. Students can benefit from understanding disciplinary features of the language differences or how science language differs in science in relation to other subject areas.

Applied to science, it becomes clear that *all* learners need assistance and feedback in making sense of, using, and producing a range of science-related graphics, linguistic features, and interactional patterns associated with particular scientific and engineering practices. This negotiation of academic science discourse is a social, cognitive, and cultural process, not merely a product or outcome achieved individually. It is also a relative and dynamic process that requires students and teachers working together to make sense of tools and knowledge through language. This is a social practice informed by institutional goals, cultural expectations, and social interactional demands.

The science texts, for example, require making sense of dense clauses, hierarchically structured information, and a mixture of general academic vocabulary and highly specialized terms within the context of making sense of scientific practices. SSTELLA in this regard addresses discipline-specific language and literacy patterns associated with scientific and engineering practices, which may contrast with academic discourses used to communicate different and particular meanings in other subject areas like language arts, history, and mathematics. The language of science, however, can be quite different from the classroom language of science yet continually approximated by teachers to advance curricular goals.

Darian (2003) refers to the language of science, an unmarked way of expressing scientific thinking, as complex and highly varied across audiences, participants, and purposes. Scientific definitions and examples in texts are often expressed through the use of figurative language, visuals, and cause-and-effect statements. According to Lee, Quinn, and Valdés (2013), the language of the science classroom "is grounded in colloquial or everyday language but moves toward the disciplinary language of science" (p. 228). Figure 7.1 describes students' language use and tasks in the science classroom where science teachers need to address and plan for and even distinguish from other disciplinary uses (Lee et al., 2013, p. 230). This perspective proposes that the work of science teachers in supporting language and literacy is much more than addressing vocabulary development or grammatical forms. All students use language and literacy in classrooms across a

Features of the classroom language	Students' Language Use and Tasks		
	Oral	Written	
	Receptive/Productive	Receptive	Productive
Modality	Whole-classroom participation (one-to-many) Small group participation (one-to-group) Interaction with individual peers (one-to-one) Interaction with adults within school contexts (one-to-one)	Comprehension of written classroom and school-based formal and informal communication	Production of written classroom and school-based formal and informal written communication • Written reports • Science journal entries
Registers	• Colloquial • classroom registers • disciplinary language and terminology	• Science-learners written registers • disciplinary language and terminology • disciplinary discourse conventions	
Examples of Registers	Classroom registers: • Comprehending oral directions • Asking for clarification • Participating in discussions Learner-appropriate science discourse registers and conventions used for: • Describing models • Constructing arguments • Providing oral explanations of phenomenon or system	Classroom, school, and science-learner written registers: • Textbooks • Lab or equipment manuals • Writing by other students • Internet materials • Science-oriented trade books • Science press articles • Syllabi • School announcements • Formal documents (e.g. classroom assignments, quarterly grades, assessment results)	

FIGURE 7.1
The language of the science classroom (Lee et al., 2013)

range of modalities face-to-face with someone else or in small groups, and in large-group contexts. *Modalities* also refers to the functions of language use including producing and interpreting language and literacy in science activities (i.e., oral, written, etc.).

Students in the science classroom are exposed to a range of oral and written contexts or modalities. Students are engaged in working one-on-one or in large classroom arrangements with peers and adults using formal and informal forms of communication. There are a range of styles of talk used by teachers and students in the science classrooms including colloquial, classroom, school, science discourse, and disciplinary registers. This range of registers of language use means that teachers need to communicate expectations for using appropriate language across these contexts and supports while giving directions, checking for understanding, describing models, and even providing written/oral explanations of a scientific concept. The language of the science classroom is very much a hybrid language, but one that is best addressed and supported by focusing on authentic scientific practices such as developing and using models, developing explanations and designing solutions, and engaging in arguments from evidence.

The language of science classrooms is replete with varied language functions that suggest relationships between concepts and pieces of information including creating categories for groups of information and translating information in terms of cause and effect and responding to focal questions. The language of science relies on and includes how language is used in multimedia texts and various inquiry experiences to express abstract ideas. That is, using, interpreting, and creating visual representation of information and science concepts are significant and indispensable literacy practices and not at all peripheral or optional to the work involved in science. The challenge here is also for teachers to create opportunities for students to engage in using the language of science without displacing the nature of scientific practices or eclipsing the inquiry process. Teachers can provide language support to ELs without watering down the content or hypermediating literacy activities (Gutiérrez & Stone, 2002; Moscovici, 1999).

Some perspectives related to supporting ELs in content areas suggest an explicit focus on linguistic features of the classroom language of science (i.e., Schleppegrell, 2004). However, the SSTELLA model does not require that secondary science teachers deconstruct grammatical features of the language and literacy demands of science activities nor to teach them explicitly as a primary way for giving support to ELs. In fact, strategies like explicit grammar instruction to promote writing with adolescents can even have a negative effect on writing outcomes for students (Graham & Perin, 2007).

Here we echo Janzen's (2008) review of the research for teaching ELs in the content areas concluding that science teachers "must be aware of instructional approaches that can effectively engage all students" including ELs with varying levels of English language proficiency and academic backgrounds (p. 1029). Promising practices for teaching science to ELs involve promoting scientific investigations that are student centered, involve all students, and support access to the language and literacy tasks attached to science activities. Supporting ELs in both science and literacy tasks does not require that all science teachers use the primary language, but rather be aware how ELs' primary language may support students' understanding of the classroom language of science. Moreover, some attempts to integrate both literacy and science development through vocabulary-centered approaches may inadvertently simplify language and content complexity such as those approaches where teachers focus explicitly on science vocabulary instruction as a way to support academic language for ELs (Bruna, Vann, & Escudero, 2007).

ELs need opportunities to use science in action where they can give and receive feedback on their speaking, listening, reading, and writing functions for real-world scenarios. Supporting language and literacy in science means sometimes engaging in firsthand investigations, and on other occasions, it means engaging in secondhand investigations (Cervetti, Pearson, Bravo, & Barber, 2006). This point is underscored by Hull and Moje (2012), who note that to learn literacy well, "students need meaningful purposes for engaging in literate practice and opportunities to use literacy for a broad range of life activities related to goals and desires beyond the moment of instruction" (p. 54). The following example illustrates some possibilities and challenges in promoting English language and literacy development in science for all students.

Interaction 1: Mrs. Bird's Lesson on the Big Bang

Interaction 1 provides a context for discussing the challenge of addressing language and literacy development while using scientific and engineering practices. This lesson draws from our team's observation of Mrs. Bird and her ninth grade students, including some ELs, in California. The ELs in this class are considered intermediate English language learners (ELLs) by the California English Language Development Test (CELDT). The lesson focuses on understanding the chronology of the universe according to the Big Bang cosmology. Students address a chronology of the universe in terms of "epochs" of time and what students already know about atoms.

The lesson begins with a warm-up activity called the "bell ringer" that reminds students about the composition of atoms and changes that occur in elements from previous conversations in the class. After the bell ringer, students engage in a sustained activity for the remainder of the lesson involving a reading about the chronology of the universe that is divided up among classmates where pairs take on reading and summarizing one or two epochs on an index card that is later placed on a class timeline of events. The lesson objectives are listed on the board and procedures for each step of the lesson are projected on the screen as the activities unfold. Most of the activity takes place between pairs and with the teacher joining groups of students to monitor, give feedback, and assist students on a range of questions from vocabulary comprehension, to instructions of the activity, writing and paraphrasing readings, and then drawing the epochs.

Mrs. Bird lists two learning objectives on the dry erase board to frame this lesson. She lists the learning objectives for this lesson, where students will be able to (1) "describe the timeline of the universe and the major events that occur through completing a class timeline and analysis questions" and (2) "explain the theory of evolution through the use of different forms of evidence and by using content vocabulary." Therefore, Mrs. Bird communicates the big idea of the lesson involving the students being able to describe the timeline of the universe to then explain a theory of evolution that relates this timeline using evidence identified in the reading and key vocabulary. Students' main task during the lesson while working in pairs is to understand and interpret a reading related to the chronology of the universe that draws from a Wikipedia page (see http://en.wikipedia.org/wiki/Chronology_of_the_universe). A simple analysis of the readability of this text suggests that it is at grade level. However, this does not mean that some students in class, ELs and non-ELs, will not have difficulty with the text or the writing tasks attached to it.

Textbox 7.1 displays the instructions flashed on the overhead screen provided to the students as they worked in pairs reading sections of the selected Wikipedia handout. This jigsaw reading activity is the principal activity that extends to a final culminating activity where students create index card summaries of their reading section that are then hung on a yellow string in the back of the room (steps 5–6 of overhead slide). The string hanging in the back of the room is intended to represent the timeline of events related to the Big Bang. The directions given to students ask that they first read their Wikipedia section silently and then work with a partner to create a short summary on their index card of what they understood from their era. After completing the short summary, students are asked to draw a picture on the backside of the index card visually representing their era including a time stamp of their era after the Big Bang.

Textbox 7.1

Universe Timeline Activity Directions

1. Silently read your assigned section.
2. With your partner create a two- to three-sentence summary of what happened in your era using your own words, and write it on the lined side of your index card.
3. Brainstorm a picture of what your era might have looked like.
4. Draw that image on the back of the index card.
5. Make sure you have your era written down and the time after the big bang it occurred, and then place your index card on the yellow timeline in the correct place.
6. Walk the timeline and answer the five analysis questions in your notebook.

The lesson most closely relates to a core scientific and engineering practice of *developing and using models* (scientific and engineering practice #2) (NGSS Lead States, 2013), where students work on developing, revising, and using a model "to illustrate and/or predict the relationships between systems or between components of a system" (appendix F, p. 6). However, the teacher does not refer to drawing of Big Bang activities in the universe as "models" (or the eventual construction of a timeline in the classroom) nor does Mrs. Bird urge students explicitly to approximate their illustrations of their era.

Interestingly, both *era* and *epoch* are used in this activity interchangeably by the teacher, which might have caused further confusion for the students. Bybee (2011) describes the use and construction of models as a critical experience that allows students an opportunity to "simulate a world not yet seen" (p. 34). The manner in which students are asked to interpret the key events in the universe and then represent their understanding of those events is at the heart of what it means to authentically address language and literacy in science learning.

Mrs. Bird's lesson is clearly attending to specific science concepts by attempting to support students' comprehension of a science-related reading and by attending to key vocabulary. The goal of providing language and literacy support for students in science is to increase access to the language of science without restricting the nature of the scientific enterprise. Teachers can *amplify not simplify* (Bravo, 2010; see also Walqui & van Lier, 2010) science activities as they integrate language and literacy. For example, Mrs. Bird does appear to enhance student access to the science content through a combination of general SDAIE strategies described earlier and discipline-specific strategies, such as:

*   using visuals, contextual cues, graphic representations, paraphrases, and some definitions to help students comprehend new vocabulary;

- recognizing students' developing scientific understandings using "every-day" words but encouraging students to use key terms as appropriate for the instructional activity;
- providing opportunities for student to read or write focusing on scientific/engineering practices (e.g., asking questions and defining problems, developing and using models, planning and carrying out investigations, analyzing and interpreting data, etc.); and
- using strategies to support discipline-specific writing (e.g., constructing models, drawing graphic representations of data, etc.).

To what extent does Mrs. Bird support the use and comprehension of the language of science while focused on developing and using models? Throughout the lesson, Mrs. Bird moves around the classroom from group to group providing assistance to students, especially ELs having difficulty with the reading and writing summaries. Table 7.1 is an excerpt from the reading handout distributed across pairs during this activity.

TABLE 7.1
Excerpts from Wikipedia Page Reading

Grand unification epoch
Between 10^{-43} second and 10^{-36} second after the Big Bang
Main article: Grand unification epoch
    As the universe expanded and cooled, it crossed transition temperatures at which forces separate from each other. These are phase transitions much like condensation and freezing. The grand unification epoch began when gravitation separated from the other forces of nature, which are collectively known as gauge forces. The non-gravitational physics in this epoch would be described by a so-called grand unified theory (GUT). The grand unification epoch ended when the GUT forces further separated into the strong and electroweak forces.

Hadron epoch
Between 10^{-6} second and 1 second after the Big Bang
Main article: Hadron epoch
    The quark–gluon plasma that composes the universe cools until hadrons, including baryons such as protons and neutrons, can form. At approximately 1 second after the Big Bang neutrinos decouple and begin traveling freely through space. This cosmic neutrino background, while unlikely to ever be observed in detail since the neutrino energies are very low, is analogous to the cosmic microwave background that was emitted much later. (See above regarding the quark–gluon plasma, under the String Theory epoch.) However, there is strong indirect evidence that the cosmic neutrino background exists, both from Big Bang nucleosynthesis predictions of the helium abundance, and from anisotropies in the cosmic microwave background.

Lepton epoch
Between 1 second and 10 seconds after the Big Bang
Main article: Lepton epoch
    The majority of hadrons and anti-hadrons annihilate each other at the end of the hadron epoch, leaving leptons and anti-leptons dominating the mass of the universe. Approximately 10 seconds after the Big Bang the temperature of the universe falls to the point at which new lepton/anti-lepton pairs are no longer created and most leptons and anti-leptons are eliminated in annihilation reactions, leaving a small residue of leptons.

Mrs. Bird helps by reading aloud to students who need support and by deciphering unfamiliar words and complex constructions in the text such as references to "gauge forces" and "phase transitions" (see Table 7.1). Mrs. Bird repeatedly asks students to put the reading into their own words and, in some cases, she helps students by rephrasing terms so that students can write their summaries. Unfortunately, the lesson remains focused more on students reading and comprehending the jigsaw sections and definitions and posting the index cards on the timeline instead of opportunities to reflect on using and creating relevant models or even discussing, explaining, and sharing ideas surrounding the big ideas of the Big Bang and scientific models.

Figure 7.2 illustrates students' posture during the lesson as they worked mostly silently for most of the period. As the teacher walks around answering questions, several EL students have difficulty with key terms such as "gauge forces" and "transitions."

Another clear challenge for Mrs. Bird and classrooms like this relates to providing appropriate support for students in accessing authentic texts. While jigsaw activities like the one used here helped some students complete shorter reading tasks, and it also provided the teacher an opportunity to assess and monitor student comprehension of the text, sometimes shorter texts (as in jigsaw sections of a reading) can further restrict student access to the

FIGURE 7.2
Students' posture during the lesson

big ideas. The text used in this example however, is so restricted that, despite being shorter reading sections, it appears to create more challenges for students grappling for more context on the science content. ELs certainly benefit from varied types of support from the teacher as provided by Mrs. Bird.

However, deeper development of scientific ideas requires more elaborate engagement in the range of written registers available like lab or equipment manuals, sharing students' writing between students, and examining scientific articles and news stories (see figure 7.1). How does this example promote the development of language and literacy in science? EL's benefit the most from opportunities to use multiple modes of language and literacy in science classrooms. Table 7.2 describes the ways in which Mrs. Bird's lesson only partly addresses SSTELLA's language and literacy development practices. This lesson example reaches a Level 1 (from a range of 0-3) in both promoting student interaction and use of authentic science literacy tasks while providing slightly more support for vocabulary at a Level 2.

TABLE 7.2
SSTELLA in Example 1

English Language and Disciplinary Literacy Development	
Promoting opportunities for English language development for ELs through student interaction	Level 1: All students work in pairs or individually on a reading task and on briefly sharing their timeline index cards, but most interaction is limited to silent work. Students receive little to no support in how to work in pairs and working collaboratively.
Promoting opportunities for English language development for ELs through vocabulary support	Level 2: The teacher attends to key vocabulary as necessary to support students' understanding of science concepts and uses visuals and graphic representations including supporting the use of everyday words to learn new terms. Yet attention to science vocabulary is not done to support scientific sense-making and scientific/ engineering practices.
Pressing for authentic science literacy tasks	Level 1: The teacher provides opportunities for students to read, write, and/or discuss texts but the focus is not on scientific/engineering *practices*.

Interaction 2: Mrs. Lara's Lesson on Karyotypes

The following description of interaction 2 provides a context for discussing the overlapping literacy demands and opportunities associated with a science lesson. Science vocabulary is often considered a primary, if not the sole, challenge for ELs and non-ELs for engaging in reading, writing, and discussions in science. However, language and literacy tasks in science involve more than acquiring science-specific terminology or even specific generic academic vocabulary.

This lesson draws from an observation of Mrs. Lara teaching biology to both ninth and tenth grade students in Texas with a large number of ELs in her classroom. Similar to Mrs. Bird, this teacher designs a lesson focused on supporting both science learning objectives and language learning objectives. Mrs. Lara writes her language and content objective on the dry erase board before every class. The writing of language and content objectives is a requirement by some schools to address language and content objectives linked to state standards for English language arts (sometimes English language development EL standards) and science. In this case the teacher writes a lesson biology objective where "students will be able to analyze karyotypes to determine genetic abnormalities" and in the case of the language objective she writes that "students will use new vocabulary in descriptions and classroom communication."

The lesson begins with students picking up their journals as they walk into the classroom, where they are asked to write down the objectives of the day. The teacher also reads the language and biology objective for the day. They then engage in a classroom routine guided by a task written on the dry erase board as a warm-up activity. Students have a baggie already resting on their tables containing the "warm-up of the day." Students are asked to match the suspect DNA fingerprint to one at the crime scene in their plastic baggies containing DNA cutouts.

Students are then asked to answer two questions: (1) How did you determine the match? and (2) How else could DNA fingerprinting be used? Mrs. Lara rotates through each pair of desks repeating the instructions. In some cases, the teacher reviews the previous lesson on DNA fingerprinting for students who missed the class. After ten minutes of students working individually or in pairs, the teacher addresses the entire class, asking for student responses to each of the two questions.

As the teacher repeats student responses, she reinforces key concepts through hand and arm gestures that parallel the key ideas. Figure 7.3 describes the teacher's modification of her speech patterns by including arm and hand gestures. These examples reference key concepts previously discussed on DNA bands and matching procedures.

As illustrated in the lesson transcript excerpt (figure 7.4), Mrs. Lara immediately provides extrasensory or paralinguistic support to augment student understanding of the science content by using her hands and arms to visually stress questions and examples related to the activity. The teacher and students engage in conversations about DNA fingerprinting including determining paternity, distant relatives, and common ancestors including reviewing pundit's squares and DNA fingerprinting. Students engage in the lesson then shift into a focus on karyotypes.[2] Students are asked to copy down the definition of *karyotypes* from an overhead slide while the teacher asks students if they like puzzles like Candy Crush or other puzzles on Facebook, which according to Mrs. Lara are much like how karyotypes are organized. Figure 7.4 describes how Mrs. Lara transitions the discussion into the lesson topic about karyotypes with a clear focus on continuing to use paralinguistic cues while also supporting students' understanding of the nature of karyotypes as a form of literacy that can be organized and read by others.

Paralinguistic Moves	Teacher Speech	
Putting together open hands to stress DNA match	"How did you determine the match? They were identical what?"	
Moving hands apart with two fingers touching	"Remember, those bands of DNA"	
Raising cupped hands in quick upward motion that signify DNA bands	"Those bands that are created"	

FIGURE 7.3
Teacher modification of her speech patterns by including arm and hand gestures

1. Teacher	This is what it normally looks like, the definition is right here (pointing to the dry erase board). Looks like a hot mess, right? Looks like a whole bunch of worms got thrown on the page.	
2. Student	DNA?	
3. Teacher	That's your chromosomes which are like your DNA but tightly coiled (spinning her hands quickly over and above each other) and it forms those chromosomes.	
4. Teacher	So that is all the chromosomes but it's a hot mess, it looks like a bunch of worms thrown on the page	
5. Student	Yeah	

FIGURE 7.4
Mrs. Lara transitions the discussion

| 6. Teacher | So because we're human and we like to organize and sort, what we do is organize and sort these. We pull out the largest ones first and then we go all the way down to our smallest one, |  |

| 7. Teacher | and then we match them up just like pairs of shoes. Imagine you had a big pile of shoes you wanted to pull out your Nike Kicks and put them together in the pile, and then you wanted your boots, so you match up by color and put them off to the side. |  |

| 8. Teacher | So we do the same thing here but instead of matching them up by color we match them up by those bands (pointing to the screen) on the chromosome. |  |

| 9. Teacher | And so it ends up looking like this (changes the slide). |  |

FIGURE 7.4
(*Continued*)

After noting male and female karyotypes with students, Mrs. Lara begins a new set of slides where students are asked to examine karyotypes on the screen to determine if they are "normal" human male karyotypes or abnormal ones. Here Mrs. Lara reminds students about genetic mutations caused by insertion or deletion of the chromosomes. She tells her students, "Today you're going to learn how to read those karyotypes and what it's going to look like." Upon looking at the next slide, where Mrs. Lara asks if students can tell what is abnormal about the picture, one students says that they can't tell if "it's a boy or a girl" in reference to a monosomy X female or Turner syndrome. The lesson continues with a series of teacher-guided questions about related abnormalities that can be detected by examining karyotypes including student examples from their family and from popular culture. So, while Mrs. Lara engages students in secondhand investigations, examples like these can be rich literacy contexts for ELs.

Cervetti, Pearson, Bravo, and Barber (2006) refer to secondhand inquiry texts as valuable forms of literacy because they provide text that "can provide data in which the reader is challenged to draw conclusions and develop claims" and where students can "investigate phenomena that are not easily modeled in classrooms" (p. 230). Literacy in science is often visual literacy going beyond words and including many visual forms. A basic definition of *literacy* across cultural and professional communities can even be considered any form of "communication through visually decoded inscriptions" (Besnier, 2001, p. 136). The following passage describes this aspect of visual literacy in science by researchers conducting science education research at the Lawrence Hall of Science, testing the synergies between literacy and science instruction.

> In science, the diversity of visual elements extends from photographs to highly complex charts, tables, graphs, and diagrams. These visual representations often carry new information that supplements and supports printed text, and sometimes literally offer *re*-presentations of textual information in a visual format. Both forms of representation—visual and print—are used to communicate complex arrays of ideas, evidence, and claims about natural phenomena. (Cervetti et al., 2006, p. 239)

All students including ELs need support in reading and discussing visual representations of science to make connections across concepts and even test preliminary understandings of information related to past science experiences at home and in school. In summary of interaction 2, there are several overlapping language and literacy demands where Mrs. Lara provides support in reading science texts. She engages students in a quick-write activity during the warm-up to review past science material and activates prior knowledge related to the new lesson. Mrs. Lara attends to varying levels of EL proficiencies by modifying her speech and by using paralinguistic cues to explain key instructions and points in the lesson. Table 7.3 describes the ways in which interaction 2 address mostly (level 2) English language and disciplinary literacy development by attending to varied modes of using language and literacy to make sense of scientific ideas.

TABLE 7.3
SSTELLA in Example 2

English Language and Disciplinary Literacy Development	
Promoting opportunities for English language development for ELs through student interaction	Level 2: All students work in pairs, individually, and as part of a large group matching DNA bands and collecting reading karyotypes. There are some opportunities for varied forms of student interaction (class discussions, partner or small-group interaction, or student presentations), but little or no support is provided for all ELs to engage in this participation through wait time, modeling, and/or role-playing.
Promoting opportunities for English language development for ELs through vocabulary support	Level 3: The teacher attends to key vocabulary as necessary to support students' understanding of science concepts and uses visuals, hand/arm gestures, and graphic representations including supporting the use of everyday words to learn new terms. This attention to science vocabulary is done to support scientific sense-making and scientific/engineering practices including classification of DNA patterns and reading DNA models.
Pressing for authentic science literacy tasks	Level 2: The teacher provides opportunities for students to read, write, and/or discuss texts with a focus on scientific/engineering practices. The teacher uses several strategies including idiomatic and everyday phrases and examples to connect to scientific understandings.

Addressing Student Interaction and Literacy in Science through Translanguaging

Interactions 1 and 2 describe typical scenarios in teaching ELs in science as teachers attempt to integrate English language and disciplinary literacy development into their lessons. The major challenge remains addressing the multiple modes of language use in the service of science learning. Increasingly educators are recognizing the importance of unexpected scaffolding opportunities within linguistically diverse spaces for engaging and sustaining student learning in the classroom through translanguaging exchanges.

According to Garcia and Wei (2014), *translanguaging* refers to using language practices as action in learning or *languaging* "between systems that have been described as separate" such as "English," "Spanish," "Chinese," and so on, that in turn creates changes in how interactional structures unfold socially, culturally, and cognitively (p. 43). This phenomenon is something that naturally occurs in social interaction between bilingual, multilingual, and monolingual speakers including mainstream classrooms, but one that can be used to further contextualize science learning and draw from existing linguistic resources from students. Therefore, shifts between languages are potentially more than code-switching but rather opportunities for reorienting student-to-student and teacher-to-student interaction to a common context and reviewing previous out-of-school knowledge to academically relevant knowledge as well.

Using translanguaging practices in the classroom can help create more productive learning contexts in science. A translanguaging practice can be used by bilingual and monolingual secondary school teachers to differentiate instruction, connect previous knowledge to academic goals, and engage student participation in key activities. This is an important point because regardless of a teacher's familiarity with languages other than English, all teachers can provide language support to ELs. ELs come from a range of English language proficiencies and academic backgrounds that need to be supported. In fact, translanguaging has been found to be a more common pedagogical practice in diverse secondary school classroom settings than in mainstream elementary classrooms (Garcia & Wei, 2014).

Learning new science language and content relies on building on previous communicative and cognitive resources. According to Garcia and Wei (2014), learning language and content is more than listening and producing new forms of language but rather "it is important to engage and interact socially and cognitively in the learning process in ways that produce and extend the students' languaging and meaning-making" (p. 79). In the case of secondary school classrooms with diverse students, including ELs with multiple home languages, translanguaging can be used by teachers even when the teacher uses primarily English as the language of instruction. The pedagogical functions of a translanguaging pedagogy can include: "1) the contextualization of key words and concepts, 2) the development of metalinguistic awareness, and 3) the creation of affective bonds with students" (Garcia & Wei, 2014, p. 111). In the case of science classrooms, translanguaging offers varied opportunities for students and teachers to work together while using multiple registers, languages, and language modalities to accomplish scientific and engineering practices.

The following exchange in table 7.4 focuses on translanguaging exchanges between a high school science teacher (Mr. Green) and a student (David) while the teacher addresses the entire class. This exchange was reported in a study by Langman (2014) examining pedagogical language practices in secondary school science classrooms as forms of language policy in action. The teacher begins the exchange with an attempt to review and build on a previous lesson on parallel and serial circuits. The exchange begins with a statement and question by the teacher in line 1 indicating that the activity they are about to begin is a review from before and also by asking for questions. This leads to a real-life question from David as he makes sense of circuits in line 4.

TABLE 7.4

Ln#	Speaker	Talk
1	Teacher	Alright. Pretty little simple review of yesterday's stuff. Anybody got any questions about that? Looked pretty much the same as yesterday
2	David	(inaudible)
3	Teacher	Yes?
4	David	Hmm, the houses have have a paral . . . a series?
5	Teacher	I'm sorry?
6	David	The houses.
7	Teacher	Mhm.
8	David	Does, have a paral . . . a parallel system and a series system?
9	Teacher	Uh, we're gonna be using the parallel, that way if something goes wrong with one system, you can still use the other one, right?
10	David	Yes but when the [pause] the . . .
11	Teacher	When the lights, like if a, a big bunch of power and all the lights go out, you mean?
12	David	Yeah.
13	Teacher	Okay, we'll be talking about that, uh, it's called fuses, and we'll be talking about that on Friday.
14	David	Okay.
15	Teacher	It's a protection so there's not too many electrons flowing.
16	David	Mhm.
17	Teacher	If too many get to flowing it gets hot, right? And you might possibly burn your house down, or something like that. So there's something called a fuse, F-U-S-E, which we'll talk about later on this week

Excerpt 8: High School Translanguaging about Parallel and Serial Circuits

This kind of exchange is a form of translanguaging pedagogy as it demonstrates how a teacher genuinely accepts David's questions and contributions on the matter of circuits as related to scientific sense-making while not shutting down his contributions as nonstandard, invalid, or unrelated. This is important because students need to be supported in trying out new science vocabulary and making observations. David is seen here still acquiring the language of parallel and series circuits with "the houses have have a paral . . . a series?" (line 4) and "Does, have a paral . . . a parallel system and a series system?" (line 8).

Despite David's developing level of key terms here, Langman (2014) explains that the teacher treats David's language as "standard, acceptable, and normal" (p. 194) in a case where often nonstandard English is corrected primarily and language feedback becomes the focus of the teacher's attention or students' contributions are rejected as unrelated to the discussion. In this scenario, the teacher treats David's question as a valid, science-related question that leads to several back-and-forth clarifications including the agreement that homes use parallel circuits. A diverse set of language registers are allowed to coexist in this exchange for the sake of scientific sense-making that in turn reinforce the nature of scientific inquiry and the inclusion of diverse identities in the classroom.

Conclusion

SSTELLA addresses authentic scientific language and literacy embedded in science and engineering practices. Literacy is already part of scientific meaning making for students and scientists alike. Greater and more careful attention to how EL students interact with each other around scientific and engineering practices in language production and reception will lead to more effective and complex learning of scientific ideas for all students.

Notes

1. These strategies, however, need to be considered carefully to sustain the nature of science activities being addressed.

2. The given definition for *karyotypes* by the teacher is "a picture of a group of chromosomes cut out and grouped together."

References

Besnier, N. (2001). Literacy. In A. Duranti (Ed.), *Key terms in language and culture* (vol. 11). Malden, MA: Wiley-Blackwell.

Bruna, K. R., Vann, R., & Escudero, M. P. (2007). What's language got to do with it?: A case study of academic language instruction in a high school "English Learner Science" class. *Journal of English for Academic Purposes, 6*(1), 36–54.

Bybee, R. W. (2011). Scientific and engineering practices in K–12 classrooms. *Science Teacher, 78*, 34–40.

Cervetti, G. N., Pearson, P. D., Bravo, M. A., & Barber, J. (2006). Reading and writing in the service of inquiry-based science. In R. Douglas (Ed.), *Linking science & literacy in the K–8 classroom.* Arlington, VA: NSTA Press.

Darian, S. (2003). *Understanding the language of science.* Austin, TX: University of Texas Press.

Duff, P. (2000). Repetition in foreign language classroom interaction. In J. K. Hall and L. S. Verplaetse (Eds.), *Second and foreign language learning through classroom interaction* (pp. 139–59). Mahwah, NJ: Lawrence Erlbaum.

Garcia, O., & Wei, L. (2014). Translanguaging. *Language, Bilingualism and Education.* Basingstoke: Palgrave.

Goldenberg, C., Rueda, R. S., & August, D. (2006). *Sociocultural influences on the literacy attainment of language-minority children and youth.* Mahwah, NJ: Lawrence Erlbaum.

Graham, S., & Perin, D. (2007). A meta-analysis of writing instruction for adolescent students. *Journal of Educational Psychology, 99*(3), 445.

Gutiérrez, K., & Stone, L. (2002). Hypermediating literacy activity: How learning contexts get reorganized. *Contemporary Perspectives in Early Childhood Education, 2*, 25–51.

Hull, G. A., & Moje, E. B. (2012). What is the development of literacy the development of? *Commissioned Papers on Language and Literacy Issues in the Common Core State Standards and Next Generation Science Standards, 94*, 52.

Janzen, J. (2008). Teaching English language learners in the content areas. *Review of Educational Research, 78*(4), 1010–38.

Langman, J. (2014). Translanguaging, identity, and learning: Science teachers as engaged language planners. *Language Policy, 13*(2), 183–200.

Lee, O., Quinn, H., & Valdés, G. (2013). Science and language for English language learners in relation to Next Generation Science Standards and with implications for Common Core State Standards for English language arts and mathematics. *Educational Researcher, 42*(4), 223–33.

Lemke, J. (1990). *Talking science: Language, learning, and values.* Norwood, NJ: Ablex.

Moje, E. B. (2007). Developing socially just subject-matter instruction: A review of the literature on disciplinary literacy teaching. *Review of Research in Education, 31*(1), 1–44.

Moscovici, H. (1999). *Shifting from activitymania to inquiry science—what do we (science educators) need to do?* ERIC document 444825.

NGSS Lead States. (2013). *Next Generation Science Standards: For states, by states.* Washington, DC: National Academies Press.

Olson, C. B., Kim, J. S., Scarcella, R., Kramer, J., Pearson, M., van Dyk, D. A., Collins, P., & Land, R. E. (2012). Enhancing the interpretive reading and analytical writing of mainstreamed English learners in secondary school: Results from a randomized field trial using a cognitive strategies approach. *American Educational Research Journal, 49*, 323–55.

Perry, K. H. (2012). What is literacy? A critical overview of sociocultural perspectives. *Journal of Language and Literacy Education, 8*(1), 50–71.

Schleppegrell, M. J. (2004). *The language of schooling: A functional linguistics perspective*. Mahwah, NJ: Lawrence Erlbaum.

Shanahan, T., & Shanahan, C. (2008). Teaching disciplinary literacy to adolescents: Rethinking content-area literacy. *Harvard Educational Review, 78*(1), 40–59.

Tharp, R. G., & Gallimore, R. (1991). *The instructional conversation: Teaching and learning in social activity. Research report: 2*. Santa Cruz, CA: National Center for Research on Cultural Diversity and Second Language Learning.

Walqui, A., & van Lier, L. (2010). *Scaffolding the academic success of adolescent English language learners: A pedagogy of promise*. San Francisco, CA: WestEd.

III

APPLYING SSTELLA PRACTICES
TO CURRICULAR AND
ASSESSMENT PLANNING

8

Explaining the Antibiotic Resistance of MRSA

A Biology Unit to Integrate Scientific Practices with Disciplinary Literacy Overview

Edward G. Lyon

I N THIS CHAPTER, we shift from detailing core instructional practices of the Secondary Science Teaching with English Language and Literacy Acquisition (SSTELLA) framework to modeling how science teachers can integrate practices when planning instruction centered on big ideas from the Next Generation Science Standards and literacy practices from the Common Core State Standards for English language arts. The biology unit described in this chapter, "Explaining the Antibiotic Resistance of MRSA," was developed as part of the SSTELLA Project to exemplify a SSTELLA-informed science unit for novice teachers during their science method course and the mentors of novices as part of professional development. In chapter 9, we deconstruct the unit to help readers understand particular instructional moves that align with the SSTELLA framework.

Introduction: Setting the Unit Context

The overarching goal of "Explaining the Antibiotic Resistance of MRSA" is to help students make sense of a core science idea (how species change by natural selection) by engaging them in the practices and discourse of scientists, while simultaneously assisting students in disciplinary language and literacy development through the interpretation of three contrasting texts (see chapter appendices) as well as the production of an evidence-based scientific explanation. The unit frames the core idea of natural selection through the specific phenomenon of bacteria strains that are increasingly resistant to antibiotics such as penicillin and methicillin, and can have serious consequences for public health in the United States.[1]

This unit is intended for a mainstream high school biology class that would range from intermediate English learners (ELs) to redesignated (i.e., former) ELs and English-only students (chapter 9 offers strategies for assisting beginning EL students who may be in your class and in need of increased support). Content in the unit builds from previously learned concepts (either in middle school or earlier in the academic year), such as basic principles of genes and genetic inheritance. The entire unit could occur between two and three weeks depending on possible extensions (as written, approximately two weeks). We focus on the beginning and the end of the unit to help teachers make sense of the unit's trajectory: how content was framed throughout and how students make progress toward the culminating task—developing a written explanation to a particular audience.

Narrative Description for the
"Explaining the Antibiotic Resistance of MRSA" Unit

After writing a response, students share with a partner, and then the teacher invites two students to share with the class: a student who responded with "yes" and another student who responded with "no." Students might share personal stories about a friend or a family member who came to the hospital to get better, only to get sick with something different. The teacher asks follow-up questions to the class, such as "Do you agree with . . ." and "What kind of evidence would support your response?" The teacher tells students that we will not come to a consensus answer yet, since this real-world problem, like most, is complex. However, everything we will be learning in the upcoming weeks will help us address this question.

The teacher proceeds to show a short video clip (www.youtube.com/watch?v=bevhCDOoYeE#t=30) that depicts a newscaster from 2005 reporting on the increased presence of a "superbug" called *Methicillin-Resistant Staphylococcus aureus* (or MRSA). The clip ends with a reporter asking an expert: "What causes these so-called superbugs?" The teacher stops the clip there and stresses to the class that they will be exploring this phenomenon—"What causes superbugs"—which will help them understand the big idea: "How do species change over time?" The teacher reviews and records on a poster important concepts introduced in the video clip, such as "the species of interest," "MRSA's relationship to this species," and "antibiotics." This poster will remain visible throughout the unit. The word *resistance* is introduced through a political cartoon that plays on the multiple meanings of the word *resistance*: "to protect from antibiotics" and "to stand up to a political organization or power."

"BIG IDEA" for LEARNERS

Species change over time through the process of natural selection, a process which is influenced by four factors: *population growth, hereditable genetic variation, competition, and differential survival (i.e., survival of the fitter)*

STANDARDS

Next Generation Science Standards (NGSS)

HS-LS4-2. Biological Evolution: Unity and Diversity

Students who demonstrate understanding can:

> Construct an explanation based on evidence that the process of evolution primarily results from four factors: (1) the potential for a species to increase in number, (2) the heritable genetic variation of individuals in a species due to mutation and sexual reproduction, (3) competition for limited resources, and (4) the proliferation of those organisms that are better able to survive and reproduce in the environment.

Common Core State Standards (Literacy in Social Sciences, Sciences, and Technical Subjects) Connections

Writing 2	*Write informative/explanatory texts, including the narration of historical*
(grade 9-10)	*events, scientific procedures/ experiments, or technical processes.*

UNIT DESCRIPTION

Day 1.

The first day of the unit begins with the teacher displaying an anticipatory question:

> Recall an experience with hospitals, such as when you…
>
> > (1) were injured,
> > (2) waited for your brother, sister, or cousin being born, or
> > (3) visited a sick family member or friend.
>
> Also think about your own knowledge of hospitals.
>
> Do you think someone could be harmed from bacteria while staying in a local hospital? Write your response **with a reason** in your science notebook.

Someone (would / would not) be likely to get an infection while staying in a local hospital. My reason is that .... hospitals are very (kron, they tend to make visitors put handitizer on before entering a patients room, or have contact with a patient. Also after leaving you leave you put handitizers.

FIGURE 8.1
Sample High School Student Response to Anticipatory Question

The teacher concludes the day by showing an abbreviated timeline to be re-visited later in the unit (see table 8.1) indicating four key points related to the MRSA "superbug." The teacher then facilitates a discussion about key concepts from each historical event (How are bacteria discovered? Revisit the word *resistance*.) then asks students to individually create an outline (via a timeline, bulleted list, storyboard, etc.) to provide a tentative explanation about *how* the species *Staphylococcus aureus* changed (from 1880s to present) so that over 60

TABLE 8.1
Initial Antibiotic Resistance Timeline

Late 1880s	1941	1961	Present
Staphylococcus aureus first identified by scientists	First resistant form of *Staphylococcus aureus* identified (resistant to penicillin)	First case of MRSA reported (resistant to penicillin and methicillin)	Over 60 percent of *Staphylococcus aureus* is resistant to methicillin (MRSA)

percent of the species is methicillin resistant (visuals or charts could help represent "0 percent" and "60 percent"). The student outlines should have both visuals and descriptions (or captions) to indicate this change. It is critical for the teacher to note that "this is just an initial model that we will revise toward the end as we gather new information." Students should not be expected to actually explain the events but rather should use this as an opportunity to explore what they already know and what questions they might still have.

Next, the teacher models on a document camera—drawing a picture of a colony of bacteria on a petri dish to represent *Staphylococcus aureus*—and then probes the students to consider how they could represent this new "variation" of the species that was identified in 1941 and what words/phrases they could use to describe what happened in between. The teacher posts all students' initial models on the walls so that students can engage in a "gallery walk" where they view each other's models. The teacher closes class by pointing out the variation in students' models (both the content and how they decided to represent). Hypothetically, the teacher might note one student's (one of his EL's) phrases: "How did bacteria get protected?" The teacher states: "This is exactly the type of questions scientists ask and why we need to seek some evidence over the next two weeks to answer the question."

Days 2–6

Over the next week (and possibly longer with extensions), the teacher engages students in multiple activities that help students make sense of four factors that, according to Darwin's theory of natural selection, influence how species change over time. The teacher draws on commonly used activities for high school biology, but sequences and discusses them in a way that allows students to continuously seek new evidence to refine their initial model of how *Staphylococcus aureus* changed over time. This sequence of activities (accompanying the various influential factors) was informed by an article in *The Science Teacher* by Passmore, Coleman, Horton, and Parker (2013). Suggested activities are depicted in table 8.2.

TABLE 8.2
Suggested Activities Related to Factors Influencing Natural Selection

Influential Factor	Class Activity
population growth	**Fish simulation:** http://sepuplhs.org/high/sgi/teachers/fishery_sim.html Students explore factors that influence population growth of Avril gulf tuna.
hereditable genetic variation	**Sunflower seeds:** students pick a seed from a bowl, examine it closely, return it to the bowl, and try to find it again to discuss general observations of variation in living things.
competition	**Game "Oh Deer":** Students engage in an outdoor simulation where they pretend to be either a deer or a resource (water, food, shelter). Deer must procure resources to survive, competing against their classmates who are also deer—helping understand the factor of competition.
differential survival	**Wormeater game:** students are given a utensil and have to "hunt" for worms (rubberbands) to understand how adaptations make a variant more fit and able to survive and reproduce. Students analyze and discuss trends in the data collected.

Day 7

At the conclusion of day 6, students have the tools needed to revise their explanatory model accounting for the antibiotic resistance of MRSA. Now, for the last three days, students will be organizing what they know to revise and use this explanatory model. The teacher hands students a summary graphic organizer (table 8.3) and gives students (already situated in groups of four) a number (1, 2, 3, or 4). Students are familiar with this routine and know that the teacher will ask them to write down some key points (starting with population growth) and a description of the class activity. Each group puts their heads together to discuss what they wrote. The teacher proceeds to ask

TABLE 8.3
Influential Factors Graphic Organizer

Influential Factor	Key Points (words, diagrams, pictures)	Class Activity
population growth		**Fish simulation**
hereditable genetic variation		**Sunflower seeds**
competition		**Game "Oh Deer"**
differential survival		**Wormeater Game**

FIGURE 8.2
Influential Factors Word Web

one of the numbers from each group (e.g., 2s) to contribute a key point, which the teacher records on a word web (depicted above). The same protocol proceeds through all four influential factors. Throughout, the teacher probes students about connections between the various factors so they understand the bigger picture—the mechanism of natural selection.

The teacher reminds students: "Our goal is to use what we have learned these influential factors to explain our initial problem—how the particular species *Staphylococcus aureus* has changed so that over 60 percent are resistant to multiple antibiotics. In other words, 'What causes this so-called "superbug" called MRSA?'" The teacher then passes back students' initial explanation outlines as well as a table (table 8.4) with some new information.

TABLE 8.4
Revised Antibiotic Resistance Timeline

Late 1880s	1941	1959	1961	Present
Staphylococcus aureus **first identified by scientists***	**Penicillin available in the United States and England** First resistant form of *Staphylococcus aureus* identified (resistant to penicillin)	**Methicillin available in the United States and England**	First case of MRSA reported (resistant to penicillin and methicillin)	Over 60 percent of *Staphylococcus aureus* is resistant to methicillin (MRSA).

*Bolded texts indicates new information given to students.

The teacher instructs student to now add to or revise their initial outlines based on what they have learned about natural selection and the new information presented in the timeline. Students share their revised models in groups as peers (with sticky notes) provide feedback as they have done before—with statements such as "Why did you include penicillin here?" A few students are asked to share their revised models with the class, which gives the teacher an opportunity to again see variation in student thinking and provide any needed feedback.

Day 8

On day 8, the teachers explains that they will turn their explanatory models (via the outline) into an actual written explanation that reflects the language that scientists use. They will also be supporting ideas with evidence, and communicating in a way targeted for a particular audience. The teacher passes out one of three texts (see appendices A–C) to each group and instructs students to (1) take out highlighter and pencil, (2) silently skim through the text, (3) use reading strategies learned through the year to help comprehend the text. For instance, students might underline main ideas or circle unknown words, or write questions in the margins. The texts will be reread for deeper meaning later.

The teacher then asks students already in groups of four to read the texts again with the following roles that they have used before (and rotate between articles).

1. *Reader (read the text aloud)*—checks group for comprehension after each paragraph
2. *Claim finder*—identifies and summarizes the claim of the text ("What is the major assertion or idea being conveyed?")

3. *Evidence finder*—identifies and lists any evidence of support of the claim
4. *Audience predictor*—predicts who the audience of this text might be (with evidence!)

Groups record their thinking on larger whiteboards.

The teacher emphasizes that the goal is not so much to "gain knowledge" about MRSA, but rather to compare/contrast different ways of communicating information. In this discussion, the teacher aims for students to understand "scientific explanations" as a common form of communication in science with particular structure and norms, such as some claim (or assertion) to address a question or problem, evidence to support the claim, and statements that elaborate on the importance of the evidence and link evidence and scientific principles to the claim (i.e., reasoning). They will also discuss that there is always a purpose (implicit or explicit) for the explanation—conveyed for a particular audience.

Students may come to see the text "*Staphylococcus aureus* Infections" as written for a general audience wanting basic information about *S. aureus*, including its transmission. They may point to factual information, but lack data to support the information and not really account for *how* something happens or a causal relationship. In contrast, the text "New Answer to MRSA, Other 'Superbug' Infections: Clay Minerals?" might be a summary for other scientists, policy makers, or even science teachers who already have background information, but are more interested in new discoveries (as opposed to what we already know). Students may also note evidence in the form of citations, but still a lack of empirical data. The final text presents the most evidence in the form of actual data and trends, and student might discuss how the description of how data were collected support the explanation.

The teacher then hands out a rubric that helps students see criteria for being successful when explaining science phenomena—which they will do all year long. The rubric includes criteria for *sense-making* (accuracy describing each influential factor in the context of MRSA and connecting ideas), *discourse* (providing a clear claim that is supported with evidence), and *writing* (that is clear, cohesive, and appropriate for the given audience).

The teacher instructs students individually to take their revised explanatory models and write a full explanation, including:

- an introductory sentence that helps readers understand the purpose of their explanation;
- a claim that directly answers the prompt "How did the species *Staphylococcus aureus* change over time so that, currently, over 60 percent are resistant to the antibiotic methicillin?";

- historical information and evidence from the various instructional activities to *support how* this happened; and
- a closing sentence to summarize their explanation.

Furthermore, the teacher discusses how the explanation is to be written in a way that is:

- cohesive (ideas flow logically; transition phrases help connect ideas);
- coherent (concepts defined/described as needed; proper spelling, punctuation, grammar used); and
- purposeful (in structure and tone) for a particular audience (in this case, a school newsletter).

Day 9

On day 9, students individually complete draft explanations. The teacher instructs them to switch the draft with a partner and displays a checklist to aid in providing feedback, which students can then use to go back and revise their explanation one final time. As closure, the teacher (from looking at preliminary work) asks three students to share explanations on the doc-u-cam as the teacher engages students in feedback about the various explanations in reference to the rubric and the learning objective. He then instructs students to describe how their thinking about how species change and bacterial infections has differed from when they started the unit. He also asks them to go back to give a brief answer to the very original question: Considering what you have experienced and know about hospitals, would someone be likely to get an infection (from bacteria) *while* staying in a hospital?

Summary

In this chapter, we described a high school biology unit developed to exemplify the SSTELLA framework: integrating all four practices so that students can use core ideas in science and productively use language while participating in authentic tasks. The next chapter deconstructs the unit to make it clear how SSTELLA practices were exemplified as well as illustrates how to plan your own SSTELLA-informed unit. In chapter 10 we connect instructional planning via the MRSA unit to assessment planning to ensure evidence of student learning is used to support students' science understanding and language development.

Appendix 8.A

Text 1: "*Staphylococcus aureus* Infections"

(Source: www.merckmanuals.com/home/infections/bacterial_infections/
staphylococcus_aureus_infections.html)

Staphylococcus aureus *is the most dangerous of all of the many common staphylococcal bacteria.*

These bacteria are spread by having direct contact with an infected person, by using a contaminated object, or by inhaling infected droplets dispersed by sneezing or coughing.

- Skin infections are common, but the bacteria can spread through the bloodstream and infect distant organs.
- Skin infections may cause blisters, abscesses, and redness and swelling in the infected area.
- The diagnosis is based on the appearance of the skin or identification of the bacteria in a sample of the infected material.
- Thoroughly washing the hands can help prevent spread of infection.
- Antibiotics are chosen based on whether they are likely to be effective against the strain causing the infection.

Staphylococcus aureus is present in the nose of adults (temporarily in 60 percent and permanently in 20 to 30 percent) and sometimes on the skin. People who have the bacteria but do not have any symptoms caused by the bacteria are called carriers. People most likely to be carriers include those whose skin is repeatedly punctured or broken, such as the following:

- People who have diabetes mellitus and have to regularly inject insulin
- People who inject illegal drugs
- People who are being treated with hemodialysis or chronic ambulatory peritoneal dialysis
- People with skin infections, AIDS, or previous staphylococcal bloodstream infections

People can move the bacteria from their nose to other body parts with their hands, sometimes leading to infection. Carriers can develop infection if they have surgery, are treated with hemodialysis or chronic ambulatory peritoneal dialysis, or have AIDS.

The bacteria can spread from person to person by direct contact, through contaminated objects (such as telephones, door knobs, television remote controls, or elevator buttons), or, less often, by inhalation of infected droplets dispersed by sneezing or coughing.

Methicillin-Resistant Staphylococcus aureus (MRSA): Because antibiotics are widely used in hospitals, hospital staff members commonly carry resistant strains. When people are infected in a health care facility, the bacteria are usually resistant to several types of antibiotics, including all antibiotics that are related to penicillin (called beta-lactam antibiotics). Strains of bacteria that are resistant to beta-lactam antibiotics are called Methicillin-Resistant *Staphylococcus aureus* (MRSA). MRSA strains are common if infection is acquired in a health care facility, and more and more infections acquired in the community, including mild abscesses and skin infections, are caused by MRSA strains.

Appendix 8.B

Text 2: "New Answer to MRSA, Other 'Superbug' Infections: Clay Minerals?"

(Source: www.nsf.gov/discoveries/disc_summ.jsp?cntn_id=132052&WT .mc_id=USNSF_51&WT.mc_ev=c lick")

Researchers Discover Natural Clay Deposits with Antibacterial Properties

FIGURE 8.3
Are the best medicines hidden in the Earth? French green clays are used for healing Buruli ulcers.

Superbugs, they're called: Pathogens, or disease-causing microorganisms, resistant to multiple antibiotics.

Such antibiotic resistance is now a major public health concern.

"This serious threat is no longer a prediction for the future," states a 2014 World Health Organization report, "it's happening right now in every region of the world and has the potential to affect anyone, of any age, in any country."

Could the answer to this threat be hidden in clays formed in minerals deep in the Earth?

Biomedicine Meets Geochemistry

"As antibiotic-resistant bacterial strains emerge and pose increasing health risks," says Lynda Williams, a biogeochemist at Arizona State University (ASU), "new antibacterial agents are urgently needed."

To find answers, Williams and colleague Keith Morrison of ASU set out to identify naturally occurring antibacterial clays effective at killing antibiotic-resistant bacteria.

The scientists headed to the field—the rock field. In a volcanic deposit near Crater Lake, Oregon, they hit pay dirt.

Back in the lab, the researchers incubated the pathogens *Escherichia coli* and *Staphylococcus epidermidis,* which breeds skin infections, with clays from different zones of the Oregon deposit.

They found that the clays' rapid uptake of iron impaired bacterial metabolism. Cells were flooded with excess iron, which overwhelmed iron storage proteins and killed the bacteria.

"The ability of antibacterial clays to buffer pH also appears key to their healing potential and viability as alternatives to conventional antibiotics," state the scientists in a paper recently published in the journal *Environmental Geochemistry and Health.*

"Minerals have long had a role in non-traditional medicine," says Enriqueta Barrera, a program director in the National Science Foundation's (NSF) Division of Earth Sciences, which funded the research.

"Yet there is often no understanding of the reaction between the minerals and the human body or agents that cause illness. This research explains the mechanism by which clay minerals interfere with the functioning of pathogenic bacteria. The results have the potential to lead to the wide use of clays in the pharmaceutical industry."

Appendix 8.C

Text 3: "MRSA Spreads in Households"

(Source: www.scientificamerican.com/article/mrsa-spreads-in-households)

Genome sequencing has revealed how a strain of Methicillin-Resistant *Staphylococcus aureus* (MRSA) spread through parts of New York City. Although MRSA is often associated with public spaces such as hospital and gyms, researchers say that private homes helped to fuel its travels in the New York neighborhoods of Manhattan and the Bronx.

The study, published in the *Proceedings of the National Academy of Sciences,* suggests a framework for other investigations into how pathogens colonize and infect communities.

Researchers examined the prevalence of the USA300 strain in northern Manhattan and the Bronx, where it has caused an epidemic of skin and soft-tissue infections in recent years. In 2009, it was responsible for around 75 percent of community-acquired MRSA infections in northern Manhattan.

Anne-Catrin Uhlemann, a microbiologist at Columbia University Medical Center in New York, and her colleagues sequenced the genomes of 400 samples of MRSA collected from 161 people between 2009 and 2011, and compared them with samples from healthy people (many healthy people carry *S. aureus* bacteria, which could be MRSA). They also gathered data on study participants' medical histories, antibiotic use and home locations to identify a network of USA300 transmission.

"This is an elegant and productive use of whole-genome sequencing in an epidemiological investigation," says microbiologist Alexander Tomasz of the Rockefeller University in New York.

Evolving Infection

Uhlemann and her team estimated the similarity between MRSA samples by checking how many different single-nucleotide polymorphisms (SNPs)—single-letter changes in their genomes—they had, and working out how fast these changes accumulated. The researchers calculated that the USA300 strains diverged from their most recent common ancestor around 1993. Although 85 percent of the samples were closely related to two known reference USA300 genomes, others were more diverse.

The team found that some of the samples originated in California and Texas, suggesting that USA300 was introduced into New York multiple times, rather than having one local ancestor.

Samples from people in a single household tended to be more similar to each other than to samples from other households, which implies that individuals within a home frequently exchange *S. aureus*. But people were also getting infected outside the home: "There were some households where we found multiple kinds of USA300, which is quite surprising," says Uhlemann. "It suggests some kind of outside reservoir, such as a link to a hospital or a gym." It seems that the USA300 strain spread in public spaces first, but it is now prevalent in households as well as hospitals. Further studies are needed to evaluate how hospitals might be involved in spreading the bacteria back into the community, say the study authors.

Uhlemann and her colleagues also found that nearly two-thirds of their bacterial samples were either fully or partially resistant to fluoroquinolone antibiotics, which are often prescribed for routine bacterial infections. The drug gets excreted onto skin surfaces, which the authors suggest may have contributed to the resistance in USA300: the bacteria get exposed to low levels of the antibiotic and can evolve ways to survive it. "We have to limit our antibiotic use because the consequences may really be a lot of collateral damage," says Uhlemann.

This article is reproduced with permission from the magazine Nature. *The article was first published on April 21, 2014.*

Note

1. More details about enacting the unit, including background about unit content, can be found in Lyon (in press). The antibiotic resistance of MRSA: Teaching natural selection with literacy development for English learners. *Science Activities: Classroom projects and curriculum ideas.* Another example of using MRSA to frame text-based inquiry can be found at Greenleaf, C., Brown, W., Goldman, S. R., & K., M. (December, 2013). READI for science: Promoting scientific literacy practices through text-based investigations for middle and high school science teachers. Paper presented at the National Research Council Workshop on Literacy for Science. Washington, D.C. Access on April 13, 2016 at http://sites.nationalacademies.org/cs/groups/dbassesite/documents/webpage/dbasse_086023.pdf

References

Aikenhead, G. S. (2006). *Science education for everyday life: Evidence-based practice.* New York, NY: Teachers College Press.

Council of Chief State School Officers. (2012). *Framework for English language proficiency development standards corresponding to the Common Core State Standards and the Next Generation Science Standards.* Washington, DC: Author.

Cummins, J. (1980). The cross-lingual dimensions of language proficiency: Implications for bilingual education and the optimal age issue. *TESOL Quarterly,* 175–87.

Lyon, E. G. (forthcoming). The antibiotic resistance of MRSA: Teaching natural selection with literacy development for English learners. To be published in *Science Activities.* Retrieved January 30, 2016, from https://teel.sites.ucsc.edu/wp-content/uploads/sites/162/2015/11/Antibiotic-Resistance-of-MRSA-lesson.pdf.

Michaels, S., & O'Connor, C. (2012). *Talk science primer.* Cambridge, MA: TERC.

Passmore, C., Coleman, E., Horton, J., & Parker, H. (2013). Making sense of natural selection. *The Science Teacher, 80*(6).

Rivet, A. E., & Krajcik, J. S. (2008). Contextualizing instruction: Leveraging students' prior knowledge and experiences to foster understanding of middle school science. *Journal of Research in Science Teaching, 45*(1), 79–100.

Windschitl (2008). What is inquiry? A framework for thinking about authentic scientific practice in the classroom. In J. Luft, R. L. Bell, & J. Gess-Newsome (Eds.), *Science as inquiry in the secondary setting* (pp. 1–20). Arlington, VA: NSTA Press.

9

Deconstructing the "Explaining the Antibiotic Resistance of MRSA" Unit

Sara Tolbert and Edward G. Lyon

Overview

This CHAPTER BREAKS DOWN the "Explaining the Antibiotic Resistance of MRSA" (referred to throughout as "MRSA") unit from chapter 8 as a way for readers to both (1) gain a deeper sense of the reciprocal and synergistic relationship of Secondary Science Teaching with English Language and Literacy Acquisition (SSTELLA) practices in the context of actual instructional planning and (2) inform how science teachers might use SSTELLA practices when planning their own science instruction. Throughout, we revisit key features of each SSTELLA practice as detailed in previous chapters and embed activities to encourage science teachers to approximate SSTELLA-informed instructional planning, which could be discussed in contexts such as method courses, professional development workshops, or new teacher induction programs.

Introduction: Relating SSTELLA to Lesson and Unit Planning

Common questions we have encountered from novice teachers in SSTELLA-participating science teacher education courses as well as experienced teachers during SSTELLA professional development sessions include, "How do I use the SSTELLA practices to construct a science lesson or unit?" and "Is there a SSTELLA lesson plan format like the 5E model?"[1] Simply put, the

SSTELLA framework is not a prescribed step-by-step model for planning instruction. We encourage teachers to use SSTELLA with a variety of lesson types to inform practice across a variety of curricular and student contexts. In other words, the SSTELLA framework is a *tool* to inform practice, from lesson planning, to teaching and learning, to assessment, and professional reflection. Teachers across university sites and districts need to have the flexibility to meet their own practitioner, community, and institutional needs.

Contextualizing Science Activity: Framing the Unit through the Phenomenon of "Superbugs"

Recall that *Contextualizing Science Activity* refers to both how the core ideas in science are embedded within a larger relevant context, as well as how students' lived experiences are elicited and shared in ways that create opportunities for them to bring in their own cultural, linguistic, and cognitive resources while making sense of science. While contextualization is important for all students (e.g., Aikenhead, 2006), it is particularly important for students who are English learners (ELs). Connecting abstract concepts to meaningful and tangible contexts or events improves both content learning and language development (Cummins, 1980; Rivet & Kracjik, 2008).

A teacher planning for a contextualized science unit, then, will need to reflect carefully on how the big ideas in science can be communicated through a meaningful context, such as investigating a discrepant event, developing and using a scientific model, or solving real-world problems that are also *relevant* to students, their families, and/or their communities. Students become investigators who seek to understand the causes of the particular phenomenon under study, and/or research possible solutions to a complex real-world problem that may be happening locally or globally. For example, students might use big ideas around the water cycle to propose a school-wide action plan to curtail rising water shortages.

It is not challenging to find some form of contextualization in science lessons, especially ones that deal directly with more observable fields of science, such as ecology. However, the context can end up being (1) more relevant or interesting to the teacher than students (how many students will connect Darwin's finches to their personal lives?) or (2) merely a "hook," meaning an isolated instance of contextualization (usually, but not always, at the start of a lesson) that is not consistent throughout the lesson or unit to bridge together concepts and bring out a purpose for engaging in the learning activities.

In the MRSA unit, students sought to understand and explain the antibiotic resistance of the species *Staphylococcus aureus*. Whereas core ideas related to natural selection are often taught in decontextualized ways (e.g., communicated as abstract concepts to be learned for the sake of "knowing"), this overarching question requires students to make sense of natural selection in the context of a real-world issue that can have serious consequences for public health. Other relevant contexts might include understanding how/why (1) the efficacy of influenza vaccines differs from other vaccines or (2) species in the *local* environment have particular characteristics (adaptations) different from other environments (e.g., Redwoods on the coastal range of northern California vs. Saguaros in the Sonoran dessert). Framing the lesson within a relevant context not only helps students understand the science, but also helps students see how they can use science knowledge in personal, democratic, and community-related decision making. Using MRSA as the context for our investigation of natural selection allows us to bring in other socially relevant sources of information, such as local news stories (e.g., via YouTube), and socially relevant readings.

Framing the lesson within a relevant problem or issue, however, is only partially contextualizing the learning experience for students with various cultural, linguistic, and social backgrounds. Students must also have opportunities *to contribute* their lived experiences (i.e., experiences beyond the science classroom, particularly those experiences often overlooked, ignored, and even marginalized in science classes) throughout the science unit. Students draw on their own experiences and funds of knowledge to make sense of and critically analyze the science they are learning in the classroom. Providing opportunities for students to share their lived experiences creates a space where all participants are positioned as valuable contributors to the construction of science understandings.

In the opening MRSA lesson, students are asked to reflect on their experiences, or family members' experiences, in hospitals to consider the likelihood of someone developing an infection while staying in a hospital. The experiences that students share during this activity are ones that both students and the teacher can refer back to throughout the unit, so that students make and see connections between what they are studying and how it relates to their own lives. Also, the teacher might learn ways that community and family members can be invited as participants during the unit. For example, students might have family members who work in medical institutions, in which case, a parent might be invited to the science classroom to share his/her knowledge of MRSA and how hospitals/clinics are working to reduce the risk of MRSA infections.

Activity 9.1 for Science Teachers

Textbox 9.1

Consider another core science idea listed below for various disciplines (you can refer to the *Framework* [NRC, 2012] for more details about the core idea):

Physical science: *How do substances combine or change (react) to make new substances?*
Life science: *How do organisms interact with the living and nonliving environments to obtain matter and energy?*
Earth science: *How and why is Earth constantly changing?*

1. What anchoring phenomenon (e.g., MRSA in the natural selection unit) could be used to contextualize the core idea?
2. What are two or three specific ways you can connect the core idea to students' lived experiences? (Some general categories include connections to the local ecology, home-family-community connections, socio-scientific issues, current events, and pop/youth culture.)

Scientific Sense-Making: Facilitating Student Modeling of "How Species Change over Time?"

In a SSTELLA-informed lesson or unit, students use scientific and/or engineering practices to engage with core ideas in science. It is very important that the lesson or unit's big idea, as well as expectations for learning (e.g., how students will demonstrate their understanding of the big ideas), are consistently and clearly communicated to students, particularly EL students. While EL students are capable of engaging in complex inquiry activities, their success in these activities can be quite dependent on the extent to which they are clear about the context of the investigation and the resources needed to competently engage in the inquiry task (e.g., not just materials, but the science concepts, writing practices, and heuristics).

In the case of the MRSA unit, the teacher communicates the big idea— "How do species change over time?"—to students in multiple and strategic ways: The anticipatory question communicates a context to be explored (bacterial infections in hospitals). The teacher connects student experiences with hospital to the big idea, stating, "We will not come to a consensus answer yet, since this real-world problem, like most, is complex. However, everything we will be learning in the upcoming weeks will help you address this question." Thus, students know there is a purpose to the various activities they will engage in, beyond "knowing facts" and "doing schoolwork."

The YouTube video addresses the particular phenomenon—the emergence of "superbugs"—which will need to be explained via the concepts being explored over the next week. Students can begin understanding that they need to connect an observable phenomenon—"increased prevalence of antibiotic resistant bacteria"—to an unobservable explanation—"evolution by natural selection"—which in turn will allow them to understand a core idea in biology: "how species change over time through natural section." Throughout the unit, the teacher communicates daily learning objectives, criteria for successfully meeting objectives, and provides opportunities for students to connect activities to prior learning and conceptions. In turn, this explicit communication and reflection can deepen student understanding of the big idea. Examples include:

- Developing an initial outline of MRSA's emergence (communicates that throughout the lesson students will be emulating what scientists do, such as test, revise, and explain models with new data)
- Reviewing the natural selection factors and associated activities (connects prior learning to the big idea)
- Providing and discussing the rubric (so students know important features of a written explanation, as well as how they will meet the learning objective)

Throughout the unit, students make sense of natural selection by engaging in two primary scientific practices: developing/using models and constructing explanations. Identifying the scientific practices is important when teaching ELs since each practice demands its own (although overlapping) set of cognitive and linguistic tasks. We chose to focus on models and explanations given that they form, as Windschitl (2008) notes, the core knowledge-building activities of scientists. Ultimately, scientists defend explanations of natural phenomena and represent their thinking via a model (which could be in physical, mathematical, or explanatory form).

To enhance sense-making, SSTELLA emphasizes that the role of students is to take partial or full responsibility for planning and carrying out the particular scientific practices. For instance, the teacher could have provided students with a prescribed protocol for how to represent the emergence of antibiotic bacteria, such as copying text or visuals onto a "timeline." But scientific modeling, as emphasized in the Next Generation Science Standards, does not mean that students merely replicate a diagram in the textbook (such as use everyday items to replicate a physical model of the cell). Instead, students develop their own initial model given what they already know—in this case some historical information and prior knowledge from previous units, courses, and learning outside of the classroom. The initial model allows students to begin making their thinking visible and organized. The practice of developing scientific models allows ELs to represent ideas and use language in a variety of ways, increasing access to the content.

Students then engage in a variety of hands-on, minds-on activities in which they explore different factors influencing how species change such as population growth (fish simulation), competition for resources ("Oh Deer!" game), and differential reproductive success (wormeater activity). The activities not only support student understanding via scientific practices of their own (e.g., interpreting data and communicating information), but also serve the purpose of providing evidence that students can refer to and even use as their model of MRSA's emergence is revised. Thus, the activities become a context for doing science: refining models and explaining a phenomenon, as opposed to just "knowing about" natural selection. Students can now revisit their initial timeline with a deeper conceptual understanding to tie together various events via a cause-and-effect relation (which in itself is a cross cutting concept in science). For instance, the introduction of antibiotics (a selective pressure) allows particular traits (in this case, antibiotic resistance) to be selected for and allows individuals possessing that trait to survive and reproduce at a higher rate.

A critical role of the teacher is to help facilitate student sense-making through learning contexts that connect content to the practices of scientists. Thus, the teacher does not just ask questions about natural selection, but helps students see how various concepts, like genetic variation, might inform how they represent and explain a real-world issue. Several supports depicted in the MRSA unit facilitate sense-making, particularly for ELs. Such supports include:

- Graphic organizers (timeline of events, summary of influential factors, deconstruction of articles)
- Multimedia (YouTube video)
- Visuals (from PowerPoint slides, political cartoons)

Activity 9.2 for Science Teachers

Textbox 9.2

1. Considering both the core science idea and the anchoring phenomenon you generated previously, what might be the one "big idea" for learners?
2. What other scientific models (again, physical, graphical, mathematical, explanatory) might be related to the big idea? Find or describe (1) an activity that can help students explore/develop an initial model, (2) an activity to collect data to test/refine the model, and (3) an activity to critique and analyze the initial model.
3. For each activity you describe, list ways to support intermediate/advanced ELs as they engage in the activities. What might you do differently to support a beginning EL that is newly arrived in the United States?

Scientific Discourse: Facilitating Discipline-Specific Communication and Science Understanding through an Explanatory Model

In SSTELLA lessons, the teacher and students engage in discipline-specific forms of communication (e.g., constructing evidence-based explanations) to both deepen students' understanding of content and enrich opportunities for productive use of language. Talk is critical throughout this process. The teacher can help students use the discourse of science while talking through (1) purposeful questioning to elicit student ideas, (2) follow-up probing so that students elaborate on their ideas, and (3) recasting to connect student talk to each other. In all cases, students' everyday use of language is valued as a resource to bridge the ways that scientists reason about and communicate ideas.

In the MRSA unit, the primary discursive activities are to evaluate and construct scientific explanations about antibiotic resistance. The unit calls on the teacher to help students understand what counts as evidence in science and *how* claims are supported from evidence. Students learn to analyze evidence and claims from a variety of texts before constructing their own explanations. The assumption for this unit is that students have not had much exposure to supporting causal explanations with evidence, although students might have previously been asked to describe "what is happening" for a particular demonstration or investigation (e.g., a feather and penny drop at the same rate in a sealed vacuum). Classroom activities centered around just describing what is happening limit opportunities to connect evidence to claims being made, which is central for doing science, as well as attending to causal mechanisms that account for the phenomenon.

By engaging students in the identification of claims and evidence from different texts, the teacher might bring out different notions of what an explanation is, including its various components, which can be used as a resource for future lessons. Of particular concern is how the structure and communication of an explanation may depend on the audience/purpose of the text. For example, the article "*Staphylococcus aureus* Infections" in chapter 8 presents information, but there are no accounts of how infections occur or data to back up the information. The text, nevertheless, is suitable for a layperson to quickly glance for answers, recognizing that as critical consumers of information, readers should be cautious about the legitimacy of such texts. In this case, the Merck index is a widely accepted and used authority on chemicals, drugs, and biologicals. Conversely, in the article "New Answers to MRSA" the text discusses an actual research study that offers new insights to the scientific field and references other sources (e.g., World Health Organization) to legitimize claims made. Once again, though, the authors present no empirical evidence to strengthen the claims. In this case, the text serves as a "research brief" to inform a variety of audiences (e.g., policy makers, teachers) who may communicate the findings to others, but perhaps not use the text itself to substantiate further claims.

Students then apply their understanding of structure and purpose of scientific explanations, drawing on evidence (the MRSA timeline) and scientific principles (natural selection) to draft their own evidence-based account of the emergence of MRSA. Students review each other's draft explanations (another form of assistance) with attention to conceptual understandings and the structure/function of the explanation.

On multiple occasions, students would be engaged in a purposefully planned and sustained science talk. For instance, on day 7 the science talk further clarifies students' developing ideas about the four key factors related to evolution. During this science talk, the teacher probes students to say more about their ideas, and rephrases students' contributions as they encourage other students to contribute to the development of science understandings. Through the science talk, students are "thinking with others" to more deeply explore the concept of natural selection (Michaels & O'Connor, 2012).

Activity 9.3 for Science Teachers

Textbox 9.3

1. Go back to the anchoring phenomenon you listed in activity 9.1. What explanation would you expect students to produce related to the phenomenon?
2. List two or three strategies to assist students in developing/evaluating their explanation (refer back to chapter 7). How would you adjust this assistance for beginning ELs newly arrived in the United States?
3. List two or three open-ended, meaningful questions that might open up a science talk around explaining the phenomenon of interest.

English Language and Disciplinary Literacy Development: Attending to Productive Use of Language through Analytical Tasks and Language Functions

Recall in chapter 2 that EL students are by no means a monolithic group. EL students bring a variety of prior experiences, sense-making resources, language proficiencies, and academic backgrounds to the science classroom. Recall also from chapter 1 that understanding language development and science learning as synergistic and reciprocal processes requires moving away from the idea that students must acquire "native-like" proficiency in English. Instead, the focus of disciplinary language and literacy development is more on supporting students to use language purposefully and productively to engage in various analytical tasks (e.g., determining which variables need to be controlled or making decisions about how to most effectively display data) rather than a flawless use of grammatical structures. When using the SSTELLA framework to plan science lessons, teachers should evaluate the type of analytical tasks in which students will be expected to engage, as well as the disciplinary-specific receptive and productive language functions, the modalities, and the registers that students will be expected to use during the lesson.

During the MRSA lesson activities, students engage in the scientific practices of constructing explanations, developing and using models, and obtaining, evaluating, and communicating scientific information. The analytical tasks and language functions associated with the scientific practice of constructing explanations for the MRSA unit are described in table 9.1.

Once the analytical tasks and associate receptive and productive language functions have been identified, teachers should consider the modalities ("characteristics of the 'channels' through which language is used") and registers ("colloquial and classroom registers, discipline-specific language and terminology, and disciplinary discourse conventions") that students would likely use or encounter as they participate in the lesson activities (Council of Chief State School Officers, 2012, p. 31). In the MRSA unit, students engage in multiple language modalities, such as communicating in small groups and as a whole class, interacting one-on-one with peers and the teacher, and interpreting and producing texts. Additionally, students will use multiple language registers as they participate in the lesson activities.

For example, the teacher and students will likely use primarily colloquial registers as they communicate with one another their experiences about acquiring infections in a hospital, but also as they communicate with one another in small groups to make sense of the analytical tasks. Students will need to use classroom registers as they comprehend teacher instructions, ask for clarification, and participate in small- and whole-group discussions. Also, "learner-appropriate science classroom discourse registers and conventions" will be used to analyze and evaluate evidence, and to construct oral and written explanations (Council of Chief State School Officers, 2012, p. 35). Students will comprehend and use discipline-specific language and terminology as they discuss what they have learned about the four factors related to natural selection, and in the development of their written MRSA explanations.

After considering the nature of the tasks and the language functions involved in the analytical task(s) of the lesson, teachers can begin to think about what type of scaffolds should be provided so that EL students can success-

TABLE 9.1
Focal Scientific Practice (Constructing Explanations) for the
MRSA Lessons Series, with Analytical Tasks and Language Functions

Analytical task	• Develop explanations. • Analyze the match between explanation or model and a phenomenon or system. • Revise explanation based on input of others or further observations.	Students read articles about MRSA to find and evaluate evidence for the claims presented in each article. Students must use evidence from multiple sources to develop and revise their own explanatory models regarding the evolution of MRSA.
Receptive language functions	• Comprehend questions and critiques. • Comprehend explanations offered by others. • Comprehend explanations offered by texts. • Coordinate texts and representations.	Students listen to and comprehend explanations related to the four key factors of natural selection both in small groups and as a whole class. Students read and comprehend explanations about the evolution of MRSA from multiple perspectives—including a variety of informational texts about MRSA, as well as their peers' written explanations about the evolution of MRSA
Productive language functions	• Communicate (orally and in writing) ideas, concepts, and information related to a phenomenon or system (natural or designed). • Provide information needed by listeners or readers. • Respond to questions by amplifying explanation. • Respond to critiques by countering with further explanation or by accepting as needing further thought. • Critique or support explanations offered by others.	Students communicate their initial ideas related to MRSA evolution in small groups and as a whole class. Students must select and use key pieces of evidence from multiple sources to write an evidence-based explanation regarding the development of an antibiotic-resistant strain of *Staphylococcus aureus*. Students also critique the written arguments of others, that is, arguments presented in the informational passages students read during class, as well as the written arguments of their peers.

Source: Adapted from Lee et al., 2013.

fully engage in the tasks. It is important to remember that supports will vary depending on the language proficiency, backgrounds, and prior experiences of the individual students in the science classroom. Therefore, there is not a single overarching set of supports that will be appropriate for all EL students in the classroom. This is not to say that teachers must develop an individualized set of supports or scaffolds for each EL student and for every lesson. On the contrary, recognizing the diverse sense-making resources that students bring to science learning, as well as the focus on use of disciplinary language practices in the context of doing science, teachers can facilitate purposeful collaborative science learning experiences that encourage widespread student-student interaction, where students support and learn from each other. In working together to solve science problems or understand scientific phenomena, students develop disciplinary language and literacy skills for science.

It is insufficient, however, to view language supports for EL students as simply a matter of assigning students to work with peers who share a common home language status. While home languages are valuable scientific sense-making resources, students also need to be supported and encouraged to use the language of *instruction* (typically English, unless in a dual immersion setting) so that they can have access to both. During the MRSA unit, students are provided with extensive structured opportunities to interact with each other in linguistically heterogeneous groups, through think-pair-shares, science talk in both small-group and whole-class formats, reciprocal teaching, and paired peer-editing activities. EL students can be further supported during these activities through attention to flexible and purposeful grouping (i.e., thinking purposefully about ways in which group formations support students' social, academic, and linguistic development; ensuring that group compositions are not static). Note that during the reciprocal teaching activity, students rotated through group roles, so that all students had an opportunity to lead the group in reading, finding evidence/claims, and determining audience/purpose.

While providing extensive opportunities for collaboration, teachers should also consider how to make sure that EL students have access to the task or activity by providing particular language supports that are task-specific. In the MRSA unit, students used text annotation strategies and graphic organizers during their group reading of the MRSA articles. These graphic organizers and annotation strategies supported students in their use of multiple modalities (comprehending and communicating information from a text) and multiple language registers (discipline-specific terminology, disciplinary discourse conventions, etc.).

The teacher scaffolds students' analysis of *multiple* forms of text, including a cartoon in which antibiotic resistance has a double entendre, a newscast, a policy brief, a timeline, and other types of nonfiction texts used to communicate MRSA to different audiences and with different purposes. To support student use of productive written language functions, students first read and analyze, with support, several different types of explanations before they construct their own explanation related to MRSA. Students are provided with a rubric to guide them in the writing process, with attention to conceptual understandings related to natural selection, explanation quality, and writing coherence. Students engage in peer editing to further refine their ideas and improve the quality of their writing.

As you can see here through this deconstruction of the unit, vocabulary is not the central focus of instruction. In this way, the development of both language and science understanding is inseparable. Vocabulary is used in context to support the development of an explanatory model, versus being presented in a more decontextualized manner (e.g., frontloading technical scientific vocabulary at the beginning of a new chapter, or copying terms and definitions from the glossary). Students *review and use* key science terms and phrases (antibiotic resistance, survival of the fittest, population growth, heritable traits, etc.) in context as they construct explanations related to the role of natural selection in antibiotic resistance.

Graphic organizers and multiple representations of core ideas through video, photos and drawings, and varied text complexities ensure that all students understand the context of the investigation as well as the core ideas needed to construct evidence-based explanations about antibiotic resistance. Notice that only a few key vocabulary words and phrases are introduced or reviewed during the lesson. Students identify and try to collectively define new words as they read informational texts. In other words, students—*not* the teacher—are simultaneously and actively engaged in doing the language work *and* the sense-making work in the classroom. The teacher's role is to support the students' sense-making process.

Activity 9.4

Textbox 9.3

Go back to one of the activities you described in activity 9.2.

1. What type of language functions (receptive and productive) do you anticipate students would engage in?
2. List three to five supports that help intermediate/advanced ELs engage in the identified language functions. Consider supports related to (a) how students interact/participate with each other, (b) developing and using vocabulary (beyond defining terms), and (c) writing authentic science texts (refer back to chapter 8).
3. How can you adjust some of the previously listed supports for beginning ELs newly arrived in the United States?

Conclusion

In previous chapters, we discussed in detail features and the importance of each SSTELLA practice, while providing suggestions for implementation in the secondary science classroom. In this chapter, we demonstrated the synergistic and reciprocal relationship among the SSTELLA practices to inform science lessons and units. The chapter offers one way to integrate SSTELLA practices, but the SSTELLA framework is designed as a tool to *inform* a variety of lesson-planning classroom implementation decisions, not prescribe them. While the SSTELLA framework informs instructional planning for all learners, we argue that the SSTELLA framework is particularly useful when considering a linguistically diverse science classroom to help students learn science and develop language through contextualized science learning experiences.

Note

1. "5E" refers to a model of lesson planning in which teachers plan instruction through five stages: engage, explore, explain, elaborate, and evaluate. The 5E model was originally developed by BSCS in 1987 to promote inquiry-based science. More information can be found at http://bscs.org/bscs-5e-instructional-model.

References

Aikenhead, G. (2006). *Science education for everyday life: Evidence-based practice.* New York, NY: Teachers College Press.

Council of Chief State School Officers. (2012). *Framework for English language proficiency development standards corresponding to the Common Core State Standards and the Next Generation Science Standards.* Washington, DC: Author.

Cummins, J. (1980). The cross-lingual dimensions of language proficiency: Implications for bilingual education and the optimal age issue. *TESOL Quarterly*, 175–87.

Michaels, S., & O'Connor, C. (2012). *Talk science primer.* Cambridge, MA: TERC.

Rivet, A., & Krajcik, J. (2008). Contextualizing instruction: Leveraging students' prior knowledge and experiences to foster understanding of middle school science. *Journal of Research in Science Teaching, 45,* 79–100.

Windschitl, M. (2008). What is inquiry? A framework for thinking about authentic scientific practice in the classroom. In J. Luft, R. L. Bell, & J. Gess-Newsome (Eds.), *Science as inquiry in the secondary setting* (pp. 1–20). Arlington, VA: NSTA Press.

10

Responsive Approaches to Assessing English Learners in Science Classrooms

Edward G. Lyon

Overview

IN THIS CHAPTER, I explore how assessment consists of yet another set of teaching practices, interconnected with instruction that simultaneously support English learners' (ELs') science learning and language and literacy development when informed by the Secondary Science Teaching with English Language and Literacy Acquisition (SSTELLA) framework. I refer to the Antibiotic Resistance unit from chapter 8 to discuss how a responsive approach to assessment involves (1) *contextualizing* assessment and (2) using assessment to *scaffold* both students' sense-making and disciplinary literacy practices, all while making sure ELs can fairly demonstrate what they have learned in science. The chapter's goal is to develop a professional understanding of responsive approaches to assessment in addition to specific guidance so that science teachers can:

- choose or develop a progression of assessment activities throughout a unit that align with learning goals and how science is learned;
- address influences of language and culture while assessing science; and
- interpret and use evidence gathered from assessing to support ELs' science learning and literacy development.

Introduction: The Role of Assessment in Secondary Science Classrooms

When starting your teacher education program, what were your first images or thoughts on hearing the word *assessment*? Perhaps standardized testing, evaluation, accountability, quizzes, multiple-choice questions? If you thought about any or all of these words, then you are not alone with other teachers entering the profession and even some who have been teaching for years.

So far, the SSTELLA framework has been used to inform responsive instruction that supports students, particularly ELs, as they learn core ideas in science and develop disciplinary language and literacy. Implicit in these instructional practices is the notion that students need to be aware of their progress in learning science and language/literacy development, as well as what they still need to do to continue making progress. To make judgments about student learning, teachers can observe and interpret a wide range of student work, including talk, writing, performance during an investigation, multimedia products, or other representational forms. The process of collecting and interpreting evidence of what students know and can do and then *doing something* with that evidence is the very essence of what it means to assess student learning.

With knowledge of alternative purposes for assessing and tools for collecting and interpreting student work, novice secondary science teachers can move beyond viewing assessment as an evaluative "test," and see the valuable instructional role that assessment serves in science classrooms (loosely referred to as using assessment formatively). However, Heritage (2007) also notes, "Even if teachers have all the required knowledge and skills for formative assessment, without the appropriate attitudes toward the role that formative assessment can play in teaching and learning, their knowledge and skills will lie dormant" (p. 145).

Dispositions need to be developed that place students at the center of the assessment process. To develop dispositions, knowledge, and tools in support of using assessment formatively, it benefits novice teachers to see in practice various approaches to assessing student learning, such as what happens when students are only asked, orally or in writing, to recall science facts without deeper thinking. Furthermore, explicit discussion and analysis of issues related to language, culture, and equity while observing assessment in action can help teachers make sense of common tensions in terms of what it means to assess responsively in multilingual classrooms, such as:

- Is it more beneficial to "simplify" the language, content, and overall expectations when assessing, or keep language, content, and expectations rigorous?
- Do I interpret how students use language or just their understanding of the concepts? Can I do both? How?

Both tensions will be addressed by the end of the chapter as we offer insight as to how assessment fits into planning a SSTELLA-informed instructional unit (as summarized in chapter 9).

What Does It Mean "to Assess"?

Educators often dichotomize assessment: it is either summative (used to report what students have learned) or formative (used as a tools to support students' continued learning). In both cases, the verb *used* is critical since it is not the activity itself (a project, a lab, an essay) that determines whether an assessment is formative or summative, but rather the process of how the teacher *uses the information* gathered by assessing (Black & Wiliam, 1998).

In this chapter, we refrain from labeling assessment as just formative or summative, because the purposes may be even more nuanced. Instead we focus on a variety of classroom activities that serve the overarching purpose of eliciting and using (1) student ideas about science, (2) student experiences outside of the science classroom, and (3) evidence of student progress toward meeting targeted science learning goals, which includes developing disciplinary language and literacy. For instance, teachers might be eliciting students' funds of knowledge for future lessons, probing for a particular student conception before teaching it, or checking progress or mastery of a targeted objective. All types of assessment activities work together as a system to ultimately make informed decisions about students for a variety of reasons and stakeholders. Scholars in assessment at the classroom level (e.g., Bell and Cowie, 2001; Heritage, 2007; McMillan, 2007; Ruiz-Primo & Furtak, 2007) best describe this system as a cyclical process in which the teacher keeps asking three essential questions (Hattie, 2012):

- "Where am I going?" (i.e., the learning objective);
- "How am I doing?" (i.e., what progress have students made?); and finally
- "Where to next?" (i.e., what can be done, given this evidence from assessing, to help students meet the learning objective?)

The cyclical nature of assessment connects to SSTELLA in two important ways. For one, assessment is viewed as a way to check progress toward a big idea, which frames an entire series of lessons. Second, assessment is a way to scaffold students' sense-making and language and literacy development. Teachers can structure critical checkpoints in learning a complex concept or literacy task, as will be expanded on later in the chapter.

Fair Assessment for English Learners: A Start to Responsive Assessment

Researchers have identified features of content-area assessments, often focusing on multiple-choice or short-answer questions found on standardized tests, which do present challenges for ELs, including sentence structure complexity, unfamiliar vocabulary and cultural references, and idiomatic phrases (Abedi & Lord, 2001; Martiniello, 2008; Shaftel, Belton-Kocher, Glasnapp, & Poggio, 2006).

 To win a game, Tamika must spin an even number on a spinner identical to the one shown below.

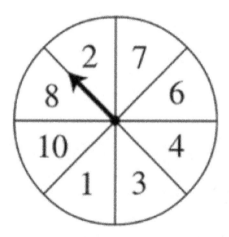

Are Tamika's chances of spinning an even number certain, likely, unlikely, or impossible?

A. certain

B. likely

C. unlikely

D. impossible

FIGURE 10.1
Source: Martiniello (2008)

For example, while studying how language influences ELs' performance in math, Martiniello (2008) found that the item in figure 10.1 (from a state-mandated test for fourth graders) advantages non-ELs over ELs. In fact, non-ELs were *twice* as likely to answer this question correctly, even when students from the two groups had equivalent mathematics proficiency. Why? Any ideas? First, the item consists of complex sentence structures with multiple prepositional phrases ("to win," "on a spinner," "to the one"). Second, fourth graders are unlikely to know many words used in the item, such as *even, spinner, identical, likely,* and *unlikely.* Follow-up interviews with Spanish-speaking EL students confirmed that students did not know the word *spinner* although the visual helped to identify the object. More interestingly, the students did understand the words *likely* and *unlikely* in the mathematical context of probabilities (the content being assessed).

However, unfamiliarity with many of the other words prevented them from demonstrating their knowledge. In essence, if the problem were re-worded (not changing the level of content being assessed), ELs would be more likely to convey their actual understanding of the content. Besides rewording text, studies suggest that strategies such as providing a glossary of terms, supplementing text with a visual, bolding/bulleting information, or organizing information with a graphic organizer may improve ELs' accessibility to the text—while keeping content rigorous (Siegel, 2007).

Language proficiency is just one influence that can shape student responses. Each student's ways of knowing and reasoning (influenced by their culture and experiences) shape how they respond to a question or task—which might be at odds with the intended way to respond. Thus, Solano-Flores and Nelson-Barber (2001) argue that assessment developers (including teachers) should also consider students' cultural worldviews, cultural communication and socialization styles, and lived experiences and values. They provide a clear example from a science item as part of the 1996 National Assessment of Educational Progress (NAEP) given to students across the United States.

The item presented two diagrams: diagram A depicted rough, jagged-looking mountains with a narrow river running through them, while diagram B depicted smooth-looking mountains with a wider river running through them. The question asked students to circle the picture that shows the mountain and river as they look "now" (instead of millions of years ago). The item is assessing students' knowledge of erosion—expecting students to understand that through millions of years weathering changes the shape of mountains, essentially smoothing them out. Certainly, students need opportunities to learn the concept being assessed (erosion), since this conceptual knowledge influences how they respond. However, when interviewing students asking them to explain how they arrived at the chosen answer, one student, who circled diagram A (the "wrong" answer), told the researcher that she had not previously learned about mountains (and erosion) in her science coursework.

Without the opportunity to learn the core concept, how did she make sense of the item? The student did not guess. The student explained that she had never seen mountains that look like diagram A (smooth) before—only ones that look like diagram B (rough). Thus, based on her lived experience, the student reasoned since she has only seen rough-looking mountains, rough-looking mountains must be the ones that currently exist.

This example signifies several important aspects of assessment. First, even though a student might answer a question "wrong," she could still exhibit a logical line of reasoning (we want students to reason!)—it just might be using different assumptions and ways of knowing (i.e., epistemologies) to justify the response. Second, lived experiences (not just cognitive underpinnings) shape the reasoning process—and thus eventual student outcomes. We encourage teachers to be cognizant of their students' diverse experiences, which we can draw on as resources during instruction and while assessing. Students must have opportunities to learn the content being assessed, as well as experience the context (examples used, type of activities). Finally, students need tasks that allow showing how they are thinking/reasoning as opposed to tasks that just call on "final answers."

To understand how to plan assessment in ways that address language and literacy in secondary science classrooms, we deconstruct the Antibiotic Resistance unit from chapter 8 through the three essential questions introduced earlier: "Where am I going?," "How am I doing?," and "Where to next?" In each section, connections are made to fairly assessing ELs.

"Where Am I Going?": Framing Assessment through Big Ideas and Learning Objectives

Figure 10.2 illustrates how the cyclical nature of assessment fits into big ideas as discussed in chapter 4 and exemplified in the Antibiotic Resistance unit from chapter 8.

The first important feature of figure 10.2 and in planning assessment is the identified "big idea." The big idea from the Antibiotic Resistance unit was to explain "how species change over time through natural selection" via the contextualized scenario of antibiotic-resistant bacteria in hospitals. Big ideas frame what students should ultimately be able to explain. Big ideas also communicate to students how they are working toward explaining natural phenomenon, not recalling factual knowledge. While big ideas

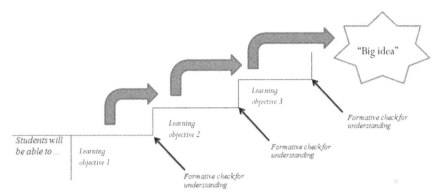

FIGURE 10.2
Source: **Adapted from Furtak (2009) Formative Assessment for Secondary Science Teachers**

focus on the "science" to be taught and learned, teachers utilize "learning objectives" to communicate how students are going to "demonstrate" what they have learned through desirable intellectual activities. For instance, instead of "know about igneous, metamorphic, and sedimentary rocks," a learning objective might state: "develop a model that explains the relationship among igneous, metamorphic, and sedimentary rocks." Thus, in addition to specifying important conceptual elements to understand, learning objectives also communicate what students will do with the concepts. For example, the Antibiotic Resistance unit's culminating learning objective was for students to:

> **Explain** how the species *Staphylococcus aureus* has changed so that currently over 60 percent are resistant to methicillin

The first part of the objective, *explain,* indicates the intellectual activity students will engage in. This activity is observable (we can collect evidence of students explaining), is clear (there are only a limited number of ways to explain, as opposed to expecting students to "know about" a concept), and integrates the core idea of biological evolution with a scientific practice—constructing explanations.

The Next Generation Science Standards (NGSS) are already written in a way that clarifies what students are expected to do (the scientific/engineering practice) and the core idea being promoted. Thus, they are a good source to align your own culminating learning objectives. The Antibiotic Resistance unit's objective was aligned with the following NGSS high school life science performance expectation:

Students who demonstrate understanding can:

Construct an explanation based on evidence that the process of evolution primarily results from four factors: (1) the potential for a species to increase in number, (2) the heritable genetic variation of individuals in a species due to mutation and sexual reproduction, (3) competition for limited resources, and (4) the proliferation of those organisms that are better able to survive and reproduce in the environment.

Textbox 10.1

Your turn:
   Consider the big idea you generated in chapter 9 as well as a specific scientific practice.

1. Craft a learning objective that communicates how students will demonstrate understanding and/or application of the big idea. As you craft the learning objective, consider:

   - Is it written clearly? (Will students understand what is expected? Is it specific enough?)
   - Is it observable? (Can you actually collect evidence of this learning?)
   - Does it promote scientific and/or language practices (to increase EL access to rigorous and authentic learning)?

2. Compare that learning objective to the most closely related NGSS.

"How Am I Doing?": Identifying Language Challenges and Opportunities While Assessing

As reinforced throughout this book, ELs bring diverse cultures, languages, ways of knowing, and lived experiences to the classroom that shape how they view and learn science. These diverse experiences and ways of thinking and knowing shape how they *communicate* their understanding of science as well (Solano-Flores & Nelson-Barber, 2001). Thus, uninformed perceptions about how ELs can communicate understanding, and the role of language and culture while finding out what they know and can do (i.e., assess), may lead teachers to underestimate what ELs can do when assessed. These issues are particularly salient for assessment, since misrepresented judgments about student learning lead to consequences such as denied classroom learning supports, lower grades, and decreased access to advanced placement classes, which all in turn could affect college and career readiness in addition to student affect and motivation. This section emphasizes language as a resource for ELs to demonstrate what they know and can do in science (instead of a limitation), which means being able to identify how students might be inter-preting and using language while being assessed (i.e., language demands) and then fairly judging evidence of student learning to provide appropriate support for their science learning and language development.

To illustrate how to identify language demands and act on them, an as-sessment activity (associated with the Antibiotic Resistance unit) is described below. We are not positioning this activity as the only or best way to assess. It is just one possibility that can be used to deconstruct how to make assessment fairer for ELs. This activity best represents a culminating task (refer back to figure 10.2), while formative checks for understanding might be smaller/shorter tasks that assess just the targeted learning objective. It is important to note here that we are focusing on formally planned activities used to collect and interpret student work or performance.

Ruiz-Primo & Furtak (2007) discuss how assessment spans from these for-mally planned activities to *informal* activities done moment-to-moment while teaching (e.g., questions asked during discussion). Much of what we have dis-cussed in previous chapters, such as engaging students in instructional conver-sations engaged in science (ICES) and eliciting students' funds of knowledge, are in themselves dialogic moves to assess student learning through elicitation of ideas, which the teacher can then respond to as students deepen their under-standing of core science ideas. The advantage of planning activities ahead of time is to ensure you are gathering actual evidence of student learning in rela-tion to the objective and can decide how to interpret and use that information.

FIGURE 10.3
Banner Baywood Medical Center in Mesa, AZ

SSTELLA Science Assessment:
Exploring the Antibiotic Resistance of Bacteria

Banner Baywood Medical Center in Mesa, AZ

Recall an experience with hospitals, such as when you...

    (1) were injured,

    (2) waited for your brother, sister, or cousin being born, or

    (3) visited a sick family member or friend.

Bacteria: *Single celled organisms without a true nucleus. When harming another organism, it is called an* **infection***.*

Also think about your own knowledge of hospitals, as the one on the previous page.

If you didn't know, bacteria are single-celled organism that lack a true nucleus and reproduce very quickly with enough resources. They can live almost everywhere on earth.

Do you think someone *staying* in a local hospital **could be harmed from bacteria**?

    Write "yes" or "no" in the box below and **give a reason**

```



```

FIGURE 10.4
Bacteria

Why do we care about bacteria in hospitals?

A recent report estimated that by 2050, *untreated infections* will cause more deaths worldwide than *cancer*. The model below shows estimated deaths from infection by 2050.

Antibiotic:
Chemicals that
prevent
bacterial
growth

Bacteria that are no longer harmed by **antibiotics** are considered antibiotic **resistant**. Antibiotic-resistant bacteria, such as MRSA, can cause serious infections that even lead to death. MRSA is sometimes referred to as a "superbug."

In this activity, you will learn more about antibiotic-resistant bacteria while demonstrating how well you...

1) *interpret a science text* using knowledge about biology,

2) *understand a core biology idea*: natural selection, *and*

3) apply the process natural selection while *explaining how bacteria become resistant* to a specific antibiotic, Vancomycin.

FIGURE 10.4
(*continued*)

Part I: Reading Task

Reading Task Directions

The following text will help you understand more about antibiotic resistance. You will learn about how the natural world interacts with *technology and human society*. For example, you will learn about the potential benefits and problems with the antibiotic **Vancomycin**. The information can help you write your scientific explanation in part III. Carefully read the following text and use any reading strategies you have learned. For example, you can number paragraphs, circle key terms, circle claims made, or write notes or questions in the margins. While you read, **answer the questions on pages 3–5.**

Resisting Our Drugs[1]

Carl's work tackles the very real problem of how bacteria in hospitals evolve to become resistant to antibiotics. Antibiotics, such as penicillin, are drugs that kill bacteria or prevent bacteria from growing. When first discovered, antibiotics seemed to represent a miracle cure for human diseases like pneumonia, typhoid, and bubonic plague. However, almost immediately after introducing an antibiotic, bacteria began to "up the stakes." Resistant strains of bacteria soon evolved that could grow even in the presence of a particular antibiotic. Drugs given by doctors became ineffective at battling these resistant infections.

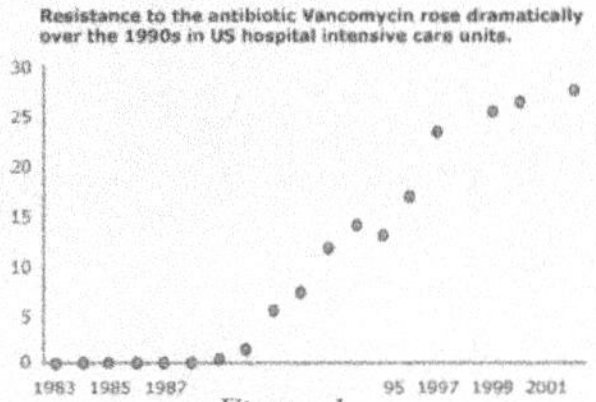

Resistance to the antibiotic Vancomycin rose dramatically over the 1990s in US hospital intensive care units.

Figure 1

The problem is much like running on a treadmill: medical researchers must sweat just to stay in the same place in their race against the bacteria. Drug companies develop and introduce a new antibiotic, only to see resistant bacterial strains evolve within a few years. Antibiotic resistance cause drug companies to develop yet another antibiotic. The new antibiotic then becomes useless against newly evolved resistant bacteria.

The cycle of drug development and the evolution of bacterial resistance is costly. Each year, over one million resistant infections occur in U.S. hospitals. Resistant infections cost an estimated 4-5 billion dollars. Resistant infections also costs human lives. And because resistant bacteria are harder to treat, antibiotic-resistant infections cause people to stay longer in hospitals and miss more days of work. For example, various sources estimate that in the U.S., we experience more than 8,000 additional days of hospitalization due to resistant salmonella strains.

FIGURE 10.5
Resisting our drugs

Circle the BEST answer to each question.

1. In this text, what does the title "Resisting Our Drugs" mean?

   a. People refuse to take drugs.
   b. Bacteria become protected from drugs.
   c. A political organization stands up to a drug company.
   d. Scientists develop new drugs.

2. Which statement best represents the author's *claim*?

   a. Medical researchers must sweat just to stay in the same place in their race against the bacteria.
   b. Resistant strains of bacteria soon evolved that could grow even in the presence of a particular antibiotic.
   c. The cycle of drug development and the evolution of bacterial resistance is costly.
   d. Resisting our drugs.

3. Which statement best represents *evidence* to support the author's claim?

   a. "Over one million resistant infections are acquired each year in U.S. hospitals."
   b. "We experience more than 8000 additional days of hospitalization."
   c. "Antibiotics, such as penicillin, are drugs that kill or prevent the growth of bacteria."
   d. Resistance to the antibiotic Vancomycin rose dramatically over the 1990s in U.S. hospital intensive care units [graph from Figure 1.

4. The author's purpose in this text is to

   a. provide an explanation about the role of antibiotics.
   b. describe a procedure to develop a new drug.
   c. discuss an experiment to test the effectiveness of drugs.
   d. identify the problem of antibiotic resistance.

A.

Questions 5-6 refer to Figure 1 from the text, shown below

5. Vancomycin is a(n)…
A. antibiotic.
B. bacteria.
C. drug company.
D. hospital.

6. What is the best *interpretation* of the data from 1990-2000?
A. The number of bacteria increased.
B. The percent of resistant bacteria increased.
C. The percent of people dying from resistant bacteria increased.
D. The percent of people dying from resistant bacteria deceased.

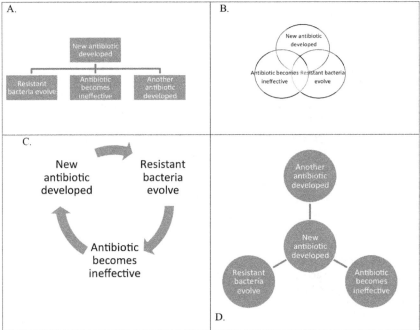

Resistance to the antibiotic Vancomycin rose dramatically over the 1990s in US hospital intensive care units.

7. In the 2nd paragraph, the author states: "The problem is much like running on a treadmill." Which model best represents this statement and ideas from this 2nd paragraph?

A.

New antibiotic developed

Resistant bacteria evolve

Antibiotic becomes ineffective

Another antibiotic developed

B.

New antibiotic developed

Antibiotic becomes ineffective

Resistant bacteria evolve

C.

New antibiotic developed → Resistant bacteria evolve

Antibiotic becomes ineffective

Another antibiotic developed

New antibiotic developed

Resistant bacteria evolve

Antibiotic becomes ineffective

D.

8. Who do you think is the main audience of this article? (*examples: scientist, doctor, general public*)? _____

Justify your answer in the lines below:

_____

_____

9. List any strategies you used to help read and understand the text

_____
_____
_____

FIGURE 10.6

Part II: Writing Task

Writing Task Directions

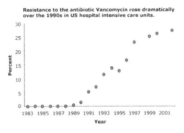

In part I, you learned about the rise in bacteria that are resistant to the antibiotic Vancomycin, represented in Figure 1 above. Your job now is to apply your own understanding about adaptation and natural selection to **explain with evidence how the percentage of bacteria resistant to Vancomycin changed from 1983 to 2001**.

Your explanation will be evaluated on 3 criteria. How well you...

- demonstrate your understanding of **adaptation and natural selection** (include related concepts such as *population, genetic variation, competition, fitness, and environment*).

- support your explanation **with evidence** and connect the evidence to the **process of natural selection.**

- write a clear and cohesive explanation. Your writing should...

  ✓ *connect* ideas through purposeful organization and transition words/phrases.

  ✓ take a *formal tone* and use a *variety* of word/sentence structure choices.

  ✓ *clearly communicate* ideas through standard writing conventions, including spelling, grammar, and sentence structure.

The next two tasks, planning exercises A and B, will help you organize and plan your explanation.

Explanation planning A

The diagram below is a *possible* representation of how a population of bacteria changes over time. In boxes (A), (B), and (C) write down any words, symbols, or pictures that will help you provide **a causal chain of events** leading to this change.

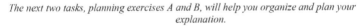

1983	1989-2000	2001

FIGURE 10.7

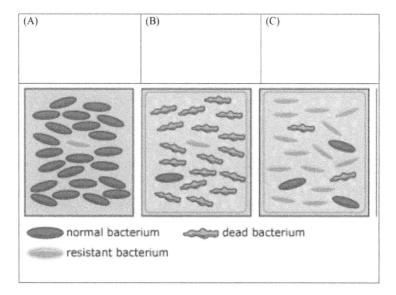

(A)	(B)	(C)

normal bacterium   dead bacterium

resistant bacterium

Explanation planning B

Remember that you are explaining *how* the percentage of bacteria resistant to Vancomycin changed from 1983 to 2001. Use the box below to organize your explanation with common explanation features.

Claim:	Some **evidence** supporting my claim:

Reasoning: Some ways that natural selection *explains the evidence*

FIGURE 10.7
(*continued*)

Your explanation

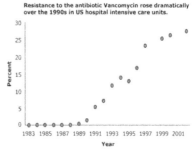
Resistance to the antibiotic Vancomycin rose dramatically over the 1990s in US hospital intensive care units.

Using your notes from planning A and B, write your explanation in the lines below: *explain how* the percentage of bacteria resistant to Vancomycin changed from 1983 to 2001. You may add pictures/diagrams to your writing.

Remember the 3 criteria:

- Demonstrate understanding of **adaptation/natural selection**

- support your explanation **with evidence** and connect evidence to the **process of natural selection**

- write a **clear** and **cohesive** explanation

Figure 11.2 MRSA Assessment Activity

Activity 11.1

Reflection questions about this assessment activity
1. How is the assessment activity framed? Does this appear relevant to "authentic science?" What about to students' lived experiences? Is it connected to how learning was framed during the unit (if Chapter 9 was read)?
2. What appears to be the focus (or foci) of the assessment – factual knowledge? Practices of scientists? Reading and writing in science? Again, how does this connect to the unit's big idea and unit learning goals?
3. Would ELs with at least intermediate proficiency be able to show what they know and can do on this assessment? Why or why not?

FIGURE 10.7
(*continued*)

Turning Challenges into Opportunities:
Increasing the Accessibility of Assessment Activities

Certainly, ELs face many challenges when being assessed, just as during instruction. However, we argue that many of these assessment challenges are in fact also opportunities to leverage in supporting rigorous, authentic, and meaningful science learning for ELs. The key is to *turn* challenges into opportunities through appropriate supports. For example, Lyon, Bunch, and Shaw (2012) studied what fifth grade students had to do with language while navigating science performance assessments—those assessments in which students engage in some authentic process or product (e.g., carrying out an investigation).

They found that students were expected to use over a dozen different texts (e.g., rubrics, procedures, reports, science notebook), as well as communicate and participate using language in multiple ways (e.g., small-group interactions, interviews with the teacher, individual reports, etc.). Although each use of language (termed a *language demand*) has the potential to disadvantage ELs, many of the language demands documented (e.g., collaborating with peers) are what made the performance assessment a more authentic and supportive assessment—providing students, including ELs, with opportunities to engage in the practice and discourse of science and even go back to revise their work.

Two key teaching moves can potentially turn language challenges into opportunities, which align with instructional moves already discussed in this book—contextualizing science assessment and scaffolding language practices.

Contextualizing Science Assessment. The Antibiotic Resistance Assessment Activity is contextualized in multiple ways. First, the entire activity is framed in a relevant real-world example via hospitals, antibiotic resistance, and drug companies. Second, students engage in an opening question to begin reflecting on their own lived experiences to make a deeper connection with the assessment activity, and perhaps the importance of what they are demonstrating. In both cases, the activity is contextualized to the *curricular* context (see chapter 8). Students have been exploring MRSA throughout the unit and it has been made clear throughout the unit that the culminating goal is to explain the emergence of antibiotic resistance. There certainly can be other ways to extend and contextualize the MRSA assessment. Students could construct the explanation in a different medium, such as a movie, a blog, and so on. They could even present their explanation to the local hospital, leading to a discussion with nurses and hospital workers closest to the actual scenario.

Activity 10.2

Textbox 10.2

Can you think about other ways to contextualize the Antibiotic Resistant Assessment and keep it aligned with instruction? (Refer back to chapter 5 for help.)

Scaffolding Students' Use of Language. As mentioned in previous chapters, SSTELLA focuses on how language is used or particular purposes (i.e., language practices), not just the structure of language (i.e., vocabulary, grammar, sentence structure). Shaw, Bunch, and Geaney (2010) applied this broader view of language to identify language demands across three dimensions:

- *Participant structure*: The various configurations set up that allow students to participate in assessment activity (either individually, interacting with other students as a group or whole class, or with the teacher)
- *Communicative mode*: How students demonstrate understanding and apply understanding (in writing? orally? performing a laboratory skill?) as well as interpret the information needed to navigate the assessment activity
- *Written texts/genre*: What type of texts do students encounter and produce as they engage in the assessment activity? These texts might represent common science genres (e.g., a lab report or written explanation, lab procedures), other texts not specific to science (e.g., a blog entry), or perhaps texts that are often associated with assessment (e.g., a rubric).

For each category, there are various norms and ways to use language that may or may not be known to students, particularly ELs. If ELs are not aware of the norm or convention, then it might be that language demand influencing their work, not actual mastery of the objective. However, the very same language demands might be what give ELs opportunities to demonstrate what they know and can do, including developing language and literacy proficiency.

Table 10.1 outlines some of language demands ELs might encounter in the Antibiotic Resistant Assessment Activity.

TABLE 10.1
Language Demands in the Assessment Activity

Participant Structure	Communicative Mode	Texts
• Pair work during introductory question (must know turn-taking norms) • Individual construction (no chance to get clarification, feedback, etc.)	• Productive (must know norms for writing an explanation) • Interpretive (if article is read to students) • Interpersonal (think-pair-share during introductory question)	• Instructions • Article • Planning graphic organizers • Written introductory task • Written responses to reading task questions • Written explanation

Ultimately, in the activity students are expected to show that they can "construct an explanation that accounts for the *methicillin* resistance of *Staphylococcus aureus.*" We identified the various language demands associated with just this one activity. In particular, note that these challenges include more than grammar and vocabulary associated with producing an individual piece of text. They include norms around the structure of text, and norms around a certain type of participation and communication. Teachers can overturn these challenges in multiple ways. This includes the role of language scaffolds, or "how specific representations and instructional strategies can be used to help students gain access to the concepts as well as to the language they need to learn" (Santos, Darling-Hammond, & Cheuk, 2012, p. 4).

- *Participant structure*: Individual work provides greater assurance of what all students can do without assistance. However, students may have learned content and engage in language practices as part of a joint productive activity throughout instruction—making the assessment activity appear more disconnected from instruction. Teachers can carefully scaffold participation throughout—promoting collaborative work, but also establishing norms so that individuals have opportunities and accountability for individual participation. As instruction continues, students may become more individually responsible for work, using group members as occasional resources. Alternatively, the assessment may be extended so that students draw on their individual explanations to present as a group to community stakeholders.
- *Communicative mode*: ELs benefit from opportunities for multimodal communication and representation, meaning that they show what they know and can do not only via written work, but also, for example, through visual representations, presentations, or another type of performance or product. These opportunities ensure a variety of ways to demonstrate understanding and open up more possibilities to draw on funds

of knowledge and connect lived experiences, especially when students can choose their mode of demonstration.

- *Written texts/genre*:

  ○ *Article*—The instructions encourage students to write in the margins to better comprehend the text. Other reading strategies might include asking them to identify claims and evidence or ask questions about the text in the margins.

  ○ *Written explanation*—Two planning exercises are included, a graphic organizer to make their thinking about the various terms and concepts visible and an organizer to structure components of the explanation—claim, evidence, and reasoning.

  ○ *Rubrics*—Teachers can display and discuss expectations for success throughout the unit, including showing the rubric itself (or a version of it). Students can even use the rubric when providing peer review on draft explanations. What type of texts do students encounter and produce as they engage in the assessment activity? These texts might represent common science genres (e.g., a lab report or written explanation, lab procedures), other texts not specific to science (e.g., a blog entry), or perhaps texts that are often associated with assessment (e.g., a rubric).

In an assessment scenario, the question becomes: *How much assistance should be given to students?* Without the graphic organizers would students, including ELs, have difficulty knowing what they are expected to do even though they do understand natural selection and how to write an explanation? Conversely, do the graphic organizers hinder independent thinking or alternative ways to write an explanation? Teachers should be cautious of *over*scaffolding. The answer is to know throughout instruction what students can do on their own and what they can do with such supports. Ideally, supports would be faded once it is clear that students can do it successfully. This is also a chance for differentiation. Perhaps by the time of the activity, some students need the support and others do not. Differentiation still promotes fairness, since ultimately the purpose of assessing is to find out what students know to support their learning (the end game isn't a grade). Students may not fully communicate what they know and can do through one form of representation (e.g., writing an explanation). Thus, providing opportunities for students to demonstrate via multiple forms of representation (talking about the explanation or supplementing the explanation with a visual diagram) can allow students to make their thinking visible. *To caution, allowing students to "make a diagram" instead of engaging in disciplinary writing or talk around the diagram prevents students from engaging in those essential language and literacy development opportunities.*

	Level 1	Level 2	Level 3	Level 4
Sense-making	*No/limited understanding of natural selection:* Able to state discrete, factual information about natural selection at best.	*Incomplete or alternative understanding of natural selection.* Able to accurately describe at least one factors contributing to natural selection, but without connecting any factor OR Able to provide at least a logical *partial* chain of events, but through an alternative conception of natural selection.	*Partial understanding and application of natural selection:* Able to use factor contributing to natural selection to provide *part* of a logical and accurate partial chain of events.	*Full understanding and application of natural selection:* Able to use factors contributing to natural selection to provide a *complete and accurate,* chain of events.
Use of Evidence	*No use of evidence:* No attempt to use any form of evidence.	*Limited/inappropriate use of evidence:* EITHER Refers to data/general trends in the graph w/o any interpretation (e.g., resistant bacteria increased) OR refers to data/general trends in the graph, but misinterprets data OR Interprets a general trend across the whole timeline in the graph generally w/o actual data.	*Partially linked evidence:* Interprets some data from the graph. May be done through actual numbers/trends. Links data as evidence to support EITHER an identifiable claim OR contributing factors to natural selection (e.g., during 1990s, *resistance to antibiotics* increased.	*Fully linked evidence:* Interprets ENTIRE data from the graph appropriately through actual numbers/trends. Links data as evidence to support an identifiable claim as well as contributing factors to natural selection.

FIGURE 10.8

Clarity and Tone of Writing	Ideas in the response are difficult to understand due to two or more of the following categories: CATEGORY 1 (TONE and STYLE): Multiple instances of… subjective/ colloquial constructions used OR ambiguous phrases/ indefinite pronouns OR tangential/off topic writing or plagiarism of a different text w/o reference/citation	Ideas are understandable but some assumptions have to be made due to one or more of the following categories: CATEGORY 1 (TONE and STYLE): Multiple instances of… subjective/ colloquial constructions used OR ambiguous phrases/ indefinite pronouns OR tangential/off topic writing or plagiarism of a different text w/o reference/citation	Ideas are clearly communicated. Meets all categories: CATEGORY 1 (TONE and STYLE): At least mostly objective language used throughout (specific data/evidence not opinion) Minor instances of ambiguous phrases/indefinite pronouns	Ideas are clearly communicated AND stylistically advanced. Meets all categories: CATEGORY 1 (TONE and STYLE): Exclusively objective language used throughout (specific data/evidence not opinion) No ambiguous phrases/indefinite pronouns
	CATEGORY 2 (RELATIONSHIP BETWEEN IDEAS): Lacks Transition devices, an introductory sentence, and a concluding sentence OR repetitious word/phrase/sentence structure used throughout	CATEGORY 2 (RELATIONSHIP BETWEEN IDEAS): Lacks Transition devices, an introductory sentence, and a concluding sentence. OR repetitious word/phrase/sentence structure used throughout	CATEGORY 2 (RELATIONSHIP BETWEEN IDEAS): At least 1 Transition Device String: First, Second, Third or To start, Next, Finally or One, Another, Last OR Single Instance: Also, Last(ly) AND no repetitious word/ phrase/sentence structure.	CATEGORY 2 (RELATIONSHIP BETWEEN IDEAS): Contains a separate Introductory Sentence, Multiple Transition Devices, AND a separate Concluding Sentence AND varied used of words/phrases/sentence structure.
	CATEGORY 3 (WRITING CONVENTIONS): Multiple instances of Sentence fragments, Run-on sentences, Lack of/improper punctuation, or Spelling errors	CATEGORY 3 (WRITING CONVENTIONS): Multiple instances of Sentence fragments, Run-on sentences, Lack of/improper punctuation, or Spelling errors	CATEGORY 3 (WRITING CONVENTIONS): Contains Complete Sentences with (minimum): Subject and predicate, beginning capitalization, and ending punctuation May contain: Minor mechanics errors (spelling – can decipher the word – and/or punctuation)	CATEGORY 3 (WRITING CONVENTIONS): Contains Complete Sentences (see level 3). May contain: Very minor mechanics errors

FIGURE 10.8
(*continued*)

Assessment itself is a scaffolding tool throughout instruction by (1) finding out what students can do on their own versus what they can do with support (e.g., via a more capable peer, graphic organizer, etc.) and then by (2) gradually fading those supports to move students toward more complex uses of core science ideas and language.

How Am I Doing?": Interpreting Students' Productive Use of Both *Core Science Ideas* and *Language*

Collecting evidence of student learning is not the same as *interpreting* that evidence to see whether students have met learning objectives. A teacher's goal is to go beyond whether students "got the idea" or "didn't" and instead interpret their partial or alternative understanding of concepts, as well as communicate understanding in coherent, cohesive, and authentic (reflecting the discourse of science) ways. Figure 10.8 displays a rubric that looks at three dimensions of the antibiotic resistance explanation. We aim to shed light on how to assess both components—recognizing how they are intimately connected with each other.

At the core of the explanation is the theory of natural selection, and how it accounts for changes in species over time. The objective of the explanation is for students to connect all four influential factors learned throughout the unit in a logical and cohesive way that demonstrates a full understanding of natural selection in the context of MRSA. Thus, when planning how you will interpret student responses, it is important to have an exemplar explanation that would fully meet the conceptual objective. From here, we can develop tentative descriptions of "partial mastery" of objectives based on what is known about student learning, including alternative conceptions—resulting in a rubric. This rubric can then be compared with actual student responses to refine the rubric.

As for use of language, we can look at the particular discourse being utilized—in this case an evidence-based explanation. The goal here is to not just look at structure (Is there evidence, a claim, etc.?), but rather how evidence is used to support the claim (Is the evidence sufficient? How is it explained?). Finally, we can take Common Core State Standards to specify how to look at the structure and crafting on the written work. Here we encourage looking beyond grammar, spelling, and so on, and instead focus on the (1) writing clarity, which includes writing conventions, but also use of transitions, an introductory and concluding sentence, and unambiguous phrases/pronouns, and (2) writing style/tone, which includes use of objective rather than opinionated/colloquial language, absence of tangential/off-topic writing, and varied use of word and sentence structure choices. This is also the opportunity to look at how the structure and tone of the writing is written appropriately for the task, audience, and purpose. Figure 10.9 displays a sample student response.

Firstly, bacteria + is well known by now by the world and how it is everywhere and how easy it is to be infected by it leading to infections or diseases. Bacteria can change even evolve and that is a problem especially for the antibiotics used to fight them. A chart on the antibiotic vancomycin and bacteria showed that within the years of 1990 to 2001 bacteria had aquired a neat 30 percent resistance to the antibiotic. This is their adaption of years exposed to the antibiotic as natural selection can explain. Natural selection is another term for survival of the fittest, in which one must evolve to survive. It's seen in any organism that competes for survival is their evolving their new traits or features improve their overall fitness that is needed to survive. This logic applies to bacteria, they become resistant to our antibiotics so they can survive.

Bacteria will continue to resistant our antibiotics to survive, that's just nature. We can continue to make our antibiotics stronger to fight, but its a costly endeavor. The bacteria will be an evergrowing threat as evolve to resist our best antibiotics and force us to implore our efforts. Natural selection is an never ending struggle for good reasons, but it's neccesary for all living things to show and learn.

FIGURE 10.9
Student Response to Culminating Explanation

"Where to Next?"

This chapter concludes by considering what next steps to take once it is clear how students are doing so that they can make continued progress toward big ideas. Key teaching practices that use evidence from assessing to support student learning include providing (1) feedback that focuses on student thinking (as opposed to correcting ideas) and encourages self-regulated learning (e.g., through peer or self-feedback), as well as (2) adapted instruction to leverage key patterns uncovered (i.e., partial or alternative understandings, language used, or funds of knowledge) in future lessons. An opportunity to become self-directed learners has been shown to be particularly beneficial for more struggling students (White & Frederickson, 1998).

Feedback and targeted next steps relate to each of the SSTELLA practices. Science instruction becomes more heavily contextualized when teachers *elicit and draw on* students' lived experiences and funds of knowledge. Students' scientific sense-making is deepened when students have an opportunity to reflect on how their thinking has changed. While engaging students in discussions about science, SSTELLA promotes dialogic strategies, such as revoicing, reporting, restating, quoting, questioning, and so on, that provide feedback to students, which they can use in the moment to deepen understanding by explaining ideas (sometimes to a different audience), clarifying ideas, applying ideas, or critiquing ideas. SSTELLA promotes assistance in engaging in argumentation and explanations, for one, through feedback on students' explanations and arguments. Finally, SSTELLA encourages teachers to provide feedback on students' use of key science terms and literacy practices to see if they are used accurately and in appropriate contexts.

Why is feedback so critical for supporting ELs? Heritage, Walqui, and Linquanti (2013) argue that effective formative assessment for ELs focuses on "languaging" (or helping students use language in more and more precise ways) as part of a joint productive activity, to accomplish some authentic task. Languaging is "always under construction, not a finished product or a fixed code" (Heritage et al., 2013, p. 12). According to them, this "under construction" nature of languaging makes formative assessment pivotal, since it allows teachers to see what is accomplished when students try various communicative events. Then, the teacher can make decisions—does the EL student not precisely communicate the explanation because of sentence structure errors? A lack of understanding about the structure and norms of an explanation? Comprehension of the science concepts needed to convey the explanation? The key is that students need opportunities to use language to accomplish authentic tasks in science—such as constructing explanations—and also need to be comfortable taking risks at using language so that they can learn from it (with help from the teacher).

Once the teacher and students have a clear sense, through feedback, of what needs to be done to fully meet learning goals, teachers can strategically plan next steps, which may apply to everyone, large groups of students (based on patterns uncovered), or individuals. Next steps do more than just "reteach" concepts. They may frame next lessons through language or experiences uncovered while assessing. Teachers may assign a task or problem that addresses a very particular alternative conception (e.g., when conceptualizing various forces acting on an object), or pair students of varying levels to discuss differing conceptions.

Summary

- Is it more beneficial to "simplify" the language, content, and overall expectations when assessing, or keep language, content, and expectations rigorous?
- Do I interpret how students use language or just their understanding of the concepts? Can I do both? How?

The goal in this chapter was to make the case for assessment as a way to identify what students know and can do (in relation to learning objectives) and allow teachers to use this evidence to support students' science learning. Assessment was framed as a cyclical process in which the teacher keeps asking, "Where I am going?," "How am I doing?," and "Where to next?" Via those three questions, we explored learning objectives and how to integrate scientific practices with core science ideas as well as tie objectives to standards and the big idea. It was discussed how to turn different challenges associated with the language demands of science assessment into opportunities for language development by contextualizing assessment activities and increasing accessibility of assessment content and language. Finally, it was discussed how to look at both students' conceptual understanding and their use of language in the service of providing them targeted feedback and adapted instruction to once again deepen their understanding of science ideas and develop language.

Note

1. Adapted from http://evolution.berkeley.edu/evolibrary/article/0_0_0/berg strom_03.

References

Abedi, J., & Lord, C. (2001). The language factor in mathematics tests. *Applied Measurement in Education, 14*(3), 219–34.

Bell, B., & Cowie, B. (2001). *Formative assessment and science education.* Dordrecht, Netherlands: Kluwer Academic Publishers.

Black, P., & Wiliam, D. (1998). Assessment and classroom learning. *Assessment in Education: Principles, Policy & Practice, 5*(1), 7–74.

Furtak, E. M. (Ed.). (2009). *Formative assessment for secondary science teachers.* Corwin Press.

Hattie, J. (2012). *Visible learning for teachers: Maximizing impact on learning.* London, UK; New York, NY: Routledge.

Heritage, M. (2007). Formative assessment: What teachers need to know and do. *Phi Delta Kappan, 89,* 140–45.

Heritage, M., Walqui, A., & Linquanti, R. (2013). Formative assessment as contingent teaching and learning: Perspectives on assessment as and for language learning in the content areas. Paper presented at the annual meeting of the American Educational Research Association, San Francisco, California.

Lee, O., Santau, A., & Maerten-Rivera, J. (2011). Science and literacy assessments with English language learners. In M. Basterra, E. Trumbull, & G. Solano-Flores (Eds.), *Cultural validity in assessment: Addressing linguistic and cultural diversity* (pp. 254–74). New York, NY: Routledge.

Lyon, E. G., Bunch, G. C., & Shaw, J. M. (2012). Language demands of an inquiry-based science performance assessment: Classroom challenges and opportunities for English learners. *Science Education, 96*(4), 631–51.

Lyon, E. G. (2013a). Learning to assess science in linguistically diverse classrooms: Tracking growth in secondary science preservice teachers' assessment expertise. *Science Education, 97*(3), 442–67.

Lyon, E. G. (2013b). What about language while equitably assessing science?: Case studies of preservice teachers' evolving expertise. *Teaching and Teacher Education, 32,* 1–11.

Martiniello, M. (2008). Language and the performance of English-language learners in math word problems. *Harvard Educational Review, 78*(2), 333–68.

McMillan, J. H. (2007). *Formative classroom assessment: Theory into practice.* New York, NY: Teachers College Press.

Pease-Alvarez, L., & Hakuta, K. (1992). Enriching our views of bilingualism and bilingual education. *Educational Researcher, 21*(2), 4–19.

Ruiz-Primo, M. A., & Furtak, E. M. (2007). Exploring teachers' informal formative assessment practices and students' understanding in the context of scientific inquiry. *Journal of Research in Science Teaching, 44*(1), 57–84.

Santos, M., Darling-Hammond, L., & Cheuk, T. (2012). Teacher development to support English language learners in the context of common core state standards. Understanding language: Language, literacy, and learning in the content areas.

Shaftel, J., Belton-Kocher, E., Glasnapp, D., & Poggio, J. (2006). The impact of language characteristics in mathematics test items on the performance of English language learners and students with disabilities. *Educational Assessment, 11*(2), 105–26.

Shaw, J. M., Bunch, G. C., & Geaney, E. R. (2010). Analyzing language demands facing English learners on science performance assessments: The SALD framework. *Journal of Research in Science Teaching, 47*(8), 909–28.

Siegel, M. A. (2007). Striving for equitable classroom assessments for linguistic minorities: Strategies for and effects of revising life science items. *Journal of Research in Science Teaching, 44*(6), 864–881.

Solano-Flores, G., & Nelson-Barber, S. (2001). On the cultural validity of science assessments. *Journal of Research in Science Teaching, 38*(5), 553–73.

White, B., & Frederiksen, J. (1998). Inquiry, modeling, and metacognition: Making science accessible to all students. *Cognition and Instruction, 16*(1), 3–118.

Appendix A

SSTELLA Practices Progression

Appendix A

CONTEXTUALIZING SCIENCE ACTIVITY

Framing

Not Present	Present
The teacher…	
does not make reference to relevant contexts.	**makes some references to relevant contexts, either…** local, ecological, home, community, social (e.g., socio-scientific issues), global, multicultural science, or other socio-cultural experiences.

Introducing	Implementing	Elaborating
Teacher references…		
• Do not contribute to a **relevant framing context** throughout the lesson. (e.g., references act as a "hook" [or series of hooks]). • Either appear **more relevant to the teacher** than the students OR their relationship with the science content is **ignored/distorted** by the teacher.	• **Frame lesson using an overarching driving question or scenario/problem in a relevant context** (see "present" list). • Appear **relevant to the students** AND their relationship with the science content is **clearly acknowledged** by the teacher.	• **Allow student contributions and/or experiences to frame the lesson in a relevant context (with teacher facilitating connection to the big idea).** • Are **driven by the students** AND their relationship with the science content is co-construct by teacher and students.

Adapting (unplanned) & Applying

Not Present	Present
The teacher…	
does not provide opportunities for students to contribute their lived experiences or funds of knowledge.	provides opportunities for students to contribute their lived experiences or funds of knowledge.

Introducing	Implementing	Elaborating
Teacher…		
acknowledges students contributions, but does not connect them to science learning.	connects student contributions to science content and relevant contexts (local, ecological, home, community, social [e.g., socio-scientific issues], global, multicultural science, or other socio-cultural experiences).	facilitates opportunities for students to **build on and respond to peer contributions**, and explicitly encourage students to connect contributions to science learning and relevant contexts.

SCIENTIFIC SENSE-MAKING THROUGH SCIENTIFIC/ENGINEERING PRACTICES

Communicating the "big idea"

Not Present	Present
The teacher...	
might communicate a general science topic, but not a "big idea" in science or a learning objective.	communicates a "big idea" in science, and a learning objective or general expectations for success (at least implicitly).

Introducing	Implementing	Elaborating
The teacher communicates the "big idea"...		
• Implicitly: Mentions only once or is stated in passing during instruction • Learning objective or expectation for meeting objective is vague or somewhat unrelated to the big idea.	• Explicitly: Draws students' attention to the big idea and connects to prior/on-going activities. • Learning objective and expectation for meeting objective are specific and aligned with the big idea with some opportunity for student reflection.	• Explicitly: Draws students attention to the big idea through a partial model or ill-defined problem and connects to prior/on-going activities • Learning objective and expectation for meeting objective are specific and aligned with the big idea with some opportunity for student reflection of how conceptions about the big idea have changed.

Pressing for MODEL- or PROBLEM-based scientific/engineering practices

Not Present	Present
The teacher plans classroom activities that....	
focus solely on recalling facts/terms or understanding science concepts.	Engage students in scientific or engineering practices with at least some momentary sense-making supports (e.g., visuals, graphic organizers, multimedia, realia).

Introducing	Implementing	Elaborating
Students engage in scientific and engineering practices through…		
• Teacher lead inquiry: Teacher provides all questions to investigate, procedures, and resources for an activity, leaving students to merely carry out, record, and report (but not share) findings (i.e., cookbook labs). • A momentary or limited support to help students make sense of the science.	• Guided or "open-ended" inquiry: Students are primarily responsible for asking questions to investigate, and/or planning the investigation, and sharing findings to other groups/the class. • The teacher facilitates connection between scientific/ engineering practice(s) and content. • Multiple supports that help students make sense of the science.	• Guided or "open-ended" inquiry that centers around testing or revising, discussing, and critiquing/reflecting on a scientific model or problem: Students are primarily responsible for asking questions to investigate, defining problems, and/or planning the investigation, and sharing findings to other groups/the class. • The teacher facilitates connection between the scientific/ engineering practice(s) and content related to the model or problem. • Multiple and sustained supports that help students make sense of the science

SCIENTIFIC DISCOURSE THROUGH SCIENTIFIC/ENGINEERING PRACTICES

Facilitating PRODUCTIVE student talk

Not Present	Present
The teacher…	
does not engage students (small group or whole class) in discussion around science ideas.	engages students (small group of whole class) in discussion around science ideas.

Introducing	Implementing	Elaborating
Discussion around science ideas…		
is limited to closed ended student responses and evaluation of student ideas.	results in brief development of student thinking, hypotheses, and/or questions about science ideas though **dialogic strategies and feedback** (e.g. revoicing, reporting, restating, quoting, questioning, etc.). All students are encouraged to talk through mixed groups, clear ground rules, group roles, etc.	results in a **sustained instructional conversation engaged in science** (ICES) about student conceptions, hypotheses, and/or questions about science ideas (w/ talk between students) with both students and teacher using **dialogic strategies and feedback** (e.g. revoicing, reporting, restating, quoting, questioning, etc.).

Pressing for scientific EXPLANATION AND ARGUMENTATION

Not Present	Present
The teacher…	
does **not** provide any opportunity for students to explain or argue about natural phenomenon (teacher might explain him/herself).	**provides an opportunity** and some assistance in showing student how to construct/critique explanations or arguments.

Introducing	Implementing	Elaborating
Opportunity to explain or argue…		
• Focuses on **components** (e.g., stating/identifying claims or evidence, or use formulaic statements, declarations), but not completely formed explanations or arguments related to the big idea. • Assistance is limited to structural components (sentence frames, reminders to use evidence)	• **Focuses on fully supported** scientific explanations or arguments related to the big idea. • Assistance helps students understand the quality (what counts as evidence?) and reason for explaining or arguing (relation to nature of science or alternative discourse forms)	• Focuses on student collaboration (whole class or small group), including **discussion, critique, and/or revision** of an explanation or argument. • Assistance helps students understand the quality and reason for explaining or arguing, and includes teacher or peer feedback on explanations or arguments

ENGLISH LANGUAGE AND DISCIPLINARY LITERACY DEVELOPMENT

Promoting opportunities for English Language Development for ELs through Student Interaction

Not Present	Present
The teacher provides…	
no opportunity for student talk related to lesson content.	opportunity for student talk related to lesson content.

Introducing	Implementing	Elaborating
Opportunity for student talk…		
happens by only by a **few students** who are nominated either by himself or herself or by the teacher.	includes **widespread student interaction** (class discussions, partner or small group interaction, or student presentations), but **little or no support for ELs to** engage in this participation.	includes **widespread student interaction** and support for ELs to engage in this participation (wait time, modeling, prep time, scaffolding roles, etc.).

Promoting opportunities for English Language Development for ELs through vocabulary

Not Present	Present
The teacher…	
avoids key science terms or uses key science terms, but provides no support for students to comprehend or use them.	provides some support for student to comprehend or use key science terms.

Introducing	Implementing	Elaborating
Vocabulary support…		
supplants opportunities to comprehend or use key science terms and is teacher-driven (e.g., copying teacher words, definitions in glossary; front-loading vocabulary).	(a) Uses visuals, contextual cues, graphic representations, paraphrases, or definitions to help students comprehend **and use** new vocabulary. -OR- (b) recognizes students' developing scientific understandings using "everyday" words but encourages students to use key terms as appropriate for the instructional activity.	(a) Uses visuals, contextual cues, graphic representations, paraphrases, or definitions to help students comprehend **and use** new vocabulary. -AND- (b) recognizes students' developing scientific understandings using "everyday" words but encourages students to use key terms as appropriate for the instructional activity. -AND- c) provides opportunities for students to demonstrate appropriate use of key science terms, with feedback from teacher on understanding and accurate use of new words.

Pressing for AUTHENTIC science literacy TASKS

Not Present	Present
The teacher provides…	
no opportunities for students to read, write, and/or discuss written texts (texts include representations such as graphs/models or multimedia texts).	**opportunities** for students to read, write, and/or discuss texts (texts include representations such as graphs/models or multimedia texts).

Introducing	Implementing	Elaborating
Opportunities for students to read, write, and/or discuss texts…		
• **Focus on science concepts and not** on scientific/engineering *practices.* • Include **no strategies** to support texts, or strategies that focus on **general reading and writing**.	• Focus on **scientific/engineering practices.** • Include strategies to **support discipline-specific writing.**	• Focus on scientific/ engineering practices and **the ways in which texts are communicated to different audiences for different purposes.** • Include strategies to **support discipline-specific writing** along with teacher/peer feedback.

Index

Abedi, J., 9, 186

Abell, S. K., xvii, xix

Abreu, G., 5, 23

Academic language, 3–8, 13–14, 26, 35, 131, 136

Achieve, Inc., 4, 7, 9, 69, 70, 71

Achievement: of ELs, 9, 11, 13, 25, 26–27; gap, 4, 8, 13; in science 12–13, 27, 66, 71, 85

Aikenhead, G, 63, 64, 170

Analytical task, 43, 96–97, 100, 111, 115, 127, 176–178

Antibiotic resistance, vi, xvii, 155, 157–159, 161, 163, 165, 167–171, 173–175, 177, 179, 180, 181, 183, 188, 189, 191, 192, 194, 195, 200, 206

Argument from evidence, 4, 40, 41, 43, 52, 92, 109, 110

Argumentation, xxi, 10, 63, 69, 105, 109–111, 115, 116, 118–122, 126, 208

Assessment: of academic language and literacy, 11–12, 183, 185; and big ideas, 88, 188; contextualized, 183, 200, 209; of English proficiency, 26, 27, 43; fair, 186, 191; formative use, 184–185, 191, 208; language

demands, 202; performance-based, 200; planning/process, xv, 163, 184, 188; and scaffolding, 201, 206; and the SSTELLA framework, 170, 185; standardized/state, xxiii, 11, 26, 187; summative use, 185

Authentic: contexts, 3, 63, 66, 71, 72; disciplinary practices, 12, 24, 26, 29, 38, 39, 41, 43, 53, 63, 111, 130, 135, 150, 163, 206; learning and instruction, xxii, 10, 35, 37, 51, 62, 84, 87, 190, 200; literacy and texts, xxi, 55, 126, 130, 131, 140, 141, 147, 180, 208

August, D., 7, 9, 21, 22, 54, 55, 88, 132

Ballenger, C., 122

Basu, S. J., 66

Batalova, J., 44

Bell, B., 185

Bialystok, E., 28, 33

Big idea: communication of, 88–90, 137, 156, 173; to frame instruction, xvi, 54, 64, 73, 79, 82, 86–87, 94, 96, 99–100, 115, 140–141, 155, 170, 172, 174, 185, 188, 190, 208–209

Bilingual: education, xii, xx, 8, 27; proficiency levels (i.e., ascendant/ emergent/incipient/fully functional), xxiii, 23–25; students, 65–66, 68, 148

Birdsong, D., 33

Black, P., 185

Bos, J. M., 38

Brown, B. A., 55, 122

Bruna, K. R., 55, 136

Bunch, George C., 4, 5, 21–24, 26, 34–36, 41, 200, 201

Buxton, C. A., 9, 62, 63, 71

Bybee, R. W., 138

California English Language Development Test, 26, 136

Carhill, A., 33

CCSS. *See* Common Core State Standards

Cervetti, G. N., 11, 136, 146

Cheuk, T., 4, 52, 110, 202

Chinn, C. A., 63

Cohen, E. G., 9, 36

Collaboration, xii, 29, 30, 37, 74, 109, 179

Collier, V. P., 33, 85

Colloquial (or everyday) language, 206

Common Core State Standards, xiii, xv, 3, 4, 39, 44, 51, 52, 59, 70, 71, 92, 93, 109, 110, 155, 206

Communicate expectations, 54, 87, 88, 93, 99, 114, 115, 122, 131, 133, 135, 172, 184, 203, 209

Communicative mode, 201, 202

Contextualization: and adapting/ applying, 74; and assessment, 183, 200, 201, 209; contrasted with decontextualized instruction, xix, 9, 41, 63, 72, 110, 180; as a doorway/ gateway, 52, 63, 72; and framing instruction/big ideas, xviii, xx, xxi, 64, 73, 62, 87, 90, 170–172, 188; and inquiry/scientific practices, xiii, 3, 11, 65, 69, 71, 84, 85, 130; and language/ literacy development, 8, 10, 39, 53,

131, 148, 181; as a SSTELLA practice, xiv, 59, 62, 64

Core science idea, 4, 10, 13, 53, 55, 94, 95, 103, 109, 110, 114, 119, 155, 172, 174, 191, 206, 209

Core teaching practices: approximating, xvi, xvii, xx, xxii, 109; experiencing/ modeled, xvi–xviii,13; noticing and analyzing, xvi–xxii

Costa, V. B., 64

CREDE, xiv, 11

Crosscutting concepts, xiii, 4, 39, 92

Cummins, J., 5, 7, 8, 170

Darian, S., 133

Decontextualized, xix, 5, 8, 9, 41, 63, 64, 72, 110, 171, 180

Dialogic, 63, 76, 109, 119, 121, 191, 208

Disciplinary literacy, xviii, 55, 72, 93, 126, 130–133, 141, 147, 176, 183

Discourse moves, xxii, 54

Driver, R., 10, 53, 54, 111

Driving question, 60–62, 73, 90, 100, 126

Donato, R., 31

Duff, P., 30, 133

Duschl, R., 9, 64, 71

Echevarria, J., 38, 96

Elmesky, R., 63

English language development, xiii, 7, 26, 27, 33, 38, 74, 112, 126, 130, 131, 136, 141, 142, 147

English Learner: and English language development, 33, 140, 142, 179, 190, 208; classification of, xxii, xxiii, 25–28, 43, 59, 80, 105; diversity of, xxii, 22, 146, 35, 124, 176; and everyday experiences, 64–66, 71; long-term, 7, 22, 27, 33, 59, 80; and opportunity to learn, 30, 51, 69; support of, xiv, 11, 23, 34–39, 60, 62, 72, 73, 75, 76, 85, 96, 97, 132, 146, 150, 156, 172, 174

English Language Learner. *See* English Learner

Engle, R. A., 120, 121
ELD. *See* English Language Development
ESTELL Project, xiv
Estrada, P., 27
Explanation. *See* Scientific explanation

Faltis, C. J., 22, 35, 37
Feedback, 31, 34, 83, 119, 131–133, 136, 137, 150, 161, 163, 208, 209
Fillmore, L. W., 7, 22, 28
Flores, B. B., 22, 187, 190
Ford, M., 118
Framework for K-12 Science Education: Practices, Crosscutting Concepts, and Core Ideas, xiii, 4, 39, 92
Funds of knowledge, 54, 55, 66, 67, 71, 74, 103, 171, 185, 191, 208

Garcia, O., 7, 8, 12, 23, 25, 148
Gee, J. P., 66
Genre, 5, 23, 36, 55, 125, 132, 133, 201, 203
Gibbons, P., 31
Goldenberg, C., 6, 7, 22, 37, 132
Gomez, K., 53, 55
Gonzalez, N., 27, 53, 55, 66
Graham, S., 54, 55, 136
Graphic organizers, 34, 38, 43, 54, 98, 100, 117, 174, 179, 180, 202, 203
Group roles, 29, 30, 43, 122, 124, 161, 179
Groves, F. H., 64
Gutierrez, K. D., 7, 84, 135

Hakuta, K., 7, 21, 22, 33, 54, 88
Hand, B., 55
Hattie, J., 87, 185
Heritage, M., 26, 184, 185, 208
Herreid, C. F., 74
Herrenkohl, L. R., 122
Heterogeneous grouping, 36, 131, 179
Hull, G. A., 136

ICES. *See* Instructional Conversation Engaged in Science

Imperial Valley Project in Science, 11, 12
Inquiry, xiii, xiv, xviii, 3, 10, 11, 63, 75, 85, 90–92, 109, 116, 119, 135, 146, 150, 172, 181
Instructional Conversation Engaged in Science, 121–125, 137, 191

Janzen, J., 24, 26, 136
Johnson, K. E., 6, 28

Kelly, G., 54, 88
Kibler, A., 25
King, D., 62,
Krajcik, J. S., 55, 88, 115, 117
Krashen, S., 8, 10, 28

Langman, J., 149, 150
Langer, J. A., 106
Language (and literacy) development, xiii–xv, xvii, xxi, 7, 10, 11, 13, 23, 27, 28, 31, 36, 38, 39, 52, 55, 64, 66, 70, 130, 132, 136, 155, 170, 176, 183, 185, 191, 203, 209
Language demand, 200, 201
Language function, 43, 97, 111, 117, 118, 178
Language minority students, 7, 25
Language proficiency, 8, 21, 22, 24–28, 35, 38, 43, 85, 90, 125, 136, 179, 187
Lantolf, J. P., 29, 31
LASERS Project, 11
Lave, J., 84
Learning objective: communication of, 173, 189, 190; and cyclic nature of assessment, 185, 191; examples of , 88–90, 163; and discourse, 121; and scaffolding, 97
Lee, Okhee, xiii, 4, 7–10, 12, 13, 22, 23, 40, 42, 43, 52, 53, 85, 97, 110, 111, 115, 133, 134, 178
Lemke, J., 10, 54, 84, 129
Lesson planning, 59, 170, 181
Levinson, S. C., 29, 30
Limited English Proficient, xxii, 11, 25

Linquanti, R., 26, 27, 208
Literacy task, 23, 24, 129–131, 136, 141, 142, 147, 185
Local ecological environment, 68
Lucas, T., 23
Lyon, Edward G., xi, xiv, 79, 85, 103, 155, 168, 169, 183, 200

Mainstream, xiii, 6, 23, 25, 26, 28, 34, 39, 44, 132, 148, 156
Martiniello, M., 186, 187
McDermott, M., 55
McMillan, J. H., 55
Met, M., 8, 85
Meltzer, J., 24, 26
Menken, K., 24, 33
Michaels, S., 125, 178
Microteaching, xx, xxi
Moje, E. B., 54, 66, 67, 106, 133, 136
Moll, L., 7, 27, 53, 55, 66
Moscovici, H., 135
Multiple forms or representation, 179, 203
Multiple meaning words, 6
Munoz, C., 11, 33

Next Generation Science Standards, xiii, xv, xxi, 3, 4, 39, 40, 44, 51, 52, 59, 64, 70–73, 81, 84, 92, 109, 138, 150, 155, 173, 189,
NGSS. *See* Next Generation Science Standards

Oakes, J., 7, 13, 53
Ochs, E., 28
Olsen, L., 7
Olson, C. B., 55, 132
Opportunity to learn, 28, 188
Ortega, L., 29
Osborne, J., 10, 53, 93, 110–112

Participant Structure, 122, 201, 202
Participation: and language development, 36; and leveraging student experiences, 65; in science classrooms, 70 71, 85; as a SSTELLA practice, 62, 147; and student talk, 120; strategies, 123, 131, 147, 148, 202

Palinscar, A., 55
Passmore, C., 54, 94, 158
Pearson, P. D., 11, 35, 54, 55, 106, 136, 146
Pease-Alvarez, L., 7
Perry, K. H., 39, 132
Poole, D., 30
P-SELL Project, 12
Primary language, xxii, 8–10, 35, 37, 136
Productive use of language, 103, 126, 175, 176

Queen, J. A., 5, 23

Real world problems, 9, 53, 64, 71, 84, 170
Reciprocal teaching, 55, 179
Rios-Aguilar, C., 27
Rivet, A., 54, 62, 66, 71, 88, 170
Rodriguez, A. J., 10, 13, 55, 70
Rogoff, B., 30
Rosebery, A. S., 8, 10, 53, 54, 63, 65, 68
Rubric, 88, 115, 116, 162, 163, 173, 180, 200, 201, 203, 206
Ruiz-Primo, M. A., 185, 191

Sadler, T. D., 69, 71
Samway, K., 33
Sampson, V., 109, 112, 113, 118, 119
Saul, W., 8, 10, 74
Scaffold(ing): and assessing, 31, 35, 183, 185, 200–203, 206; definition of/its role, 30–32, 97; and discourse, xviii, 40, 115, 122, 124, 125; and language/literacy development, 35, 44, 64, 131, 148; over-, 117, 203; and sense-making, 54, 97–100, 173, 179; and teacher development, xix,xxi, 13
Scarcella, R., 5, 55
Schleppegrell, M. J., 4, 24, 26, 135
Seeds of Science/Roots of Reading, 11

Sense-making; and assessing, 183, 185, 208; and big ideas, 86, 88; definition of/its role, xxi, 54, 79, 84–85, 100; and discourse, 41, 63; and ELs, 64, 65, 176, 179; everyday, 64; and language/literacy development, xvii, 130, 141, 142, 150, 180; and scientific practices/inquiry, 90, 95, 96, 119, 162, 172–174; as a SSTELLA practice, xiv, 52, 72; supporting, 96–100

(Scientific) discourse: and argumentation/explanation, 117, 119, 121, 162; definition of/role, 40, 54, 103, 106, 127; and inquiry/scientific practices, 10, 11, 109, 110, 114, 115, 155, 200; and language of science, 42, 108, 129; and register, 177, 179; as a SSTELLA practice, xiv, xxi, 52, 72, 105; and student talk, 88, 111, 120, 122, 123, 126, 135, 175; support, 112, 124

Science Framework. *See Framework for K–12 Science Education: Practices, Crosscutting Concepts, and Core Ideas*

(Scientific) Explanation: activities to support, 116–120, 176, 180, 208; as a central goal of scientists, 91, 109, 110; and Common Core State Standards, 93, 97; as a core teaching practice, xvi, xvii; and language functions, 10, 43, 52, 53, 85, 110, 111, 127, 129, 135, 177, 178, 202, 203; and the MRSA unit, 155–157, 160–163, 194, 200, 202; and scientific discourse, 54, 63, 103, 105, 120–125, 175, 206; as a scientific practice, 40, 83, 84, 87, 89, 92, 94, 109, 173, 177, 189, 190; to promote scientific understandings, 111, 173, 175, 206; structure and function of, 112–115, 173, 175, 176

Scientific (and engineering) practices, xvii, 39–41, 53, 67, 81, 90, 93–95, 105, 111, 114, 124, 133, 135, 138, 173, 174, 177, 178, 189

(Scientific) Models/modeling: and discourse, 10, 109, 110, 175; examples of, 24, 60, 83, 89, 98, 99, 158, 159, 161, 162, 189; and language/literacy development, 43, 82, 84, 97, 111, 132, 135, 139, 178, 180; and model-based inquiry, xvi, xviii, 119; as a scientific practice, 39, 54, 79, 81, 85, 87, 88, 91–96, 138, 140, 170, 172–174, 177

SIFA Project, 11, 12

Socioscientific Issues, 54, 64, 69–71, 116, 118, 121, 122

SDAIE. *See* Sheltered instruction

SSI. *See* Socio-scientific Issues

Secondary Science Teaching with English Language and Literacy Acquisition: and assessment/feedback, 183, 185, 208; and contextualization, 59, 62, 63, 71; and discourse, 105, 106, 119–121, 126, 175; as a framework, xvi, xvii, 51–53; and language/literacy development, 33, 39, 41, 43, 110, 130–133, 135, 141, 147, 150, 201; and lesson/unit planning, 155, 163, 169, 170, 177, 181; practices progression, vi, xxi, 211; project goals/development, xiv, xv; and method courses, xviii–xxii; and sense-making, 85, 92, 172, 173; and supporting ELs, 23, 28, 32, 34, 37, 40, 55, 116, 184

Self-directed learners, 208

Shaftel, J., 186

Shaw, J., xiv, 85, 200, 201

Short, D. J., 7, 24, 26, 35, 36, 38, 96

SSTELLA. *See* Secondary Science Teaching with English Language and Literacy Acquisition

Solano-Flores, G., 187, 190

Solis, Jorge, v, vi, xiv, 12, 21, 22, 103, 129,

Snow, C. E., 8, 22, 23, 54, 55, 106

Stoddart, Trish, xiv, 3, 5, 9, 10, 11, 51, 53, 85,

Stoll Dalton, S., 63

Stone, C. A., 135
Student Talk, xxii, 96, 105, 120, 121, 123, 126, 175

Tellez, K., 22
Tembe, J., 33
Texas English Language Proficiency Assessment System, 26
Tharp, R. G., 30, 31, 34, 130
Thomas, W. P., 33, 85
Tolbert, S., 51, 59, 74, 79, 169
Toulmin, S. E., 112

Unit planning 73, 169

Valdes, G., 22–26, 40, 42, 133, 134
Veel, R., 54, 106
Vocabulary: and decontextualized instruction, 9, 41, 64, 109, 142; and English Learners, 24, 36, 142; and language development, 6, 40, 135, 136, 150; and the language of science, 42, 55, 64, 106, 108, 122, 133; and language structure/demands, 186,

201, 202; as a SSTELLA practice, 130, 131, 141, 147; strategies, 125, 131, 137, 138, 180; to support scientific understanding and practices, 11–12, 40, 136, 180
Vygotsky, L. S., 4, 29

Wallace, C. S., 55
Walqui, A., 25, 26, 29–32, 35, 54, 97, 138, 208
Warren, B., 8, 10, 53, 54, 63, 65, 68, 74, 84, 126
Watson, J. D., 8, 10, 53, 54, 63, 65, 68, 84, 126
Weiss-Magasic, C., 55
Wells, G., 4, 127
Wiggins, G., 54, 73, 86
Windschitl, M., xvi, 54, 91, 92, 110, 127, 173
Wood, D., 30, 70

Zeidler, D. L., 69
Zoellner, B. P., 70
Zuengler, J., 28

About the Authors

THE AUTHORS ARE ALL principal investigators and key collaborators on the Secondary Science Teaching with English Language and Literacy Acquisition (SSTELLA) Project, funded through the National Science Foundation's Discovery Research K–12 program.

Dr. Edward Lyon, Sonoma State University

Dr. Edward Lyon is an assistant professor of science education in the School of Education at Sonoma State University. He received his Ph.D. in science education from the University of California, Santa Cruz, and his B.S. in psychobiology from the University of California, Los Angeles. Dr. Lyon researches how secondary science teachers engage in instructional and assessment practices that promote authentic science learning and literacy development in multilingual classrooms. He also studies how preservice secondary science teachers become prepared to integrate science and literacy in their instruction and assessment. Dr. Lyon has been recognized for his research through the 2013 National Association of Research in Science Teaching Outstanding Paper Award, the 2013 California Council on Teacher Education Outstanding Dissertation Award, and the 2012 University of California All Campus Consortium on Research for Diversity Dissertation Fellowship. Dr. Lyon teaches courses on secondary science teaching methods and research paradigms in education.

Dr. Sara Tolbert, University of Arizona

Dr. Sara Tolbert is an assistant professor of science education in the College of Education at the University of Arizona. Dr. Tolbert received her Ph.D. in education from the University of California, Santa Cruz, and her B.A. in environmental studies from the University of Colorado, Boulder. She researches how secondary science teachers can facilitate contextually authentic science learning experiences for minoritized youth, including English learners, and how science education can be a vehicle for community engagement and social change. In 2015, Dr. Tolbert received a National Academy of Education/Spencer postdoctoral fellowship to explore how secondary science teachers expand possibilities for social justice through school science. Dr. Tolbert teaches courses on equity and social justice in math and science education, elementary (bilingual) and secondary science teaching methods, and indigenous knowledge in math and science education.

Dr. Jorge L. Solís, University of Texas at San Antonio

Dr. Jorge L. Solís is an assistant professor in the Department of Bicultural-Bilingual Studies in the College of Education and Human Development at the University of Texas at San Antonio. His research interests include the development of academic literacy practices with second-language learners, preparing novice bilingual teachers, tensions and adaptations of classroom learning activity, and understanding the academic transitions of older, school-age language minority students. He holds a Ph.D. in language, literacy, and culture from the University of California, Berkeley, and an A.B. in public policy from Stanford University. He is currently collaborating on two related projects developing effective ways to integrate science-language pedagogy with elementary and secondary school preservice teachers working with English learners and bilingual students. As a former National Science Foundation CADRE fellow, his research has been funded by the Spencer Foundation and the Center for Latino Policy Research. Dr. Solís teaches undergraduate, teacher education, and graduate courses.

Dr. Trish Stoddart, University of California, Santa Cruz

Dr. Trish Stoddart is professor of education at the University of California, Santa Cruz. She has a Ph.D. in educational psychology from the University of California, Berkeley, and M.A. and B.A. degrees in psychology from the University of Birmingham and Leeds in the UK. Her research focus is effective STEM pedagogy for English learners and teacher preparation. In her program of applied research, she uses mixed methods quasi-experimental design research to investigate the impact of preservice teacher education on the development of novice teachers' expertise in integrating the teaching of academic language and literacy and science instruction for English learners. She is the founding director of the TEEL (Teacher Education and English Learners) Center, which includes multiple projects (ESTELL, EL-LISA, and SSTELLA) funded by the National Science Foundation and the U.S. Department of Education.

Dr. George C. Bunch, University of California, Santa Cruz

Dr. George C. Bunch is associate professor of education at the University of California, Santa Cruz. His research and teaching focus on language and literacy challenges and opportunities for English learners in academic settings and on the preparation of teachers for working with them. An experienced K–12 teacher and teacher educator, he holds a Ph.D. in educational linguistics from Stanford University and an M.A. in bilingual education and teaching English to speakers of other languages (TESOL) from the University of Maryland, Baltimore County. He is a founding partner of the Understanding Language Initiative (ell.stanford.edu), designed to heighten awareness of the role that language and literacy play in the Common Core State Standards and Next Generation Science Standards. A former National Academy of Education/Spencer postdoctoral fellow, his research has been funded by grants from the Spencer Foundation, the William and Flora Hewlett Foundation, and the University of California All Campus Consortium on Research for Diversity.

CPSIA information can be obtained
at www.ICGtesting.com
Printed in the USA
FSHW022024251019
63418FS